ECONOMIC FICTIONS

ECONOMIC FICTIONS

A CRITIQUE OF SUBJECTIVISTIC
ECONOMIC THEORY

PAUL K. CROSSER

GREENWOOD PRESS, PUBLISHERS
NEW YORK

Hypotheses non fingo

Isaac Newton

CONTENTS

FOREWORD

THIS tract deals with patterns of thought. As such, it does not depend upon detailed documentation. As such, it dispenses with the procedure of minute quoting.

Quotations, this writer observes, are for the most part quotations out of context. Quotations, no matter how minute, have little relevance as far as the validation or invalidation of a basic approach is concerned. Quotations, no matter how extensive, can prove little, if anything, for or against a major premise.

The writer tries to fathom focal aspects of thought, he refers to major parts of a particular treatise.

Part I, Chapters 1, 2, 3 respectively which relate *The Rise of Economic Subjectivism* offer a critique of *Johann H. von Thuenen's Der Isolierte Staat, Karl Menger's Grundsaetze der Volkswirtschaftslehre* and *Friedrich von Wieser's Ueber den Ursprung und die Hauptgesetze des Wirtschaftlichen Werthes* and *Der Natuerliche Wert.*

Part 2, Chapters 4, 5, 6, 7 respectively which deal with *The Climax of Economic Subjectivism* present a criticism of *Eugen von Boehm Bawerk's Capital und Capitalzins, John Bates Clark's The Distribution of Wealth* and *William Stanley Jevons' The Theory of Political Economy.*

Part 3, Chapters 8 and 9 respectively which cover *The Anti-Climax of Economic Subjectivism* contain a critical evaluation of *Joseph A. Schumpeter's Theorie der Wirtschaftlichen Entwicklung* and *John Maynard Keynes' A Treatise in Probability* and *The General Theory of Employment Interest and Money.*

Part 4, Chapter 10, which deals with the *Anti-Anti-Climax of Economic Subjectivism* criticizes *Othmar Spann's Tote und Lebendige Wissenschaft* and *Philosophenspiegel.*

The systematic economic treatises which form the subject matter of this presentation constitute in themselves the embodiment of a creative endeavor. As such, they throw out a challenge to a creative criticism. In his reevaluation of the systematization efforts of the theorists under review this writer confronts fundamentals with fundamentals. It is, in this way, that the present writer attempts to bring out the essential features in the thinking of any of the theorists whose thought he sets out to explore.

Just as he had to take upon himself to select the most representative writers of the subjectivistic school of economic thought, this writer took it upon himself to choose the most representative writing of any of the selected authors.

This writer concedes that there is a place for a study of the variations in the formulations of any representative writer. He also admits that there is room for studies of the evolution of the thought of a particular writer, alongside of biographical studies of any given author.

This presentation is, however, concerned with scrutinizing essentials in a writer's major contribution. This study, in turn, tries to fathom the thought of a representative theoretician at the height of his professional career.

An inquiry of this kind can well prove to be decisive as far as an overall re-appraisal of a given school of thought is concerned.

PAUL K. CROSSER

INTRODUCTION

I

ALL science and all scientific propositions are forms of approximation of reality. The comprehension of reality is, in turn, a cognitive proposition of its own. Given a certain comprehension of reality, there are degrees to which the approximation of a specific kind of reality can be attempted.

Hypothetical postulations state the possible or probable approximation of a given comprehension of reality. Hypothetical postulations, in order to rate as scientific, are not supposed to be mere guesses or hunches. To be rated as scientific hypotheses, those propositions have to be related to known aspects of a given comprehension of reality. Hypotheses non fingo—the famed saying of Isaac Newton—continues to stand guard over the role of scientific propositions as means of relating the known to the unknown, within a given comprehension of reality.

The degree of comprehension of reality, by way of scientific propositions, can be termed—the degree of scientific truth.

In following the lead of natural science, classical political economy conformed to the stated epistemological and methodological tenets. In proceeding in the Newtonian epistemological and methodological manner, classical political economy as founded by Smith and Ricardo, discovered economic laws and established a number of generalizations which brought economic life into the sphere of scientific knowledge.

A reaction against the form of conceptualization of Smith and Ricardo, to set the chronology right, set in almost a century ago with the publication of "Der Isolierte Staat" by Thuenen. Thuenen's work, though, remained largely unnoticed at that time. Thuenen's anti-classical position which in its overtones constituted a plea for a return to self-sufficiency in agriculture, did not produce much of an echo at his time.

Not until Smith's and Ricardo's concepts had undergone a reformulation by the pen of Marx, did a general wave of criticism of Smith's and Ricardo's formulations set in. A general reaction against economic classicism came about, when some classical conceptions were incorporated into the orbit of a system of reasoning which was aimed at a radical change in the social and economic matrix which underlay the classical propositions.

The use of classical propositions by Marx, for the purpose of negating them, started off an avalanche of criticism of the classical school, its epistemology and its methods. A new kind of epistemology and methodology arose with a conception of reality of its own.

Reality became an exclusively psychologistic reality, the non-psychologistic frame of reference became fully excluded from the comprehension of reality. Any non-psychologistic range of reality came to be rated as unrealistic. The vagaries in the working of the human mind were made the sole criterion of the scientificalness of economic propositions. The factor of validation of economic reasoning retreated into the fold of mental recesses. Knowledge came to be regarded as not encompassing anything which could not be placed within a subjectivistic orbit.

In the absence of a contrasting non-subjectivistic frame of reference, the subjectivistic form of reasoning was left at the mercy of individual mental reactions. Hypothetical postulations which were based on a clear distinction between the known and the unknown, became out of order.

Within the fold of uncontrolled and uncontrollable mental reactions the known comes to be indistinguishable from the unknown. It is, therefore, understandable that psychologistic economic reasoning proceeded on the assumption that all knowledge is but an illusion and that it is inconceivable that a clear distinction can ever be established, by way of a scientific proposition, between the imaginary and non-imaginary, between fictitiousness and reality.

To comply with the proposition that the fictitious is indistinguishable from the non-fictitious, subjectivistic economic theory placed fictions in the place of hypothetical propositions. A fiction, as distinguished from a hypothesis, is a postulation which is based on the assumption that a distinction between reality and unreality or, to put it in another way, a distinction between reality and appearance, constitutes an inconceivable proposition.

Within the fold of a reasoning which is based on the presumption of fictitious propositions, there is no objective criterion left, by way of which certainty could conceivably be distinguished from uncertainty. Even the factors of probability and improbability become undifferentiated and undifferentiable in the fold of reasoning in which a fiction is supposed to serve as a major proposition.

A fiction used as a highest postulate, there should not be any doubt about it, precludes the conceptualization of uniformity and regularity. The cognitive criterion for setting the accidental and incidental apart from the non-accidental and non-incidental, is absent. The general comes to be indistinguishable from the specific, the concrete becomes undifferentiable from the abstract.

At best, a fiction can serve as guide for a rationalization. With the loss of the cognitive basis of objective knowledge, the ground is removed on the basis of which objective uniformities can be established. The cognitive prerequisite for the evolvement and testing of economic laws is lost.

The epistemological and methodological attack on the classical school of political economy by the subjectivistic economic theorizers can well be termed a systematic effort of deconceptualization. The psychologistic economic writers proceeded with the disqualification and deformation of the concepts which had constituted the theoretical arsenal of the school of economic thought which had pre-dated Marx. In bringing forward their unrelenting opposition to Marxism, the subjectivists (as well as the relativists and logico-positivists) overshot their target. They disqualified not only the Marxist propositions but the propositions of the non-Marxist classical school as well.

In proceeding with the relentless task of subjectifying economic reasoning, the psychologistic theorists dismantled the categories which had formed a constituent part of the systematization which had been offered by the classical economic thinkers and put nothing of any comparable cognitive relevance in its place.

Economic theory has been left a disarray of shambles of concepts in the wake of the cognitive wrecking drive, in which, one after another, of the subjectivistic economic theorists came to be engaged.

One can well assay the history of subjectivistic economic theory as a history of devolution of economic thought, in the course of which each succeeding subjectivistic theorist had undertaken to destroy, in the cognitive sense, that which was still left conceptually intact of the classical economic concepts by his respective subjectivistic predecessor.

Subjectivism, it should be noted, goes hand in hand with relativism; both contribute to the fragmentation of thought and, thus, form effective stumbling blocks in the path of social and economic identifiability. Relativism constitutes a potent device to relate one unidentified and, for that matter, unidentifiable factor to another. The relativistic cognitive approach can well be used to extend the range of social and economic undifferentiation to infinity.

Though relativism does form a part of subjectivistic economic theory, it does not necessarily have to serve as but an adjunct to subjectivism. Relativism does not necessarily have to play a subsidiary role, it can well assume a primary cognitive function. Relativism, for that matter, forms the basis of a school of economic thought of its own. Relativism provides the cognitive basis for the German Historical School and the American Institutional School. Both schools are anti-conceptual in the sense that their very relativistic cognitive basis effects of necessity a fragmentation of thought. Both schools of thought emphasize empirical research and shy away from generalization. The difference between the two schools lies more in the area of selection of empirical material than in the analytical approach itself.

The German Historical School is, as its name indicates, interested in historically relevant material, historical relevance being in the stated context a relevance which emphasizes the pre-capitalistic past and expresses a definite nostalgia for the reestablishment of an admixture of dated feudal economic forms and early mercantilistic practices. The American Institutional School is basically a-historical, in the sense, that it does not select data with regard to a specific socio-historical pattern. The American Institutional School is rather eclectic in the selection of data and does not have any notions about a preference of one historical period over another. One outstanding American institutionalist, Thorstein Veblen, tried to introduce an a-historical approach, in the sense, that he attempted to overextend the historical range of economic inquiry by bringing in anthropological issues. At the same time Veblen placed great emphasis on the change of attitude, which brought the subjectivistic factor into great prominence in American institutional thinking.

The relativistic schools per se, the German Historical School and the American Institutional School are not dealt with in the body of this critical exposition. Relativism, as has been stated, is only treated as subsidiary cognitive factor in this critical exposition.

Another school of modern economic thought, the logico-positivistic, is accorded an intermediary place within the scope of this volume. Logico-positivism is, in a sense, an antidote to subjectivism. Logico-positivism is characterized by a strictness of form, as against the formlessness which constitutes the characteristic of subjectivism. Logico-positivism, though, is but strict as far as the outer contours of its propositions are concerned; logico-positivism is, in turn, characterized by a lack of content, and social and economic content in particular.

Subjectivism, to advance an overall appraisal of its position at this turn, constitutes a form of comprehension which stops short of the conceptual. The subjectivistic form of comprehension does not advance beyond the range of the strictly perceptual. Logico-positivism, on the other hand, does advance to the level of conceptual propositions, though the range of the conceptual is confined to a narrow formalistic scope.

Logico-positivism presents a symbiotic development. From the logical postulations of economic reasoning, as they have been advanced by Cairnes, there follows a path to the positivistic proposition of Comte. The logico-positivistic integration which has but recently been attempted by Wittgemtein, resulted in an ever growing stream of formalistic economic reasoning.

The mathematical school of economic thought can be well regarded as but a subsidiary branch of logico-positivistic economic thinking. Use of higher mathematics, it should be noted, constitutes but a particular form through the application of which analytical economic aspects can be demonstrated. In that sense, mathematics can well be treated as an auxiliary branch of any pattern of economic thought. It should be admitted, though, that mathematical reasoning as such belongs most properly within the formalistic frame of logico-positivism with which it shares a common cognitive approach.

An outgrowth of logico-positivism can be seen in operationalism. Operationalism can be adequately termed a set of manipulative devices which are applied to a managerial framework, as such operationalism lies outside the scope of national economic inquiry.

Logico-positivistic economic writing is dealt with in the present exposition by way of interpolation; it is introduced in the treatment of the works of Keynes. The works of Keynes demonstrate that logico-positivism as any other cognitive approach does not remain simon-pure in its application. Subjectivistic as well as relativistic cognitive elements are interwoven in Keynes' application of the logico-positivistic approach. It is in the latter sense, by way of a demonstration of the interrelation of logico-positivistic, relativistic and subjectivistic elements in economic thinking, that Keynes is treated in this exposition.

II.

The general framework of subjectivistic writing was provided by Thuenen. Thuenen postulated the factor of social and economic isolation which furnishes the background for all subjectivistic economic thought. Thuenen's method of isolation is not in any way identical with the method of isolation as it had been applied by the classical theorists. The proposition of ceteris paribus, which the classical writers employ, constituted but a device by which a given economic factor was subjected to but temporary isolation. The principle of ceteris paribus, as it had been employed in the classicists use of the method of isolation constituted but an intermediary factor in the analysis. It was understood, that the artificially isolated factor was to resume its character as one of the interrelated aspects of social and economic life, as soon as the analysis of the isolated factor had been completed. In that sense the analysis remained only temporarily out of touch with social and economic reality, the intermediary of an isolated analysis was to provide a testing ground for a more comprehensive understanding of the real, the non-isolated factors of social and economic life.

Not so, in Thuenen's conception. Thuenen applied the method of isolation as a deliberate fiction. He posited an isolated factor or factors with the stipulation that the isolation is to be undertaken not as a temporary analytical expedient, but as a final step which sets the isolated factor, once and for all, apart from the flow of social and economic life. He severed all communication lines between the isolated factor and the outer world. He did not conceive the method of isolation as a proposition by which one factor was temporarily severed from other interrelated factors. He conceived of isolation as a means of disqualifying the factor of social and economic interrelation as such. In that sense, the method of isolation was not designed to play the role of a mere analytical tool; it was supposed to become a means for the evolvement of the conception of fictitiousness; it was to become a means by which reality was to be turned into unreality. In Thuenen's conception, subjectivistic schemes were supposed to replace the very comprehension of the reality of social and economic existence. His scheme constitutes a deliberate escapist attempt. Thuenen is trying to eschew the complex problems with which he was confronted in real life.

All the subjectivistic writers take Thuenen's method of isolation for granted; they regard the social and economic vacuum which Thuenen established in his "isolated state" as a preconditioning factor of their reasoning. Menger, who placed the factor of individualistic reactions in the center of his discussion argues as if the factor of an interrelated existence of individuals was entirely absent in social and economic life. Menger presumes that the inner recesses of the individual human mind are the only testing grounds of social and economic living.

Menger's presumption that a cognitive distinction between a conscious and unconscious individual, between an individual who is awake and a sleep-walker is unavailable, can be made to stand only under the assumption that a realistic social and economic background which can provide an objective frame of reference is supposedly non-existent. The same can be said of Menger's presumption that a cognitive criterion is not available by which imaginary attributes of economic goods can be distinguished from non-imaginary properties. If the inner recesses of the human mind are to be permitted to function as the sole guides of economic reasoning, there is no way left by which mental aberrations can be distinguished from normal mental processes, as Menger himself admits.

Menger is to be credited with having laid the groundwork for the disqualification of the analytical tools by which the objectivistic classical writers gained an understanding of the processes of production, consumption and exchange. The comprehension of the process of production is blocked by the introduction of a continuous referral device to be known as complementary goods. Production becomes a never ending labeling device. Causation is replaced by classification.

Consumption, which constitutes Menger's basic proposition, rates as a factor which is at the mercy of an indeterminate play of emotions. Consumption is basically presented by Menger as a chain reaction based on an inexplicable irrational fear of an imaginary scarcity.

Wieser seconded Menger in the effort to subjectify and fragmentize economic thought. Wieser's focal conception of marginal utility is based on the proposition of a ceaseless division of particles into particles and so on and so forth, ad infinitum. The very ceaselessness of that division makes a specification of a particle and, moreover, any kind of measurement of a particle or particles, inconceivable.

Boehm-Bawerk saw it as his special task to prevent a social and economic identification of the factor of means of production. He centered his deconceptualization effort on the social and economic disqualification of the category of interest which, in turn, enabled him to prevent a social and economic identifiability of the concept of capital.

John Bates Clark erected a terminological barrier of his own to prevent a social and economic identification of the category of capital, he introduced an indeterminate conception of marginal utility of labor to promote his own brand of social and economic unidentifiability.

The indeterminateness in the interpretation of social and economic data reaches a high point in Jevons. His advancement of socially and economically unidentifiable conceptions, brings him to a point where he argues in circles. His exposition of what he calls exchange ratio and final degree of utility are no more than exercises in redundancy.

Schumpeter's literary performance is in a sense anticlimactic. His a-historicism coupled with his intuitionism make economic reasoning dispensable. In that sense, Schumpeter, it might be said, wrote an epitaph on the demise of economics as a science.

Othmar Spann's literary offering is, in turn, anti-anti-climactic. The irrationalist anti-scientific position which Schumpeter had advanced leaves the door open for a comprehension, as the one advanced by Spann, which does not permit any feasible distinction between an entity and a non-entity. Spann's reduction of human comprehension to the level of a recording of inexplicable inner voices forms the most advanced post on the road towards indistinguishability between human consciousness and unconsciousness, in the sphere of economic comprehension.

In Keynes, lack of social content, the major cognitive characteristic of the logico-positivistic school goes hand in hand with the lack of form, the outstanding characteristic of the subjectivistic pattern of economic thinking. In that sense, it can be said, Keynes has combined the cognitive factors which are operative in the dissolution of economic thought.

Keynes' attack on the classical propositions, his criticism of the differentiation of monetary and non-monetary income by the classicists, his special stricture of the distinctive marks which the classicists had attached to their comprehension of real and nominal wages, is but aimed at emptying those propositions of any social and economic content. In that sense, Keynes is properly a logico-positivistic thinker. His analysis of saving and investment, his exposition of what he calls propensity to consume and predilection to invest places him squarely, in turn, within the subjectivistic fold with formlessness in social and economic comprehension as its attendant mark.

III.

Subjectivism with its relativistic counterpart, as well as the logico-positivistic variation, to attempt an overall appraisal, does not constitute a way of comprehension which is strictly limited to the sphere of economic theory. Economic life constitutes but one of the many manifestations of human life and, as such, presents but one of the many spheres to which the subjectivistic form of comprehension, its relativistic counterpart as well as the logico-positivistic variation are applied. Subjectivistic, relativistic and logico-positivistic conceptions have invaded all spheres of social science. Subjectivistic, relativistic and logico-positivistic conceptions in the sphere of economics do, therefore, not present anything exceptional, they constitute but a manifestation of prevailing patterns of thought as applied to a specific sphere of inquiry.

Nor are subjectivistic, relativistic and logico-positivistic conceptions limited to the sphere of social science. Natural as well as social science have become subject to subjectivistic, relativistic as well as logico-positivistic forms of conceptualization and deconceptualization.

Nor are subjectivism, relativism, and logico-positivism forms of comprehension which are strictly limited to the sciences. Those forms of comprehension are applied to the arts as well.

Neither should it be assumed that the spheres of either social or natural science, on the one hand, and the arts, on the other hand, present independent and unrelated manifestations of diverging forms of comprehension. The manifestations of the forms of comprehension in the sciences and the arts are closely related to each other.

The application of subjectivistic, relativistic and logico-positivistic conceptions in the sphere of the sciences is reflected in the application of the subjectivistic, relativistic and logico-positivistic conceptions in the sphere of the arts as well as vice versa.

Impressionism, which represents subjectivistic formlessness in art has its counterpart in scientific treatises in nautral as well as social science.

Wieser's formulations, as they have found expression in his major work, can well be termed a potent manifestation of impressionism.

Expressionism with its characteristic lack of content can likewise be detected in the arts as well as the sciences. Menger's performance can for instance be found constituting a major expressionistic exercise.

Schumpeter, in turn, can well be termed as a surrealist, the formlessness of his conceptions is the outgrowth of his irrational-ism. In that sense, it can be said, he runs true to the surrealistic form.

Spann, on his part, can well be regarded as an expounder of the artless way of life, if art goes hand in hand with science, artlessness goes hand in hand with a non-scientific postulation.

Mysticism, and Spann is an expounder of it, is supposed to refer to something incomprehensible. Mysticism is therefore unable to relate any specifiable form of either expression or impression, as Spann demonstrates it.

All forms of comprehension, and the subjectivistic, relativistic as well as the logico-positivistic forms of comprehension are no exception, are, in turn, but derived from philosophical system-atizations. In that sense forms of comprehension, whether they are applied in the sciences or in the arts, are, as it had been stated at the outset of this introductory essay, but ways of com-prehension of reality.

Though, subjectivism, relativism and logico-positivism constitute definite patterns of comprehension in the sciences and the arts, the stated division of patterns is primarily one of a methodological range.

Within the epistemological range there is a greater variety of modes than the stated three-fold methodological division.

As far as the sphere of epistemological propositions is concerned, the galaxy of economic writers who have been dealt with in the present exposition, represent the following variations in thought.

Thuenen's conceptions, it can be said, reflect the supra-natural-ism of Schelling. At the time when Thuenen made his entry into the literary scene Schelling had made a philosophical bid for eliminating the cognitive dividing line which sets objectively con-ceived generalizations apart from subjective perceptions. In Schell-ing's metaphysical conception science became undistinguishable from revelation. Intuition as a wholly unqualified proposition came to rule supreme. In expressing a deliberate contempt for the ma-terial in the world, Thuenen fully subscribes to the subordination of the non-metaphysical real to the metaphysical ideal. He thus eliminates the distinguishing marks between the non-fictitious and fictitious.

Menger, it can be stated, advanced on the slippery cognitive road on which Thuenen tread. By placing the thought prerequisites of time as well as causation beyond the range of the specifiable Menger has torn down the cognitive safeguards which stood in the way of an unqualified validation of subjective notions. Menger has thus placed his ultimate conceptions in the fold of a voluntaristic comprehension. His drive to override reflections by sensuality, according to which fictions and fictitiousness constitute a superior form of reality, lands Menger squarely in the range of Schopenhauer's comprehension. In Schopenhauer's metaphysical conception to which Menger implicitly subscribes, the illusory world is the real world.

Wieser's denial of the feasibility of coherence in human expressions and interhuman communication, places him squarely in the anti-rationalist fold of Nietzsche. His refusal to recognize a common interhuman denominator on which a comprehension of value can be based is fully in accord with Nietzsche's stand as expressed in "Beyond Good and Evil."

Boehm-Bawerk, on his part, reflects in his ultimate conception, the dual influence of Neo-Kantianism and Neo-Positivism. In viewing mere appearances of life in general and outer manifestations of social and economic life in particular, as the only signifiable factors in human comprehension, Boehm-Bawerk aligns himself with the latter day reinterpreters of Kant and Comte who misconstrued major propositions of Kant's and Comte's thought.

John Bates Clark, on his part, reflects a kind of epistemological Primitivism. Clark does not recognize any necessity for making a cognitive distinction between signification and designification, with the result that there is no way of differentiating between meaningfulness and meaninglessness in Clark's presentation. In a sense, Clark echoes the obscurantist reverberations of the Scottish Common Sense School and, in turn, anticipates the obscurantism of Pragmatism.

Jevons' form of comprehension, bears, in turn, many an epistemological mark of John Stuart Mill. Jevons, it should be noted however, is more subjectivistic than Mill. Mill, it can be said, is predominantly a subjectivist in his writing, Jevons, in his turn, is exclusively subjectivistic. The objectivistic factors which continue to hang by a thread in Mill's exposition, are completely cast off by Jevons. With Jevons the dissolution of objectivistic economic thinking had come to a full turn.

Schumpeter's presentation, on its part, bears all the marks of Bergson's epistemological position. Bergson's anti-intellectualism, his attack on reflection, his disqualification of memory, are fully represented in Schumpeter's espousal of intuitionism. With Schumpeter the anti-rationalist position which had initially been taken by Wieser comes to fruition with a complete turn towards irrationalism.

Keynes' conceptions, on their part, bear the earmarks of Husserl's logical postulations. In squaring the logical, non-logical and il-logical, Husserl has made it cognitively unfeasible to distinguish between those three aspects of human comprehension. Without any acknowledgment of any direct influence of Husserl, Keynes nevertheless applies Husserl's devices.

Spann, who made the irrevocable step from irrationalism to a-rationalism in economic comprehension, expresses a mode of thinking which had but recently been reformulated by Heidegger. His denial of rationality and irrationality as its counterpart, can well be linked to the a-rationalist Existentialist position which propounds a flight into Nothingness.

Part 1

The Rise of Economic Subjectivism

CHAPTER 1

ISOLATION

ECONOMIC fiction made its literary debut in the shadow cast by a rambling philosophical structure. A feeling of intellectual despair permeated the literary climate at a time when economic fictitiousness made its first distinct appearance. An emotional reaction had swept over Europe in the wake of reverses suffered by rational thought and radical action. A mood of disillusionment had come to impress itself upon the literary mind; the conceptual strictness and intellectual discipline of rationalism had made way to a looseness of an indiscriminate sensualism.

In Central Europe a destructive intellectual movement had been set into motion to force a revocation of the concessions which German metaphysics had made to the French Enlightenment. The movement to reverse Kant by eliminating the physical from the metaphysical went hand in hand with an onslaught against the priority claims of natural science.

At the time when Thuenen had come to clamor for literary recognition, Schelling had disavowed the conceptual differentiation between the natural and the supranatural; the would-be inheritor of the mantle of Kant, refused to draw a line between objective generalization and subjective perception – science was to become indistinguishable from revelation, intuition as a kind of catch all was to rule supreme.

Although the author of "Der Isolierte Staat" did not touch upon the subtleties of Schelling's sophistry, he nonetheless willfully submitted to the overall influence exercised by the latter day metaphysician. Thuenen is wholeheartedly accepting the subordination of the qualified real to the unqualified ideal, he is fully subscribing to Schelling's disqualification of the material world.

In advancing methodological views of his own, Thuenen does not hesitate to demand that objectified abstractions be denied validity while deliberate fictions are to be viewed as expressions of truthfulness. Wistful schemes drawn in social and economic isolation are to rule supreme. Fenced off concoctions are to be made safe against any analysis which would admit the existence of social and economic forces. Any inquiry into the real pulse of social and economic life is to be held off through the posting of rules against the asking of embarrassing questions.

With a selfassertiveness bordering on the naive, Thuenen prefaces his major treatise with a bold announcement that he is deliberately departing from reality. The selfprofessed schemer makes it perfectly clear that he is determined to prevent any disqualification of unrealistic postulations. Preconceived notions are to be made to prevail over any conceivable countering causes and contradicting effects.

Thuenen does not care to honor the attributes which distinguish a fruitful inquiry from a hopeless search. The utter futility of adding artificialities to artificialities does not seem to disturb him. The lessons of the historical struggle against the pitfalls of reasoning appear to go unheeded with the author of "Der Isolierte Staat." The condemnation of cobwebs, the denunciation of empty syllogisms, the demonstration of the necessity to evolve a hypothesis in close proximity with a proven thesis, the entire range of the methodological upsurge identified with the names of Francis Bacon and Isaac Newton, has obviously not registered with the selfadvertised recaster of economic thought.

Thuenen's uncritical reliance on willful guesses and whimsical hunches, the full scale embracement of wishful thinking by the initiator of economic fictitiousness reflects the methodological undercover attack against Descartes and Spinoza. The proclamation of the inherent supremacy of the human mind was met by a relentless opposition; the call for a rule of reason has been under a continuous barrage from Malebranche on until Condillac. An incessant stream of words has been hurled at the radical exponents of ration-

2

alism – reason was to be made to resubmit to the reign of unreason.

Thuenen's eagerness to advance nonarguable pre-suppositions to the place of arguable suppositions, his unqualified preference of the unprovable as against the provable, his overt leaning on intuitive feeling are sure indications of the vogue of irrationalism which had come into high gear with the supplications of Schelling.

Let one imagine, the selfprofessed schemer opens up, a vast and teeming city being situated in the very midst of a fruitful cultivated valley. Let one presuppose, Thuenen goes on, the urban center and its surrounding area are completely lacking any flowing water – not a single river, not a canal is to be found in the city and its adjoining countryside.

The countryside, Thuenen continues, is supposed to be surrounded by an unapproachable forest. The forest, the author of "Der Isolierte Staat" would like to make believe, is of such density, as to foredoom any and all attempts to establish some kind of human communication within its confines. All efforts to build a road are to be viewed as coming invariably to nought. Even the endeavor to secure a footpath is to be held as being of no avail.

The impenetrable forest is, in turn, supposed to form an unsurpassable enclosure for the imaginary countryside lying in its very center. The forest is supposed to serve as an insurmountable fence which is to prevent the countryside and the city in its midst to establish any communication with the rest of the world.

The impenetrable forest is supposed to seal the social and economic insulation of the countryside. The impenetrability of the forest is to serve as a deterrent for the inhabitants of the enclosed countryside against their ever attempting to break the social and economic fences which Thuenen has in store for them. The supposedly impenetrable forest is to make it, moreover, inconceivable for the countryside it encloses, to receive any urban supplies from any other source, save the one city which is placed within its range. For the single city, in turn, it should appear inconceivable to obtain any agricultural produce, save from the presumably insulated countryside.

By forcing a complete social and economic isolation upon his imaginary countryside, and the city placed within its scope, Thuenen maintains, he has created the most ideal situation. By

3

compelling the inhabitants of the imaginary countryside and the residents of the single city it is supposed to contain, to limit the range of their economic communication to an exchange of their respective products, Thuenen considers he has laid down the rules for the attainment of a most perfect social and economic amalgamation.

To assuage those who might be inclined to doubt that he has proffered a workable supply stratagem, Thuenen is willing to offer a followup proposition. Those who might be inclined to argue that a complete insulation of the countryside and the single city in its midst is a sheer impossibility, since such isolation would necessitate the cutting off of the isolated population from any outside supplies of salt and minerals, Thuenen is willing to reassure. He proffers to place coal mines and salt pits within the range of the social and economic enclosure.

The distribution of the said mineral resources within the isolated social and economic orbit is not supposed to allow for either surpluses or shortages. Since neither an export to the outside world, nor an import from the world outside, are supposed to take place, the supply of mineral resources is at no time to exceed the ever present demand of the population within the enclosure. The demand for mineral resources is, in turn, at no time to be either greater or smaller than the available supply. The potential as well as the actual output of the coal mines and the salt pits within the insulated social and economic range, is supposed to insure, at all times, a mineral supply which allows for neither opulence nor want.

It is presumptuous, Thuenen is willing to confess, to assume that a countryside of any appreciable size is dependent upon the products of a single city. The very placement of the one and only city in the exact center of the surrounding countryside presents but a flight of fancy, Thuenen does not shy away from stating. A number of large and small cities the author of "Der Isolierte Staat" does not refuse to take notice, are usually found to be spread over any sizeable territory. To presume that a one and only city and its adjoining countryside are deprived of navigable means of communication as he is about to demand, involves an added remoteness from social and economic reality, Thuenen recognizes.

Nonetheless, the author of "Der Isolierte Staat" does not refrain

4

from insisting that the one and only city he has in mind is to be thought of as completely lacking any navigating facilities. The imaginary city is to be pictured as an urban settlement through which neither a river nor a navigable canal is found to flow.

Thuenen is quite frank when he proclaims that he is not willing to have any parts of his scheme empirically contested. The sketch he offers of either the city or the countryside does not grow out of generalizations which are founded on the socially and economically extant, Thuenen does not care to deny. The godfather of economic fictitiousness is not averse to confide that he is trying to eschew the socially and economically existing by indulging in fantasies. The author of "Der Isolierte Staat" is not unwilling to reveal that he is departing into a dream world to evade a realistic dealing with social and economic problems. Thuenen is prepared to concede that he is attempting to devise subjectified escape routes as a way of working off the impact of fundamental social and economic maladjustments on his own person. He does not at all dispute that he is anxious to give expression to a personal fancy instead of finding answers to social and economic questions which had come to trouble him.

Thuenen is not at all shy in revealing the source of his tribulations. The author of "Der Isolierte Staat" is not at all constrained to state that he has become perplexed by the commercialization of agriculture. The inaugurator of economic fictitiousness does not hold back his woes, he does not shrink from detailing his difficulties in making ends meet in running an estate. Thuenen is not at all hesitant to make it public that his cost calculations have gone astray. He is not at all unwilling to admit that the unpredictability of the market has upset his bookkeeping.

How ideal the socio-economic situation would be, were certainty to come to reign where uncertainty has become rampant, Thuenen sighs. How pleasant, how dignified the life of an agriculturalist could become were a ban declared on the social and economic indignities caused by the market. How sedate a social setting could be created, Thuenen escapes into daydreams, if the existing economic imbalance could be disposed of by discounting it. How serene an economic atmosphere could come to prevail if the perplexities of intake and outgo could be simply side-tracked. What perfection could be attained if all economic distress could be removed by the simple device of not registering it. What a delight it would be, Thuenen spins his cobweb, if economic questions involved in the selection of agricultural products could be entirely overlooked by way of having all problems relating to the selection of agricultural products treated as the exclusive domain of agrochemistry. What an enchantment could be lent to agricultural pursuits if the social problems connected with the distribution of agricultural products could be fully removed by having all problems arising in the disposition of products relegated to the province of a transportation device.

Were an agrochemical analysis be made to stand for an economic inquiry, were technical transportation schemes, in turn, to take the place of social investigations, neither a critical economic situation, nor a threatening social condition could ever come to be realized as such, to interpret Thuenen's train of thought. Under the presumption that social and economic problems are denied means of expression, Thuenen is correct in assuming that no contravening factors could ever be detected, were production to be regarded as bearing the marks of no other factor than productive intensity. No contradictory evidence could, under the stated presumption, be uncovered were products, in turn, to be graded on no other basis than the one of expended effort. Nor could anything contrary come to manifest itself, with the stated presumption in force, were transportation facilities to be rated as nothing but a technical extension of a production arm. Hence, keeping the stated presumption in mind, Thuenen is right in concluding that no contrariety could ever be cited against the identification of an efficient operation of transportation with the selfperpetuation of a production scheme.

With social and economic comprehension barred, within the just stated context, neither social deviations nor economic disturbances could ever be made to mar a perfect functioning of Thuenen's scheme. With social and economic conceptualization deferred until further notice, Thuenen can well entertain himself with the gracing of his model of perfection by picturing it in symmetrical lines. He can well serve his sense of aesthetic appreciation by demanding that the cultivation in the isolated countryside be specially molded in the form of evenly shaped belts.

Belts containing products of differing cultivation intensity are supposed to surround the urban center at varying radiuses. Belts containing products of comparatively high cultivation intensity are to be conveniently placed at a comparatively short radius from the city limits. Belts, in turn, containing products of comparatively low cultivation intensity are on their part to be appropriately located at a comparatively longer radius from the town. Since the location of production is supposed to be determinable on no other basis than the relative productive intensity, Thuenen does not see any reason why he could not insist that the spacing of production is but a matter of geometrical precision.

Since nothing but productive intensity is supposed to count in the spacing of agricultural production, the symmetry of the scheme could hardly come to be upset, Thuenen is free to presume. Since moreover, cultivation as well as transportation are supposed to be governed by no other factor than the principle of technical efficacy, no methodological or logical obstacles could be placed in the way of having the symmetry of production belts matched with symmetrical transportation lines, Thuenen considers himself free to reason.

In continuing to amuse himself with the adding of one perfection to another, Thuenen suggests a selfperpetuating transportation scheme. A transportation line of a comparatively shorter radius is supposed to serve a production belt of a comparatively higher production intensity, while a transportation line of a comparatively longer radius is supposed to feed a production belt of a comparatively lower production intensity, in Thuenen's perfectionist design.

In keeping with the presumption that the cultivation of the right kind is always located in the right place, it pleases Thuenen to visualize trains carrying products leaving and arriving just in time to prevent either gluts or shortages. The perfect location of production belts and its respective transportation lines, Thuenen radiates with contentment, can well be invoked to provide a guarantee against social maladjustments and economic dislocations. The perfect location of production belts and its transportation lines, Thuenen appears to be more than pleased, can well be cited to furnish an unquestionable assurance of a perfect balance between production and consumption. Thuenen feels particularly confident

7

that by directing the attention of the dwellers of the isolated urban center to the perfect location of the production belts and the respective transportation lines, they could be persuaded to presume that they can, with impunity, disregard the economic aspects as far as such aspects have any relation to either the quality or the quantity of the agricultural produce which the fenced in surrounding countryside is supposed to supply to them. The author of "Der Isolierte Staat" feels equally sure that a reference to the perfect location of the production belts and their respective transportation lines can make the populace of the one and only city in the isolated countryside believe that an ever normal granary has been established for their benefit.

Were it not for some disconcerting afterthoughts, Thuenen could have rested his case. Were it not for the undercurrent of his motivation, Thuenen could have well sounded off with an exclamation. Were it not for his recurring desire to attain a degree of economic security for himself, Thuenen could have well completed his scheming by recounting the pleasurable experience he had derived from gazing at lines drawn in symmetrical proportion. Were it not for his personal longing to enter upon the threshold of economic stability the inaugurator of economic fictionalism could have well left the literary arena with an invitation to share his aesthetic pleasure.

Since, however, he did not wholly lose sight of the reason for his escapades, since he did not fully forget that his entrancement with a fairyland was born out of the intolerable conditions then prevailing in North German agriculture, the author of "Der Isolierte Staat" did not entirely brush aside the realization that his embracement of fictions was brought about by the dismal outlook of operating a marginal estate. Thuenen remains particularly conscious that he has been confronted with the problems of managing an estate which was not his own. Thuenen is specifically mindful of the complexities involved in the managing of an estate for an absentee owner.

He views, to be sure, his assignment as a test of his loyalty to the grand seigneur. He regards himself as an appointed trustee of the owner. He tries to prove his worth by furnishing a spirited defense of rent collection. The issues involved in rent payments,

8

Thuenen would have it, have been misrepresented. The very concept of rent has been misconceived according to Thuenen. Rent, Thuenen laments, has come to be linked with social exclusiveness.

In the conception of Turgot, Thuenen registers a specific complaint, rent expresses a social privilege. In Smith's conception, Thuenen is ready with another charge, rent appears as a premium for idling. Neither Turgot nor Smith, Thuenen is at hand with a censure, have come to realize that it is not permissible to place rent in a social focus. Neither Turgot nor Smith and his disciples, Thuenen appears miffed, had been aware that it presents an intolerable affront to the rent collector to have rent regarded as but an aspect of social relations. Turgot, as well as Smith and his disciples, Thuenen is bitter, have placed a wholly unjustifiable social onus on the landlord by insisting that rent collections are socially caused.

Rent, Thuenen avers, is a phenomenon of a naturalistic order. The law of nature finds its most adequate expression in rent, the author of "Der Isolierte Staat" alleges. Rent pre-conditions any social relations as much as the surface of the soil in Thuenen's assertion. Rent, Thuenen echoes Quesnay, is to be conceived as being as much of a fruit of the soil as any plant which grows out of the earth.

Rent, Thuenen would like it to be emphasized, is not to be regarded as a reflection of social power. Rent is not to be related to property rights. Distribution of land is not to account for any rent payments. Rent collections, Thuenen insists, are to be presented as if they were rooted in nothing else but fruitfulness. Rent in that case is to be perceived as if it were nothing more than a constituent productive factor. The rent level is, in turn, to be looked upon as but an indicator of nothing else save the degree of productiveness.

Any doubting of the social justification of rent payments, any attempt to throw a social onus on rent collections, is to be out of question in view of the preconceptions Thuenen is instrumental in foisting upon agricultural production. Any attack on the social basis of rent, Thuenen would like to have it inferred, is based on the faulty proposition that human action is capable of altering the workings of the eternal law of nature. Human effort, Thuenen is led to argue, cannot change the intrinsic qualities of the soil of

9

which rent presents an unalterable manifestation. The preconception that rent is essentially productive is inviolate, Thuenen contends.

Even a partial revocation of his all-out claim that rent is essentially productive, is being ruled out of question by Thuenen. The casting of the slightest doubt on the social justification of rent by having some of its aspects declared non-productive, is being condemned by the author of "Der Isolierte Staat." Smith's critical attitude towards some factors of rent collection on the score of unproductiveness, meets as much resentment on the part of Thuenen as Ricardo's all-out attack on the unproductiveness of rent. Smith's demonstration that rent elements other than those which present either a restitution for soil improvement or a recompensation for the erection of agricultural structures, are non-productive and thus antisocial appears as repugnant to Thuenen as Ricardo's exemplification that rent in all its constituent parts tends to become an unproductive expenditure and thus turn into an unjustifiable social burden.

Just because the productivity of the soil is progressively deteriorating, just because the effect of soil cultivation is increasingly decreasing in the wake of stepped up cultivation efforts, rent payments do not turn into a social liability, Thuenen advances a counter argument. In view of the diminishing returns, in view of the growing necessity to cultivate marginal lands, rent collections come to be of increasing social benefit in Thuenen's contention. The elimination or even the reduction of rent would constitute a social evil, Thuenen feels constrained to maintain. With the abolition or even reduction of rent, much of the arable land would remain untilled, Thuenen is led to argue. Without the necessity of furnishing rent payments, extensive cultivation would come to take the place of a hitherto intensive cultivation, Thuenen ventures to guess.

The author of "Der Isolierte Staat" does, to be sure, not care to make quite clear that he is advancing an all out defense of the landlord. He does not specifically deny that there exists a social distinction between the owner and the nonowner of land. He does on the other hand, bring out that the economic benefits derived by the landlord are fully compatible with the economic gains made by the tenant. The tenant, should he be permitted to utter a sound, is to be expected to reaffirm his allegiance to his lord and master. The tenant, should he be allowed to use his voice, is to be expected to express gratitude for the opportunity he is given to manage the lord's estate as if it were his own. The true tenant is to be proud of making it feasible for the landlord to live a detached life. The true tenant is to be overjoyed at the prospect of providing the owner with means for a serene existence. The true tenant is supposed to become increasingly appreciative for having to augment his contribution to the well being of the landlord in view of the increasing scarcity of land. The true tenant is supposed to become increasingly beholden to the landlord for being left to struggle with mounting production difficulties.

In making a case the social desirability of rent, Thuenen accords rent payments the character of patrimonial loyalty tests by making them appear as the expression of an undiluted agrarian paternalism. Thuenen's disregard for the social and economic context within which rent has been analyzed by Smith and Ricardo, is, in turn, coupled with the discounting by the author of "Der Isolierte Staat" of the classicists' approach to having rent related to prices. Smith's disqualification of the intrinsic in prices is being disavowed by Thuenen. Smith's emphasis on an interrelated price analysis is termed unacceptable by the author of "Der Isolierte Staat." Smith's inference that rent presents but an effect of pricing is being flatly rejected by Thuenen. Smith's demonstration of how the level of agricultural prices is affecting the rate of rent is labeled unconvincing.

Ricardo's followup of Smith's observations on the increasing difficulty of meeting rent payments from marginal lands is branded as unfounded. The necessity for a progressive economic unburdening of the utilizer of the land, the underlying motivation of Ricardo's reasoning, is being violently opposed by Thuenen. The author of "Der Isolierte Staat" wants it to be accepted as a paramount dictum that agricultural prices are of necessity to guarantee rent payments for all arable land. It is to be regarded as an unalterable tenet that mounting agro-technical difficulties are bound to furnish added reassurance for rent claims. The pricing of the agricultural products derived from marginal lands, Thuenen would

11

like to have it particularly noticed, cannot but serve as a means of extending rental claims to hitherto neglected agricultural areas.

Everybody else but the landlord is to be made to bear the burden from rising prices, were Thuenen's approach to rent and prices to be sustained. Everybody else but the landlord is to be made to bear the mounting production costs, were Thuenen's price formulation to be upheld. Thuenen somehow finds it necessary to apologize, the superimposition of rent on the price structure, he pleads, is not to be taken as constituting an undue hardship for those who are not themselves landlords. The landlord Thuenen feels constrained to insist, does not owe his social standing to marketing arrangements. The economic share of the landlord cannot be considered as being essentially derived from the exchange of goods in Thuenen's assertion. The owner of a landed estate, Thuenen maintains, can well eschew an all out participation in money deals. The landed owner, Thuenen would like to have it inferred, can well afford to have the fury of marketing pressures hit somebody who is not a landlord.

The landed owner is not fully dependent for his income upon a scramble for pecuniary rewards in Thuenen's presumption. The landlord according to that presumption, is free to act as if a goodly part of his economic needs are met by tributary offerings. The landed gentry – again on the strength of the stated presumption, – is to be at liberty to operate its estates, as if no substantial inroads have ever been made on the basis of self sufficiency, to re-intone Thuenen's most favored motif.

Marketing, as far as it cannot be avoided, Thuenen has a secondary device ready, is supposed to be conducted with particular consideration of the privileged position of the landlord in agriculture. Exchange transactions, as long as they have to be undertaken, have to be centered around the estate. No trading is to be given any prominence, unless it is directed towards the promotion of the interests of the foremost agriculturist. No exchange deal is to be granted any import unless it is intended to uphold the social aspirations of the landed proprietor. All money deals, Thuenen brings in another aspect of exchange transactions, are supposed to revolve around agricultural produce. Expansion and contraction of monetary transactions are supposed to fall completely in line with a

12

respective increase and decrease in agricultural production. The amount of money in circulation, Thuenen would have it, is to be viewed as reflecting nothing else but the available supply of agricultural products.

In reverting to his most favored theme, Thuenen takes pains to caution that no matter how much an exchange deal should benefit the owner of a landed estate, an exchange can rate but as a forced compromise. Any money deal in particular, no matter how much the landlord might profit from it, is to be considered as but a temporary deviation. The purity of the selfsufficiency principle, Thuenen would like to make it sure, is not supposed to be affected in any basic form by any succumbing of the landed proprietor to acquisitive practices.

In redesigning the essential features of a self containing patrimony, – to move a point further in Thuenen's scheme, – the author of "Der Isolierte Staat" sees to it that the town comes to be included within the agricultural orbit. Thuenen makes sure that the town economy, he devises, does not have any specific urban features. Town production, in Thuenen's design, is predetermined by the needs of agriculture. All town products are in Thuenen's scheme, made to order for rural customers. Urban enterprises come to look as if they were designated to no other purpose than the supplementing of agricultural production implements and the augmentation of rural consumption. Urban production units are made to appear as if they were nothing else but annexes of rural home production establishments.

Thuenen is not willing to admit that the productive activity in the town might not be wholly dependent upon agriculture. He is unwilling to take cognizance that organized craftsmanship had quite successfully contested the social predominance of the landlord. The historical records of the jealous selfrule of townships, exercised by associations of master craftsmen, are left unheeded by Thuenen. The realization that the establishment of shops of master craftsmen, within town limits, forms the markstone of urban economic autonomy, has obviously not caught up with Thuenen. Thuenen's conception presumes that the craftsmen have not yet settled down. Thuenen's scheme supposes that craftsmen are still performing their work in an ambulatory fashion. In Thuenen's pre-

13

sumption, the craftsman is yet wandering from one country seat to another where he performs his work on the premises of those who place work orders with him.

Back of Thuenen's scheme, lies the presupposition of a socially submissive craftsman. In Thuenen's presupposition, the patrimonial landlord exercises an overall social rule. In Thuenen's fictitious proposition, a benevolent grand seigneur towers over the solicitous craftsman. The master servant relation which is supposed to govern the cultivation of the soil, is supposed to find its extension in the patriarchal frame drawn for all manual labor. Labor is not supposed to be performed to escape dire need. Work is not supposed to be undertaken to save oneself from starvation. Work, Thuenen would have it, is being done for the sake of proving one's loyalties. One is engaging in work in order to demonstrate one's social attachment.

In indulging in a nostalgia for a patriarchal revival, Thuenen tries his best to evade the issue of an agreed upon wage. The reward for labor, Thuenen makes it appear, does not reflect a relation between a hirer and the hired. The laborer, it would seem, is free to act as if he were his own employer. Nothing appears to stand in the way of the laborer who undertakes to compensate himself out of the fruits of his own work. The share of the laborer seems to grow in direct proportion with his exertion. The economic gain of the worker, Thuenen is eager to stress, can never amount to less, than the productive gains attained through the laborer's effort. It is not to be regarded as being customary to have wages paid out in money, Thuenen strikes a neo-romantic chord. The form of labor reward has little, if any relation, to the factor of exchange in Thuenen's conception. As a rule, Thuenen would have the laborer to be compensating himself by withholding part of the product in the effecting of which he the laborer has been instrumental.

Hard work, Thuenen remorsefully observes, might by itself not insure the laborer against privations. Even diligence, coupled with temperance, might not prove sufficient to save the laborer from abject poverty. Only continuous abstinence offers a promise of an ampler reward, according to Thuenen. Only the hoarding of the products the consumption of which the laborer is willing to deny

14

himself at present, Thuenen brings the selfsufficiency angle to bear, is apt to save the worker from the threat of starvation.

Should a distinction be made in regard to the social and economic conditions of labor conducted under a shelter and labor performed under the sky, such distinction could only be commensurate with the degree of loyalty expressed by the respective kind of labor. Should non-agricultural and agricultural labor be considered to differ in their social and economic aspects, such difference could only be viewed as an expression of comparatively less or more social attachment. Comparatively greater willingness of selfsacrifice on the part of the relatively immobile agricultural worker, can be ascribed to a greater awe with which workers in the field are imbued, Thuenen has little doubt. Working in full view of the glorified seat of patrimonial power, the worker in the field is to be expected to express readiness to vie with the worker in the town shop for the limit of privations which either of the two would be willing to endure. Neither the laborer conducting his work under the shelter, nor the worker performing his task under the sky, are supposed to be in any way concerned with the question of ownership. Ascertainment of who owns the tools or who has taken possession of the soil, is not to be considered as having any influence, whatsoever, on the fundamental attitude of either of the two sections of labor. Hence, neither of the two labor groups could ever be led to ask the question who owns the means of production and why. Neither the agricultural nor the nonagricultural labor group could be ever made to discern the web of social relations within which they are caught, Thuenen is fairly certain.

For once, Thuenen appears to be sure, the worker could not possibly relate his social position to the standing of those with whom he has no direct personal contact. It should be considered inconceivable for the worker to have a grievance against anybody else but the supervisor in the shop or the overseer in the field. Hence there should be little difficulty in settling grievances. Should the managing representative of the owner be able to make the worker feel that he is not working hard enough, and is asking too much in return, any conceivable social tension could be made to abate without much further ado, Thuenen appears to be quite certain.

15

The placing of productive labor within the fold of the visionary scheme, makes Thuenen's illusion of self-containment come to run its full course. In trying to make sure that the tranquility of the landed estate is not to be disturbed by any noise which could possibly have its origin in wage bargaining, Thuenen makes a supreme bid for having social and economic serenity radiate from a self-sufficient estate without any social and economic interference. The author of "Der Isolierte Staat" guards himself with particular care against having his harmonious scheme mared by any disagreements which could conceivably arise out of a realistic appraisal of the question of labor reward.

While he might permit a ray of reality to simmer through his portrayal of the estate owner, there is not an ember of realism left in Thuenen's characterization of the laborer. While he does not have his conceptualization of rent and prices wholly removed from the exchange nexus, not the slightest trace of the marketing phenomenon can be found in Thuenen's conceptual approach to wages. As far as the social and economic reservation is concerned, to which the landlord is being confined, a slight piercing of the selfsufficiency ring is not wholly unfeasible. Such feasibility lends itself to an interpretation – Thuenen no matter how half-hearted, was constrained to admit, – that a communication with the real world on the part of the landlord cannot be wholly avoided. As to the social and economic range in which the propertyless worker is made to operate in Thuenen's scheme, the author of "Der Isolierte Staat" has given no indication that he would be willing to consider a release of the laborer from the bonds of selfcontainment, no matter how temporary and limited such a release would come to be. There is not a hint contained in Thuenen's literary offering that work can be compensated by means other than self-reward.

CHAPTER 2

DECONCEPTUALIZATION

As against Thuenen's open admission that he is presenting fictions, Thuenen's theoretical counterpart claims he is offering a realistic proposition. As against the unabashed boasting of the author of "Der Isolierte Staat" that he is evolving an escape technique into an unreal world, Menger claims he is concerned with the encompassing of the real. Realities to be sure of a special kind, are brought into picture, by Menger. The author of what are presumed to be realistic "Principles" does not find anything objectionable in an unqualified acceptance of prima facie views. He does not consider that a disregard for any and all rules of reasoning, might clear the way for fallacies.

It is obvious, Menger opens up, that things, the material quality of which makes them suitable for the satisfaction of human wants, deserve the name of utilities. It should be likewise self-evident, that it is the very personal impression which an object makes upon an individual, that merits the signification of that object as a good. It is the objectivity and materiality to which utility refers, Menger presumes, which foredooms the term of utility to insignificance. The immateriality and spirituality which comes to the fore in the designation of a good, the author of "Principles" supposes, predetermines the signification of the denotation of a good. The attribution of objectivity and materiality, Menger would have it, makes it imperative to deprive a term to which those attributes refer of any particular meaning. The ascribing of immateriality and spirituality to any denotation is, in turn, to call for an assigning to that term of an overriding meaning.

Goods, Menger spells it out, are not to be referred to as such, on the basis of the qualities they possess, but on the basis of what one thinks those qualities are supposed to be. Goods are to merit signification as such, not on account of the effects they cause, but on account of what one thinks those effects should be. One could possibly ascribe to a good, Menger is ready to admit, a quality it does not possess. One could in turn predicate an effect the good cannot possibly have. Once the individual himself and only the individual is made the sole judge of the reality of his expressions, the criterion which holds the imaginary apart from the non-imaginary in the expression of human views, comes to be lost, Menger is willing to concede. Observations of the existent as expressed in science and presentations of the nonexistent as expressed in fiction, come to be indistinguishable. Even a differentiation between an expression of a demented mind and an expression of a generally sane person, becomes well nigh impossible, if only subjective judgments are to be heeded.

Menger's admission that he is trying to make a case for an almost complete identification of object and subject, does not deter him from insisting he is presenting unequivocal formulations. His conceding, that he is bent on being instrumental in all but merging the preceding and succeeding in human comprehension, does not appear to interfere in any way with his claim that he is laying down uniform principles. Nor does his admitted realization that he is obscuring the approaches to conceptualization, keep Menger from asserting that his presentation is keyed to a most undisguised form of causation.

Causation, to be sure, refers to personal anticipations in the view expressed by Menger. Causative links come to relate but personal expectations. Menger insists, nevertheless, that his brand of subjectified causation is not to be known by the name of imputation. There is to be no admitted distinction between objective and subjective correlation, if Menger can help it.

His approach to causation, Menger tries to explain, requires the assigning of a supreme causal factor to a personal inclination, to regard a good of having the attribute for meeting of one's more or less immediate wants. A like causal consequence is, in turn, to be attributed to a personal disposition to ascribe to a good the quality of satisfying one's more or less remote individual desires.

When he is called upon, however, to exemplify his approach, he shifts from the sphere of causation to the subject of classification. Without either an explanation or an apology, Menger proceeds to treat classification as identical with causation.

His classification of goods for instant consumption as goods of the first order and of goods for less immediate consumption, as goods of the second, third, fourth, and multiple orders, Menger parades as a patent case of causative sequence. His labeling of a good desired for instant consumption as a good of a lower order as contrasted with his terming of a good which is not being desired for instantaneous consumption, as a good of a higher order, Menger offers as a model demonstration of comparative causal efficacy. Causal correlation comes to be referred to as a sequence of labels. Causal efficacy comes to indicate an efficient form of tagging.

Menger, it should be noticed in this context, does not recognize any material production factors. He does not, moreover, abide by a conceptual distinction between production material, means of production, and finished product. In addition, the author of "Principles" does not care to differentiate between human and non-human production elements. When he comes to deal with the production process, he makes but a nominalistic reference to it. When he undertakes to project his brand of causation into the production sphere, he does little more than disqualify the specific social and economic attributes of the production process in order to fit the subject of effectuation of goods into his nominalistic scheme.

The subject of production of goods when it emerges from Menger's presentation, appears in the form of tagging and retagging of goods. Goods tagged with one number come to be slated for a retagging with another number. Goods which have been tagged with a comparatively high number, Menger insists, cause the effectuation of goods which are to be tagged with a successive lower number. Goods which have been tagged as goods of the fifth order, Menger tries to exemplify, cause the effectuation of goods which come to be tagged as goods of the fourth order. Goods which have been tagged as goods of the fourth order, Menger continues

19

his exemplification, cause, in turn, the effectuation of goods which are to be tagged as goods of the third order.

Causation in the stated exemplification, can hardly be interpreted as causing production, it is a causing to label which Menger's formulation comes to mean. The causal sequence in the proffered exemplification, contains no meaningful reference to a causal sequence in production, it is a causal sequence in labeling which Menger is actually bringing out. The formulation in which Menger presents goods of comparatively higher orders as causing the effectuation of goods of successively lower orders, but reemphasizes his identification of causation with classification. His ascribing of the successive effectuation of goods of the lowest order, to the prevailing desire to have nonconsumable goods turn into consumable goods, does not concern itself with any property whatsoever, the consumable or nonconsumable goods might actually have. It but reiterates the presumption of the author of the new kind of "Principles", that individual wishes in regard to goods can be rated as their qualities. Hence, his entire scheme of effectuation of labeling which he proffers under the name of the effectuation of goods, can well be explained as being prompted by his leading motive to avoid the granting to production of any specific relevance.

The how of the effectuation of goods, it is easy to notice, is not accorded much attention by Menger. What actually takes place when a certain kind of good transforms itself into a good of another kind, Menger does not care to elaborate in any exact manner. Nor is he willing to state anything specific in regard to the quantities which are involved in the qualitative changes which are brought about by production.

A thrown in sentence stating that for the effectuation of goods one requires a proper qualitative and quantitative correlation, is to furnish all the light which Menger is willing to turn on production factors, at this stage of his presentation. The assertion that a proper quality and an appropriate quantity of goods which are tagged by a certain number unreservedly assure a proper quality and an appropriate quantity of goods, is to provide all the explanation of production procedures which Menger is prepared to provide at this turn of his literary offering. Any further inquiry into qualitative and quantitative aspects of production is being blocked at

20

this juncture through the erection of an added terminological fence.

A new tag is to prevent any extension of a production analysis. Any uncalled for inquisitiveness into the constitutional elements of production, is to be held off with the assistance of a catchall term. The quality and quantity of sundry goods of a comparatively higher nomenclature which are supposed to effectuate a good of a comparatively lower nomenclature, are to receive the added tag of compensatory goods. The term compensatory goods can thus be made to cover any conceivable specification of the material content of production and any feasible concretization of a technical production device.

In continuing his nominalistic game, Menger makes sure the time element involved in production is denied any specific signification. Although he does not dispute that time does play a part in the effectuation of goods by goods, he is in no way inclined to treat the category of time as expression of exactness. In Menger's proclamation, the run of time is something undeterminable, as far as the process of production is concerned. Nothing more than the realization that time is neither finite nor infinite is to be regarded knowable about the time category. As for periods of time and in particular, time periods, as referred to a production process, nothing more is to be held as ever to become knowable, than the ascertainment that any production period is longer than an instant and somewhat shorter than eternity.

Objective factors cannot be permitted to account for anything approaching definiteness in the determination of time, according to Menger. Time is supposed to reflect nothing but individual preferences. Time is to relate but individual wants and personal desires.

Individual wants and personal desires, Menger emphasizes, are not to be brought into any recognizable correlation with time elements. Individual wants and personal desires are not supposed to contain any specific reference to the past. All individual wants and personal desires are to be considered as being keyed to the present. The individual bent on the satisfaction of his wants and desires, is being portrayed by Menger, as being exclusively concerned with the ascertainment of his current needs. The ascertainment of a person's current needs is, in turn, being presented by the author of the new kind of "Principles" as being undertaken by that person under the constraint of satisfying those needs out of a strictly limited supply. The ascertainment of a person's current needs cannot extend to any other correlation, Menger wants to make it doubly sure, than the correlation of a supply of goods which in the view of the assaying individual are presently available to him.

The individual who is engaged in relating his current needs to goods he considers are presently available to him for the satisfaction of those needs, is not supposed to permit himself to look into any related problems. Mindful that he is constrained to ascertain his current needs within the framework of supplies which are currently available to him, the individual is not to let his imagination wander; he is not to concern himself with the problem of the generation of goods, nor with the issue of appropriation of goods, in strict compliance with the schematic directive issued by Menger.

Menger's stricture places a particular onus on the problem of production of goods which can hardly be clarified without referring to a production which has taken place in the past. Under no circumstances is the individual who becomes engaged in the assessment of his current needs in relation to supplies, which in his view are at present available to him, to permit himself to gain a conscious realization of the subject of production of goods. The subject matter of replenishment is not supposed to exist for an individual who comes to occupy himself with the strictly limited task of assaying his current needs in relation to what appears to him as his current supplies. Nor for that matter, can the subject of acquisition of goods ever to be allowed to register with a person who is under strict orders not to realize anything but his personal wants and desires in relation to some consumable stockpile which he considers within his reach.

An individual who becomes preoccupied with the ascertaining of his current needs within the framework of supplies which appear currently available to him, Menger wants to make it sure, is to behave as a person whose whole imagination is taken up with a visualization of a ready made table. Such an individual is to act as a householder who seizes upon supplies coming to him from nowhere. Nor is any person who becomes engaged in the ascertain-

22

ment of his current needs to take stock of the future in any specific form. The individual who becomes engaged in ascertaining his current needs within the framework of what he considers are his presently available supplies, is to be disdainful of the prospect of coming to know anything in regard to the material and objective factors which could possibly account for a production of goods in the future. The stated individual is to be solely concerned with the disposition he would be willing to make at present in anticipation of imaginary future supplies which he expects to seize. The question how those imaginary future supplies are to be realized, as well as the question on the strength of what he, the individual, is supposed to seize the yet unrealized supplies, is to be considered as illegitimate as the question of how presently available supplies have come into being and on the strength of what social and economic consideration those supplies are being or have been seized.

The illusion created by the vision of an everreadied table is supposed to envelop considerations which refer to the future along with considerations which relate to the past. Under the cloud of the notion of coming from nowhere the future is to become as undiscernible as the past. The individual who preoccupies himself with the ascertaining of his current needs within the framework of what appears to him as presently available with reference to supplies, appears imbued with the disposition to deprecate his future needs in the further evolvement of Menger's scheme. The individual who submits to Menger's strictures is expected to express willingness to forego any part of what he regards as his future allotment, could that part be used for augmenting what he is disposed to view as the allotment at present available to him.

The individual who is guided by Menger's evaluation scheme is supposed to act as if he lives solely in the present. He is to conduct himself, as if nothing which is specifically related to the past affects him. He is, moreover, to behave as if he cares very little, how he shall fare in the future—he is to approach his personal evaluation of his needs and supplies, as if he were living but for the day.

Values which are being accorded to goods by persons to whom those goods appear as being subject to their personal disposition,

Menger is ready with another amplification, are likely to fluctuate from person to person as well as from good to good. One person might express preference for a bottle of champagne, another person might be inclined to favor a loaf of bread. There should be no question that any objectively conceived social and economic conditions could have any influence in the stated variations in personal evaluation. The only conditioning factor which is to merit consideration is to be identified as personal apprehensiveness.

Any single evaluator is being placed by Menger under the pressure of an underlying tension. The tension is supposed to express itself in an unyielding fear.

The disposition of goods which the individual considers are presently available to him, is supposed to be permeated by fear. Fear, he might not be able to hold on to the whole amount of what he considers is currently available for his consumption, is supposed to be as prevalent among those who try to apply Menger's evaluation scheme, as fear of being denied the consumption of any number of particles of which the whole amount appears to consist.

Fear of short supply, fear of the prevalence of scarcity, is supposed to be particularly manifest. Such fear Menger is willing to concede, is not to have any direct relation to anything real. Such fear, as the one which is expected to prevail among those who are engaged in evaluating their current needs, is not even to have any necessary relation to the actual amount or the concrete quality of a good which a person considers as being readied for his individual consumption.

Nonetheless, fear on the part of any individual evaluator, is to rate as the indispensable factor in the signification of an economic good. Should the underlying fear be permitted to vanish, should the fear of privation to be declared untenable; should the threat of short supply to be prevented from holding sway over the imagination of the individual, economic values will cease to exist, Menger ventures to predict. Should bountifulness and abundance be allowed to play a preponderant part in the personal expectations of the individual evaluator, Menger does not undertake to deny, it would become impossible for the individual evaluator to continue to pretend that he cannot conduct an economic evaluation under any other circumstances, than by closing himself in with some unrenewable supply.

The subject of economic value cannot be considered as concerning itself with anything else but unspecifiable anticipations of individual satisfaction, Menger continues to insist. It is to be held as being of no essence to relate anything definite about the way the means of satisfaction are being generated. The material to be used as well as the technique, applied in the effectuation of means of satisfaction, Menger wants to have largely discounted. The chemical as well as the physical processes which are taking place in production, are to be fully disregarded. Only the changing of hands as it applies to production instruments, is to merit some attention. Only to the outer form in which production instruments come to be available for personal use, Menger appears to be willing to grant some relevance.

In treating the recompense which accompanies the taking of turns in the use of equipment, Menger turns it into a borrowing charge. The rental charge, however, as strange as it might seem, is not supposed to be referrable to the owner. The rental charge which secures the use of the equipment, is supposed to be due to some unidentifiable property holder. The rather odd rental charge is supposed to be supplementable by another fee. A fee for the privilege of exercising a kind of trusteeship is supposed to be due in addition to the rental charge. The trusteeship fee is to insure a proper management of the equipment on the part of the entrusted individual who, for all appearances, is drawing that equipment from a common pool.

Both, the rental charge as well as the trusteeship fee, are to be chargeable to the subjective value which is supposed to accrue to the individual by virtue of his having secured the temporary use of the equipment. Both charges are to be considered deductible from the personalized value which the individual comes to be inclined to ascribe to the goods effected by the borrowed production implements. The charging and paying of the rental charge and the added trusteeship fee comes to take a form in which the individual user of the equipment attempts to square accounts with himself.

The rental charge and the trusteeship fee, Menger would like to leave the impression, refer but nominally to an appropriation in advance of use. The rental and the trusteeship fee, Menger would like it to seem, accrue not by virtue of ownership, but by virtue of usage. Menger studiously avoids the linking of primary appropriation with ownership. He prefers to refer to primary appropriation as income division. In avoiding to take a stand on the social and economic implications of ownership, Menger deprives the individual who uses the equipment which is not his own, of any socially and economically relevant criterion for making a distinction between what he owes and what he owns. To an individual who is denied knowledge of property distribution, rental charges and trusteeship fee can hardly appear explainable in any definite social and economic form. Such individual can well come to regard rental charges for the use of equipment which he does not own as one set of intangibles which he is supposed to deduct from another set of intangibles, as Menger expects him to do.

The source of a personal income is in Menger's contention of no relevance. Whether the source of a personal income is a productive or an unproductive one, is of no import, Menger insists. It is a matter of indifference whether income is derived from an amusement park or an establishment which produces daily necessities, the selfprofessed reformulator of "Principles" would have it. Nor is it to matter, whether income is being generated in industry or agriculture. Since anybody is supposed to presume that productive instruments are as freely available to him as to somebody else for temporary use, since anybody is to presuppose that any productive instrumentality, whether it is land or a mechanical implement, is readily available to him for taking turns in its operation with somebody else, only the subject of rental charges can have any bearing on the question of the origin of economic gains. The observation that rental conditions predetermine all social economic relations, should the individual acknowledge it at all, is not to be taken as his, the individual's, acknowledgement that rent presents a manifestation of a social privilege, Menger would like to make it sure. Rent, Menger reiterates, is not to represent a fee claimed by the owner. The payment of rent, Menger likes to be considered as an expression of appreciation on the part of an individual for the advantages he derives from having either land or mechanical equipment made available to him for his temporary use. Rent, in this formulation, comes to be rated as a manifestation of social solidarity.

The subjectification of the rent category, Menger proclaims, has rendered the rent controversy pointless. The entire range of questions in regard to rent which had been raised by Ricardo, has come to be ruled out of order by the author of the new kind of "Principles." What significance can there be accorded to the distinction of the social and economic factors which underlie agricultural and industrial production when rent comes to rate as an expression of individual appreciation, Menger is led to ask a rhetorical question. The social and economic aspects of the nonreproducibility of the land and the reproducibility of machines can hardly merit any signification, after rent is accorded the role of manifesting individual gratitude, Menger feels justified to explain. The social and economic immobility of the soil and the mobility of the mechanical equipment can hardly be made to count as such when rent rates come to be linked to personal inclinations, Menger has reason to conclude.

All objective factors of production, as far as the accruing of income is concerned, are to be discounted, Menger reinforces his stand. The impact of material elements in production are to be overridden, by making personal likes and dislikes assume a major importance. The bearing of raw material and technical devices is to be played down, to let personal preferences appear preponderant. Only individual anticipations are to merit attention. Only such expectations which are not related to existing goods are to be given special consideration. Only imaginary satisfactions are to be permitted to rate as formative elements in the accruing of income.

The distinction between income categories is to be regarded as but a nominal one, Menger continues. The citing of specific income concepts, should not be taken as indication that each of those concepts has a meaning of its own. The retention of rent as a separate income category, Menger cites an instance, is not to be taken as an indication that the concept of rent has retained a specific meaning. Income from agriculture is to be regarded as conceptually unspecifiable as income from industry, Menger is at pains to stress. Since income from agriculture cannot be considered as being in any way differently derived than income in industry, Menger wants it to be emphasized, none of the two income spheres can assume any significance of its own within the formulation proffered in the "Principles." Since, moreover, income from industry and income from agriculture are meant to express but an individual's fancy, to fill Menger in on Menger, it but indicates that income in its most general form is devoid of any socially or economically specifiable meaning. With the subject of income formation to be turned over to the imagination of any given individual, the income category can hardly continue to encompass something which is realizable. Rent, in the terminological context proffered by Menger, comes to indicate as unrealized and unrealizable an income as are the forms of incomes which are referred to by the categories of profit, interest and wages.

The category of wages, Menger finds it opportune to forewarn, is most susceptible to what he, Menger, considers to be a misleading interpretation. In order to have wages express something unrealized and unrealizable, it is requisite to abstain from viewing wages as a compensation for an expended effort. It is further necessary to have the comprehension of wages detached from any possible link with production expenditures. The physical requirements of the laborer are, further on, to be prevented from accounting in any way for the wage level. Wages are to be considered as being as unrelated to the needs of bare existence as any other income form. As any other form of income, wages are to express nothing else but personal expectations. As any other form of income, wages are to be expressive of nothing more than personal anticipations. Along with rent, interest and profit, wages are to be regarded as an expression of imaginary satisfactions and dissatisfactions which have no direct relation to any existing goods.

In having all income forms presented as nothing but a reflection of individual likes and dislikes, Menger feels sure he has precluded any social delineation of the flow of income. In having emotional disposition elevated to the position of an overriding income determinant, Menger is confident he has placed the factor of social division of income within the realm of the unthinkable. How could any kind of income division be sustained, should the play of personal emotions be held to account for economic gains,

Menger is led to ask another oratorical question. If variations of income levels are to be considered linkable to nothing else but personal emotional curves, what significance could there be accorded to other income factors? If all income rates are to be regarded as expressive of nothing more than the tension of personal emotional stresses, what, if any distinction, could there be made between income in the sphere of production and income in the sphere of exchange, Menger pleases himself in asking. Since formation of all income is to be regarded as being explainable in no other terms than the ones of personal likes and dislikes, should not all spheres of income be regarded as being fully analyzable in terms of personal anticipations.

Isn't it perfectly logical to have economic values generated in production, as well as economic values generated in exchange, represented as but an indication of a personal emotional reaction, Menger begs the question,—if all economic valuation is to be treated as but a form of a play of personal emotions.

A person becomes emotionally preconditioned for an exchange deal, Menger proffers a demonstration in lieu of an explanation, when the pain anticipated from yielding an expected satisfaction is being more than compensated by the joy anticipated from another expected satisfaction. Should another person come to feel the same way about his disposition to yield one expected satisfaction for another anticipated satisfaction which he expects to derive, the preconditioning for an exchange transaction is to be considered as having taken a full turn.

The exact assessment of the emotions, which condition the individual for the exchange act, should not present any great difficulties, Menger sounds hopeful. Any person who ponders upon a possible loss of a satisfaction becomes initially dejected; subsequently, in view of a prospective substitution for the sense of anticipated privation, the same person can be found to become elated as the record shows, Menger states in a matter of course manner.

The author of the new kind of "Principles" does not regard it appropriate to take it into consideration that emotions and in particular individual emotions are as unpredictable, as they are elusive. In spite of the highly presumptive conjecture of his observation on the emotional preconditioning of exchange, Menger does not shrink from the offer to demonstrate a respective exactness. He appears to be convinced, or at least he would like to sound convincing, when he insists that the exactness which can be attained in the measurement of a pain which a person imagines he will suffer, in anticipation of a dissatisfaction, and a respective comparative measurement of the overenjoyment, to which a person presumes he will be given, in expectation of a compensatory satisfaction, leaves nothing to be desired. By declaring that the pain which a person imagines he will suffer in anticipation of a dissatisfaction is to be regarded as fully measurable, as the overenjoyment of the person who presumes he can expect a compensatory satisfaction, Menger considers he has laid the ground for establishing comparative standards of measuring personal emotions. Menger does not consider that his assertion that the emotional self-conditioning of a person who is confronted with the prospect of depriving himself of a satisfaction he would derive from drinking champagne in anticipation of a greater enjoyment he could experience by consuming liquor is as fully ascertainable as the emotional self-conditioning of an individual who is confronted with the prospect of depriving himself of the pleasure he would derive from drinking liquor in expectatiion of an overenjoyment he could experience by drinking champagne, is open to the interpretation that, as far as an exact measurement is concerned, the self-conditioning in the one hypothetical case presented by Menger is as unattainable as the reverse case which he hypothesizes.

Although Menger insists that, given the relative quantity of champagne and liquor bottles, placed at the disposal of two individuals, the point at which each of the two persons will consider himself emotionally preconditioned to trade one kind of alcoholic drink for another, can be clearly determined, the author of the new kind of "Principles" does not offer any kind of proof to that effect. Proof, if attempted, would have to be based on the presumption of a person who gets to such extent caught between two conflicting emotions, as to become completely devoid of any other aspirations or interests. Even if such total isolation of an emotionally constrained individual could be conceived, Menger would have to prove, that the emotional reaction of two such individuals caught in the web of their conflicting emotions is to be precisely the same. Without such proof, anything that the author of the new kind of "Principles" says further about interpersonal exchange, cannot be considered as constituting any kind of explanation.

His subsequent observation, that as long as two individuals continue to consider themselves as being emotionally preconditioned for the indulging in an exchange deal, the pendulum which records their emotional reaction will continue to swing, most obviously avoids giving any answer to the question as to the how and why in regard to the generation of the selfconditioning by the two individuals which are supposed to become engaged in an exchange transaction. Menger's followup statement that as soon as any of the individual parties to the trading act comes to lose his specific emotional stimulus, the emotional transaction is bound to cease and that in consequence the emotional recording curve will, of necessity, flatten out, but reemphasizes Menger's unwillingness to offer any further clarification in regard to the factors which stand back of the personal emotional selfconditioning.

Menger has just the opposite of any social and economic clarification in mind, when, in his subsequent contention, he asserts that the amplitude of the emotional reaction of any individual has no direct relation to any material quality. This contention is intended to block any reopening of the question, what wider social and economic issues could be held responsible for bringing about individual emotional reactions.

Menger's proclamation that the emotional response to a perspective exchange of daily necessities cannot be considered as differing in any particular way from the emotional reaction to a suggested deal in luxuries, is based on the same unproven and, for all intent and purposes, unprovable presumption as the just proffered example which was supposed to relate the exchange of champagne and liquor between two persons. Menger himself but underscores his desire to remain in the sphere of unproven and unprovable presumptions by declaring that the prospect of trading corn for cows has to be regarded as having the same emotional effect on the trading individuals as the prospect of exchanging champagne for liquor. In some way, Menger gives himself away in this latest declaration; the socially insensitive individual with

31

which Menger presumes to deal can hardly be expected to possess any criterion for distinguishing daily necessities from luxuries, nor, for that matter, it can be pointed out to the author of the new kind of "Principles", can such socially isolated person to whom he, Menger, refers, to be able to give an account to himself of what makes for a similarity and what for a difference in any range of goods. Menger's individual who is supposed to undertake an exchange transaction in complete disregard of any social aspirations and economic interests of either himself or other individuals, can most certainly not be expected to become cognizant of what constitutes the economic difference between corn and cows or champagne and liquor; even the possibility of such differentiation in any social and economic sense, is not supposed to occur to the hermetically shut off human being.

Menger is at least consistent when he goes on stressing that the emotional urge to trade is a highly personal affair.

He remains at least true to himself when he undertakes to bar time from any meaningful relation with a trading act.

Menger could hardly elicit any surprise from those who have become aware of his bent for obfuscation, by his direction to brand any attempt to introduce nonpersonal factors into a trading analysis, as an uncalled for invasion of the individual trader's privacy.

Whether trading occurs in one period of time or another, is not to be asked, Menger would like to make it sure.

The question of whether a recorded trading act refers to the immediate or the more distant past is not to merit attention.

Nor is it to be considered of any import to ascertain whether the recording of a trading act pertains to the present.

Nor is it to be of any concern whether the record of trading is to be referable to either the immediate or the more distant future.

Any question pertaining to the time element in the comprehension of trading is to be brushed off with a reference to the instantaneousness of the trading act, on Menger's specific advice.

In barring distinctive time elements from the comprehension of recorded trading, Menger but climbs down to the conceptual level of a socially blinded individual, the fictitious image of which permeates his entire argumentation.

A person who is supposed to cater to nothing else but his most primitive desires, Menger's exposition makes it clear, can hardly be considered capable of making any socially and economically relevant distinctions between a past, a present and a future.

Along with his attack on the social and economic signification of time sequence goes Menger's drive against a socially and economically meaningful presentation of special distinctions as far as trading is concerned.

It should not be considered requisite to ask whether trading has been conducted within one social range or another, Menger would have it.

The question of whether the exchange act takes place within the range of a single village or whether the exchange deal transpires between two villages, Menger wants to be termed as irrelevant as the question, whether a trading deal involves a transaction between a village and a town.

It is further to be ruled as being of no essence, Menger insists, to record whether trading is taking place on a national or international scale.

In rooting for a know-nothing in regard to social and economic distance, Menger again descends to the level of the socially and economically castrated individual, the fictitious image of which permeates his reasoning.

If the fiction of a socially and economically emasculated person is to be sustained, to retrace Menger's line of argumentation, that fictitious individual whom Menger has invented, has logically to be excused from making a distinction between different social and economic ranges: the supposedly socially and economically emasculated individual has even to be absolved from ever realizing that such a phenomenon as social and economic distance exists, to suit Menger's fancy.

His disqualification of social and economic relevance of time and space, to restate Menger's nominalistic reasoning, is fully in keeping with his untiring effort to personalize the meaning of exchange.

The kind of timing and spacing he is willing to permit to come to the fore in trading, Menger does not mind to restress it, can hardly come to refer to anything which extends beyond the range of the factor of intensification of a personal emotional preconditioning to trade.

The kind of time and space conception with reference to an exchange deal, he is prepared to acknowledge, Menger spells it out, is not supposed to encompass more than a multiplication of the acts of exchange in terms of emotionally predisposed personal trading preferences.

The impetus to exchange, there should not be any doubt about it, is being conceived by Menger as a purely emotional urge.

Menger's individual who indulges in exchange is supposed to be motivated by an exclusive desire for emotional compensation.

To link the exchange stimulus to a desire for economic gains is not to be considered proper, according to Menger. To relate in particular the exchange deal to profit making is being ruled out of order by Menger.

Any material benefit which might accompany a trading deal is not to be regarded as being attributable to the factor of personal interchange, on the direction of Menger.

No acquisitive design should be imputed to the trading parties, Menger wants to make it sure.

The desire of material aggrandizement, Menger raises his voice, is to be viewed as being far removed from the persons engaged in an exchange act.

The parties to the exchange act are to be viewed, Menger's voice becomes shrill, as being fully immune to the temptations presented by the existence of a market.

The trading parties are to be viewed, Menger's voice is still on a high pitch, as being determined to seek nothing but the satisfaction of their most immediate wants.

Should any marketing gains to be made in the course of the exchange act, Menger moves a nonacquisitive fiction into position, they are to be listed as if they were expenses.

Should any profits accrue from an exchange transaction, Menger takes a leaf from Thuenen's book, they are to be dealt with as if they fall within the range of transportation expenditures.

The individual traders themselves are presented by Menger as frowning on any pecuniary deal.

The immediate parties to the exchange transaction are pictured by Menger as being so unpecuniary minded as to resent even the taking of a hand in drawing up expense accounts.

The setting up of expense accounts on the part of an individual trader, Menger is obviously fearsome, could conceivably lead to an interpretation that the kind of trading person which he, Menger, espouses in his exposition, comes to be engaged in the recording of his expenditures as a first step towards setting up a profit and loss account.

The individual trader is made to appear so uncommercially minded, as to even refuse to recognize transportation costs as costs of a specific range.

The identification of transportation costs as such on the part of the individual trader, Menger is by all signs afraid, could well be interpreted as an inadvertent admission on the part of the individual trader that his social and economic radius is wider than the extremely limited personal horizon within which the author of the new kind of "Principles" wants the trader to operate.

To avoid the embarrassment to the author of the new kind of "Principles" the individual trading parties who are supposed to conduct themselves as if they were operating in a social and economic vacuum, are being directed by Menger to turn the handling of the transportation task over to a specially designated group.

Menger wants to make it sure that the individual trading parties are protected from having to face an economic situation which could not be fully squared with their scruples against personal enrichment which they are supposed to have, by having the removal of goods from place to place entrusted to what he, Menger, designates as a "so-called professional trader."

The "so-called professional trader" is not to be viewed as being exactly a trader, Menger elaborates.

He does not want the "so-called professional trader" to be regarded as a person who actually engages in exchange, Menger is eager to stress.

The "so-called professional trader" Menger insists, is to be considered as someone who renders but yeomen service.

The "so-called professional trader", Menger is anxious to point out, is to be identified as the one who places the goods at the disposal of those who actually exchange them.

The motives of the "so-called professional traders" might not be as pure as those of the actual traders, Menger follows up his terminological twist. The "so-called professional trader", the author of the new kind of "Principles" makes the paradoxical statement, might not be as strictly opposed to pecuniary gains as those who actually trade. The "so-called professional trader" might not even object to the making of profits, Menger half-heartedly admits.

In deference, however, to the allergy against pecuniary practices with which the actual trader is supposed to be imbued,—Menger is trying to get out of the tangle,—the "so-called professional trader" is to have his profits listed as returned advances.

To assuage the anti-pecuniary bias which he ascribes to the actual trader, Menger wants the economic outgo of the "so-called professional trader" to be recorded in a form in which those entries are made to look as initial advances of toll payments in forming the outgo and as collections of tolls in forming the intake.

The economic gains of the "so-called professional trader" are i.e. not supposed to appear as being derived from the kind of economic activity for the performance of which the "so-called professional trader" was originally designated.

Though he initially assigned the "so-called professional trader" the role of placing goods at the disposal of those who are to become actually engaged in interpersonal exchange, the economic gains of the "so-called professional trader" appear as gains derived from the operation of tolls.

By insisting on the maintenance of the anti-acquisitive appearance on the part of the "so-called professional trader", Menger is conceivably trying to forestall the outbreak of a quarrel between his actual and his "so-called profesional trader", as to who is preventing whom from making marketing gains and who is, moreover, seducing whom into profiting from marketing.

In his first move which is supposed to obscure the social and economic significance of trading gains, to retrace Menger's hide and seek game, he insists on listing profits of the actual trading act as transportation costs.

As a second move of his terminological merry-go-round, he wants the managing of what he presents as transportation costs to be entrusted to what he chooses to name as a "so-called professional trader".

The "so-called professional trader", to make the terminological tangle worse, is, in turn, being presented as not being an actual trader at all.

The "so-called" which prefaces the denotation of professional trader, is to indicate that the professional trader is in Menger's designation but a trader by name, not a trader in fact.

The "so-called professional trader" is supposed to conduct himself as having no other interests but those of acting as transportation manager.

In a subsequent terminological twist, Menger directs the "so-called professional trader" to claim that the transportation costs which he is supposed to manage, are not transportation costs at all, but toll charges.

Menger uses the three just recounted terminological substitution moves, to have the comprehension of profits thrice removed from the range in which profits by his, Menger's, own admission, do exist.

After having arrived at the point at which he could not deny the existence of profits in connection with trade transactions, Menger takes recourse to a triple terminological screen to prevent the profit issue from becoming an acute analytical factor.

The "so-called professional trader" is being slated, moreover, for another role by Menger.

The professional trader so-called, is made to oblige as much with his appearance as with his disappearance.

Since the "so-called professional trader" is not supposed to play any decisive role in the exchange process, Menger argues, it should not be a cognitive faux pas to evolve an exchange formulation which makes no allowance for anything that the professional trader might do or might not do.

Since the "so-called professional trader" is not supposed to exercise any significant influence in the effectuation of an exchange agreement in the first place, Menger argues, it should not be considered much of a cognitive slip were he, Menger, to suggest that it be forgotten for a moment that the professional trader is not supposed to take any actual part in trading.

It could be presumed for an instant, Menger comes out with a new terminological twist, that the professional trader so-called, is supposed to act as a non-trader.

If the professional trader is made to disappear in his capacity of non-trader in advance of the evolvement of an exchange formula, Menger proffers a piece of sophistry, the entire issue of the social and economic relevance of actual trading could be sidetracked on the presumption that professional trading has been eliminated from the analytical picture.

A pricing scheme can then be evolved, Menger opens his Pandora box, which would have to make no direct reference to a socially and economically signified exchange formulation.

That in arguing for the elimination of the professional trader from his analytical picture, Menger wants to take more from the role of his professional trader than he had granted him when he had first introduced the professional trader, does not appear to trouble the author of the new kind of "Principles."

Menger seems to be solely concerned with using the ghost-like appearance of his so-called professional trader to hide the social and economic relevance of profits.

He appears, in turn, bent on the disappearance of his so-called professional trader, whom for all intent and purposes, he turns into an actual trader at this stage, for no other reason than to provide himself with an opportunity to claim a terminological alibi for the detaching of social and economic issues involved in trading from his formulation of prices.

Prices to Menger are but expressions of emotional releases.

Prices are supposed to be nothing but stopgaps in the individual's quest to get respite from his restlessness.

Prices are to be regarded as instant flashes in the unsteady flow of a person's resilient emotions.

Prices, Menger amplifies, reflect but the feelings of those who appear in the role of incidental traders (ie. not professional traders).

Prices thus come to be viewed as being indicative of the emotional stresses of the ones who are ostensibly not trading for the sake of economic gains.

A pricing deal, Menger proffers an implementation, represents but an instantaneous stand-still agreement.

A pricing deal, in Menger's conception, marks but a momentary resolution of conflicting feelings.

A pricing deal in Menger's specific description, formalizes an agreement between two individuals to console each other for the prospective loss of a satisfaction.

A pricing deal comes, in effect, to be presented as the clinching of an agreement between two persons to accept compensatory emotional satisfaction from each other.

Price negotiations come to be limited in Menger's formulation to an interaction between closeted individuals.

Price determination is presented as a restricted inter-communication between two persons who shut themselves off from any contact with the outside world.

Price negotiations in Menger's postulation, come to be preconditioned by the rarefied air of social seclusion.

Price negotiations presuppose in Menger's proposition, a serene climate which comes to be engendered by economic isolation.

Prices, Menger finds it necessary to warn, cannot be made to express material equivalents.

Prices cannot in any sense encompass material production expenditures, Menger places himself on guard.

Prices in particular cannot be brought into any causal relation with a productive labor effort according to Menger's strictures.

Whether or not a multitude of persons are involved in pricing or but a few individuals, is not to be regarded as being of any great import.

Whether or not an unlimited number of production units is taking part in making a price or but a limited number of production units becomes involved in forming a price, is not to be viewed as deserving much attention.

Whether or not, Menger is ready with an amplification, monopolistic practices or competitive devices are being applied in the evolvement of a price level, is to be considered as being rather incidental, if not totally irrelevant.

Pricing, Menger elaborates, is akin to evaluation, since both pricing and valuation are but expressions of the intensity of feelings.

Pricing, as well as valuation, are both but indicative to Menger of degrees of sensitivity.

Pricing, as well as valuation, come to relate nothing else but individual moods to the author of the new kind of "Principles."

Pricing, as well as valuation, come to reflect nothing more than the vacillation of a person's emotions in Menger's formulation.

Prices arrived at, Menger specifies, are as fleeting as attained values.

A given price is as bare of any social content as a given value, Menger stresses.

A given price is, in Menger's presentation as devoid of any objective economic context as a given value.

A person who considers himself oversupplied with precious stones and undersupplied with bread, is likely to accord an exchange value to luxuries and ascribe use value to bread, Menger exemplifies the asocial character of his value concept.

Another person who considers himself undersupplied with precious stones and oversupplied with bread, Menger continues his asocial characterization of value, is likely to attach use value to the precious stones and ascribe exchange value to bread.

Whether any given object or any part of it is being accorded use or exchange value, is not to be regarded as having any reference to any kind of social factor according to the exemplification just offered by Menger.

The categories of use value and exchange value are not to express anything but a personal sense of satisfaction and dissatisfaction, in line with the just cited demonstration.

Use and exchange value are made expressive of nothing else

but what an individual regards as his sense of satiety by the author of the new kind of "Principles."

Valuation to Menger presents but a way in which an individual tries to ascertain what are his personal preferences with regard to a good.

Valuation comes, in turn, to play the role of an instrumentality through which an individual undertakes to rate a good on the sole basis of his personal attitude.

Whether a good rates as a commodity or not, comes to be entirely dependent upon the way it affects a single person's emotions.

Should a person be emotionally disposed to accord exchange value to a good, that good will rate as a commodity, Menger exemplifies his definition.

Should, in reverse, a person be emotionally disposed to ascribe use value to a good, such good will come to rate as a mere consumable product in Menger's designation.

The material attributes of a good, Menger wants it understood, are in no way essential to the kind of rating the good receives.

Any designation of a material object as a commodity is subject to recall by that person, Menger insists.

Any designation of a material object as a consumable product is, in turn, subject to rescinding by that individual, Menger wants it stressed.

A person who is initially inclined to designate a good for exchange is free to change his mind and redesignate the good for his personal use, Menger becomes emphatic.

Any person, to take the reverse case, who is initially inclined to designate a good for personal use is at liberty to change his mind and redesignate the good for exchange, Menger emphasizes.

Menger is careful not to attach any social attribute to either the initial designation nor its reversal.

He rules out any social qualification for either of the two designations of a good; he leaves it all to the sensual predilection of a single person.

The placing of a good into the exchange flow as well as a subsequent elimination of that good from the exchange process, along with the reversal of the just stated sequence, is being presented

41

by Menger as a mere playball of the emotional predisposition of any given individual.

The realization of exchange value, the actual exchange of a commodity for a commodity, does not alter the subjectivity of any value, Menger is persistent.

Those who form an objective standard and conceive such a standard as a necessary requirement for a proper assaying of the circulation of goods, are being told by Menger that they are laboring under a misconception.

Those who, in turn, define money as a standard of value and a medium of accumulation, are being furthermore called to order by the author of the new kind of "Principles" for representing accidentals as properties.

According to Menger, the value of money is as much susceptible to personal moods as the value of any other good.

Money, in the conception he proffers, Menger wants it stressed, has no specific significance.

Money, in the formulation he advances, Menger wants it emphasized, has no particular meaning.

Monetary exchange, Menger wants it to be duly noted, is in his kind of conceptualization, as unspecifiable as non-monetary exchange.

In looking backward on what he has accomplished, Menger can be well satisfied.

By placing of the thought prerequisites of space and time beyond cognitive reach, by emptying of the categories of value and price of any social content, he can well be pleased, as he no doubt was, on having erected insurmountable road blocks on the path of the conceptualization of profit, interest, rent and wages.

Menger can well congratulate himself, as he doubtlessly did, on having sufficiently undercut the fabric of economic reasoning to make an attempt towards concretization appear as futile as an attempt to form an abstraction.

He can well pride himself on having so impaired the rules of conceptualization as to render the general as indeterminable as the specific.

By submerging the entire framework of socio-economic reasoning in an interplay of inexplicable feelings, by having all socio-economic context subverted to a medley of conflicting wishes, Menger can rest content, as he no doubt was with having successfully blocked the recognizability of a dividing line between a realistic approximation and a deliberate fiction.

By causing individualistic notions to take the place of systematic reasoning, by effecting the reduction of economic categories to a maze of willfulness, Menger can well claim credit for having perfected much subtler scheming devices than the one which had been expounded by Thuenen.

In advancing a treatment of concepts as if they were the exclusive domain of individual preferences and personal whims, Menger has moved further down the road which had been traveled by Thuenen towards the acceptance of Schelling's exposition of the intuitive as a cognitive ultimate.

In making sensuality override reflection, Menger, moreover follows Schopenhauer to whom fictions represented a superior form of reality.

CHAPTER 3

DESIGNIFICATION

THE drift into the as if under the ostentatious claim of embracing a superior reality to which Menger had given expression, continues its course under the auspices of Friedrich von Wieser.

In line with Menger's effort to prevent a differentiation between the universal and the concrete, Wieser roots for making a formulation of a concept cognitively indistinguishable from the observation of a fact.

As a counterpart to Menger's claim that he is expressing the most obvious, Wieser clamors that he is portraying the most common.

Wieser devotes himself in his essay "On the Genesis and the Principal Laws of economic value" to the dragging in of a mosaic of detail in an obvious attempt to obscure social contours.

He plays up minute observations in a poorly disguised effort to obfuscate the emergence of an economic structure.

By invoking a numberless recounting of individual reactions, by invoking a sheer endless recollection of marks left by personal introspection, Wieser is making a supreme bid for taking over the task of deconceptualization at the point at which Menger had left it.

44

In taking account of Menger's conceptual wrecking accomplishment, Wieser is keen to notice that the category of costs has been left somewhat intact.

In spite of Menger's effort to disqualify the social and economic significance of costs, the cost category could still be used as a key factor in economic analysis, Wieser observes with misgiving.

The cost category somehow withstood the initial thrust which was supposed to reduce that concept to meaninglessness, Wieser recounts with a foreboding.

In spite of the blow which was to deprive costs of any meaning, the delineation of economic expenditures could still be applied as a means of social and economic identification, Wieser finds reason to complain.

In aspiring to the role of Menger's disciple, Wieser would have had to consider himself ill-deserving of his master were he not to undertake another attempt directed at what had turned out to be a resilient category.

In vying for the place of an intellectual heir of Menger Wieser would have had to consider himself as unworthy to wear Menger's mantle, were he not to renew the assault on a category which Menger had intended to tame.

Wieser to be sure does not disappoint those who see in him the trustee of Menger's heritage.

Wieser is quite prepared to disavow any inclination to recognize objective factors in the consideration of costs.

He is in a not uncertain mood to tell anybody off who after reading Menger's "Principles" would still be hesitant to regard the cost category as but an indicator of personal preferences.

Wieser expects to have talked any economic theorizer into submission as a result of his verbal assault against the cost category.

Any economic theorist who in spite of Menger's direction might still be reluctant to treat costs as an itemizer of individual pleasures and displeasures, is taught otherwise by Wieser.

Costs, Wieser opens up his essay "On the Genesis and the Principal Laws of Economic Value" refer to but a way of recording of sensual vacilations.

Costs relate but a way of terming personal moods to Wieser.

Costs constitute but one form of itemizing personal expectations in Wieser's conception.

Costs present but one of the terminological means for detailing individual anticipations in Wieser's presentation.

Cost items by no means quantify utilized material (Aufwand) Wieser is anxious to stress.

Cost items do in no sense relate production expenditures, Wieser is eager to underscore.

Itemization of costs presents to Wieser a way of arraying expected pains against anticipated joys.

Any economic theorist who would be inclined to persist in maintaining a fundamental distinction between material and non-material costs is to be made to desist from following such a course on Wieser's instruction.

Any economic analyst who would specifically insist on seeing a basic difference between labor and material utilized in production is to be forced to relent hereafter on Wieser's direction.

Non-human and human costs are to be viewed as being essentially of the same character Wieser wants to make sure.

Material expenditures as well as human exertion, Wieser argues, are both caused by an individual desire.

The productive use of material as well as the productive effort of labor, Wieser is at pains to stress, are both geared to a personal want.

Material as well as nonmaterial expenditures, Wieser underscores it, both reflect pleasurable anticipations.

Material as well as human expenditures, are both presented as means of asserting expected joys over anticipated pains in the formulation advanced by Wieser.

In placing material and nonmaterial expenditures within the fold of personal satisfaction, it should be noted, Wieser does not mean to say that the labor effort can be explained in terms of the satisfaction which the laborer himself might derive from the act of working.

The satisfaction felt by a worker who sees himself equal to

the task he is called upon to perform is but a negligible factor to Wieser.

The sense of accomplishment felt by the laborer who finds his work has been well performed is being referred to by Wieser as an extraneous feeling.

Effective satisfaction can never be derived from any productive activity, Wieser argues.

Real pleasure can only be felt in anticipation of consumption according to the perception which Wieser is trying to advance.

Only barbarians can attribute any special significance to a human effort, Wieser contends.

Only the non-civilized can ascribe any particular meaning to productive labor, Wieser insists.

Only under primitive conditions, Wieser asserts, can expended labor be regarded as a causal factor.

Only under conditions of technological backwardness, Wieser maintains, is a general stimulation of labor absent.

Only in an epoch typified by a tremendous waste of natural resources (Raubwirtschaft) does the effectuation of labor present a problem according to the conception which Wieser is attempting to propound.

Only where a rational organization of labor is missing, Wieser reaches the height of his stated contention, is the objective result of labor linkable to the labor effort.

Only where the physical hardships of labor outweigh the satisfaction which could be possibly derived from an added product, only where pain associated in the individual's mind with added production overshadows the anticipated pleasure from the satisfaction of one's wants—Wieser reaches a point at which he is ready to invoke a subjective stipulation instead of an objective explanation—is it to be permissible to uphold a causal correlation between the result of labor and the human effort spent on it.

In the contemporary period, in the era characterized by technological advances, human exertion becomes undetectable according to Wieser's contention.

In the era in which human effort can easily be presented as a part of the work of the machine, Wieser is overstating an argument, labor loses the characteristics of an attribute of its own.

47

From its place as a specific requisite of production which labor had hitherto commanded, Wieser develops his overstatement, labor employed at the machine comes to be reduced to the role of an indeterminable production implement.

Taking the overstatement as his basic proposition, Wieser is proceeding to infer that labor employed at a machine constitutes in an analytical sense, nothing more than one of the many items in an undifferentiated recording of material and nonmaterial costs.

No protest is to be expected against the subversion of the social and economic aspects of labor on the part of any contemporary laborer, Wieser reassures himself.

In the mind of a factory worker the painful experience connected with work is far removed, Wieser contends.

The unpleasantness of work is by far outweighed, Wieser insists, by the promise of satisfaction of personal wants which the worker expects.

The contention that it lies solely within the range of the personal preference of the laborer to effectuate or noneffectuate any given productive labor effort, is being extended by Wieser to include the entire range of production.

Under the stated presumption, Wieser considers it safe to assert that productive labor is being put to use and put out of use in accordance with the preferences the laborer himself expresses for one or the other means of satisfaction.

Since no specific objective factors are supposed to be recordable, according to his dictum, Wieser considers it methodologically safe to advance the proposition with impunity that the laborer is in a position to regulate the rate of his individual employment and unemployment in accordance with his personal desires which he wishes to realize.

He finds it opportune to underscore that the stated presumptive proposition, does not invite a collision with known facts, though he abstains from presenting any evidence to that effect.

Wieser's major proposition, the linking of costs to personal desires is not without specific implications.

The submerging of costs in sensual vibrations is of singular import within the framework of Wieser's reasoning.

Costs relegated to the role of an indicator of a chain reaction of individual sensitivity, it should be realized, are well fitted to serve as a cognitive advance post for a body blow which is aimed at the subverting of the comprehension of the entire production process to subjectivistic notions.

The rule against the acknowledgement of any objective material consideration in the interpretation of costs of production, is well designed to be a forerunner of the exclusion rule for any material factors in the presentation of any production phase.

In any analytical scope in which the feeling of a person is made to rule supreme, Wieser is proud to announce, a material correlation of production factors becomes well nigh inconceivable.

In an analytical scope fenced in by individual emotions, means of production and their respective output do not appear as being causally related, Wieser observes with satisfaction.

With comprehension of production approached on the basis of subjective notions, the material effectuation of production can hardly acquire any conceptual import, Wieser is pleased to notice.

As any given product comes to be evaluated in accordance with personal moods, the material embodiment of the product, Wieser proffers a formalistic inference, can hardly come to merit any attention.

Neither forces of nature, nor social forces, are granted recognition by Wieser, it should be duly noted in the stated connection, as causative factors in production.

Contrary to the view expressed by representatives of the classical economic school, Wieser demurs from having either the soil or capital or labor represented as being causally effective in the realization of products.

Causal linkage with any specific factors appears to be detestable to Wieser.

Causal comprehension in which the cause as well as the effect might possibly be traced and linked to each other does not meet with Wieser's approval.

What man knows, what a human being could conceivably ascertain, Wieser wants to sound determined, is not to qualify as an element of effective causation.

Only what can be merely guessed, only what can be assumed to be improbable and uncertain, is Wieser willing to rate as a factor of causative efficacy.

As far as causation with regard to the production process is concerned, only the kind of causative sequence which can be attributed to unspecifiable notions of individual sensitiveness, is allowed to stand by Wieser.

In regard to the causative factor in production only such correlation which relates an undeterminable sense of personal pleasure with another, is being recognized by Wieser.

Only what will surely be found insufficient of having a significant effect in the course of production, only what is most certain to prove unreliable material in a determination of the production course, Wieser is willing to have included among the causative production factors, as can be gathered from his specific statement to that effect in his essay (*Wesen und Ursprung*—p. 174).

There is neither need nor use to try to prove anything about actual causation, Wieser asserts in the stated connection.

There is no need even to attempt to describe the actual causal sequence in the most general form, Wieser insists.

All that is required for purposes of an economic analysis is the gaining of a personal self assurance that an *apparent* causation prevails.

All that is needed for what he terms as a coherent understanding of relevant economic issues, Wieser is selfconfident, can be gathered within the limits of the most subjective of imputations.

His disqualification of any objective factors in causation is sure to serve as effective deterrent to any reconsideration of the production process within the framework of his reasoning, Wieser is reasonably confident.

Speculation about causation Wieser directs, does not have to be extended beyond the range of what an individual might be willing to present as the reason for his own pleasurable anticipations.

A comprehension which tries to assess an affected causal linkage, Wieser clamors, should not be required to penetrate beyond what any single person might be inclined to regard as the immediate antecedent of a sense of momentary satisfaction.

He has rendered the resumption of a qualitative distinction

in the causal appraisal of production factors well nigh impossible within the scope of the presentation, Wieser can well utter a sigh of relief, by having disqualified all respective causative material links in production.

To the will-o'-the-wisp to which subjectivistic imputations give rise, Wieser can rest content, all constituent production elements will come to appear as unascertainable parts of an indeterminable mixture.

In what might be taken as a kind of about face, Wieser protests, he is willing to respect the quantification aspect.

He is however quick to warn that a quantitative identification of actual production material, can under no circumstances, be tolerated.

All questions pertaining to a quantitative signification of actual amounts used and effected in production, are to be ruled out in advance.

Only within the range of consumer's goods is quantification to be held permissible.

Only such goods which come within the range of individual wants are to be deserving of quantification.

The amount of consumable goods which the individual cares to have at his disposal, Wieser appears to have a second thought, cannot be said as having no relation whatsoever to either the effecting or the sustaining of production.

No attempt is however made by Wieser to use a quantification device to arrive at any specific amount.

When he is confronted with the proposition to ascertain an actual quantity, Wieser starts to waver.

He prefers to introduce uncountable numbers, he chooses to invoke infinitesimal particles when faced with the task of presenting concrete quantities.

Any analytical device which does not square with his comprehension of production as an array of unscrutinizable shifts and unexplainable fluctuations, Wieser is determined to disregard.

Only such an analytical procedure which permits a manipulation of the qualitative as well as the quantitative aspects of production, to make it conform to the vagaries of individual desires and personal wants, merits Wieser's rating of acceptable.

His refusal to recognize socially conceived production factors, his denial to acknowledge material production elements, Wieser is quite conscious about it, is specifically intended to prevent a kind of social and economic analysis in which the effectuation of a product is being respectively linked to its social sources and its material antecedents.

Within the analytical scope he provides, Wieser concedes in a rather apologetic mood, production comes close to appearing as an act of spontaneous generation.

He is doing his utmost, as far as the social and economic disqualification of concepts is concerned, Wieser is quite aware of it, to have the process of production appear as a kind of admixture of everything with anything, in order to create the impression of the presence of an insurmountable methodological obstacle to the bringing of output in any specific relation to either an individual or a collective contribution which might have had any part in that output.

He thus prevents, Wieser can by no means be unmindful of it, the identification of any economic appropriation.

With his insistence moreover on the social disqualification of the production process, Wieser could hardly undertake to deny it, he is tending to disrupt the signification of any specific income form.

As a result profit making, rent collecting, interest taking, or for that matter wage earning, come to be deprived of any particular social meaning in Wieser's presentation.

No specific principles are supposed to be involved in the social divison of the product, Wieser does not mind to underscore it.

The product which emerges from his presentation as something or other which is cooked up in an indeterminable admixture, is being subsequently placed by Wieser at the disposal of everybody who cares to help himself to it.

Anybody who is willing to claim that he is either a profit maker, or a rent collector, or an interest receiver, or a wage earner, is to regard himself free to take hold of any kind of product or what he imagines to be parts of a product which he wishes to consume in full accord with his most personal predilections, with the gracious permission of Wieser.

Wieser astounds everybody within his reach with the extending of a claim that he has reached extreme clarity with his formulations.

Individual choice and personal preference allow for definite approximation, Wieser feels no hesitation to protest.

Anticipations of satisfactions and dissatisfactions provide a sure basis for estimates, Wieser feels no scruples to clamor.

No matter how subjective the initial anticipation of pain, no matter how intimate the subsequent expectation of joy, each such emotional vibration is subject to the most exact quantification, Wieser feels no compunction to proclaim.

Wieser's boasting of exactitude comes somewhat to grief however, when he is confronted with the problem of stating what specifically he considers subject to quantification.

The inner springs of individual emotions, the operation of personal feelings remain obscure, Wieser finds himself forced to concede.

Psychophysical inquiries have not progressed yet to the stage at which they could explain in any meaningful and significant manner the resolution of emotional conflicts, Wieser is willing to concede.

Psychophysics—Wieser remorsefully refers to Fechner in this instance—has not been yet able to offer a meaningful interpretation for the way in which an individual's feeling of dissatisfaction comes to be transformed into a sense of satisfaction.

It remains inexplicable, Wieser ruefully remarks, how it comes about that a person's pain becomes overcompensated by his joy.

There is no need, however, to wait for a clarification of qualitative distinctions, Wieser tries to console himself.

Qualitative distinctions can be easily overridden by quantitative specifications, Wieser persists.

What difference does it make, he poses an oratorical question, whether one person is a beggar and the other endowed with material riches.

It all depends, he considers he has the whole answer ready,

upon the respective attitude of the individual concerned.

A frugal poor should be expected to tend towards as much moderation in the expression of his feeling as a thrifty rich, Wieser exemplifies his all out dependence upon attitude in his conceptualization.

A starving poor should, in turn, be expected to be as much inclined to exaggerate his emotional reactions as a gluttonous man of wealth, Wieser states the reverse of the just stated exemplification.

It all depends in Wieser's inference—and all is supposed to exclude any objective social and economic considerations—upon a person's sensitivity.

It all depends, in Wieser's forced conclusion—and all in this instance is supposed to be postulated in disregard of any given social fabrique and any existing economic pattern—upon the intensity of a person's feelings.

The intensity of personal feelings, Wieser considers it opportune to caution, cannot be measured by the application of simple mathematical rules.

The degree of emotional intensity evoked by a pile of goods cannot be determined by ordinary arithmetical or regular algebraic devices, Wieser considers it appropriate to confess.

Neither subtraction nor division nor the taking of root, neither addition nor multiplication, nor raising to power can be of any assistance to a quantification of personal pains and individual joys, Wieser is prepared to concede.

Wieser does not shrink, however, from going to the other extreme and branding as preposterous any attempt to lay down any kind of uniform rule as far as a quantitative appraisal of individual emotions is concerned.

No general device is to be considered conceivable for the purpose of a quantitative elucidation of a person's sense of appreciation, Wieser protests.

It is therefore to be left to each single individual to devise his own kind of mathematical procedure on Wieser's direction.

Any single person is, on Wieser's direction, to consider himself free to devise his own peculiar way of calculating the degree of his satisfaction and dissatisfaction.

There is to be no necessity for any individual to communicate his own mathematical notion to another individual.

Nor is it to be viewed as serving any useful purpose, were any person to try to exchange with some other person, his experience with the application of his personal device for the calculation of his feelings.

The very subject of quantification of emotions demands secrecy on the part of the respective individuals, Wieser would have it.

Only the individual who separates himself from any other individual, is being viewed by Wieser as the proper person who is able to ascertain with some exactitude the degree of his own emotional response to what he is inclined to consider as his individual wants.

Only an individual who is bent on communicating with nobody but himself is regarded by Wieser as the one who is able to learn anything about the magnitude of what he imagines are his innermost desires.

Only an individual, to spell it out for Wieser, who is not quite sure of what he wants out of the social and economic world, from which he removes himself, is to be credited with a capacity for exactitude.

Only an individual who by the very subjectivity of his speculations becomes twice removed in his mind, from the society and economy in which he lives, to fill in for Wieser, is being imbued with a sense of precision.

Only an individual,—Wieser bolsters his unrealistic proposition with another fictitious claim,—only an individual who can imagine that he is an isolated husbander, irrespective what social and economic conditions are in which he finds himself, Wieser protests, is likely to arrive at some rating of his needs with reference to his emotional predisposition.

Only a person,—Wieser continues to spin his fictitious proposition,—who can act as if his entire social and economic life depends upon a stock of provisions which are placed at his disposal—irrespective of what otherwise constitutes the social and economic condition in which he finds himself—can come to know the margin of satisfaction which he is willing to forego and the margin of dissatisfaction which he is prepared to spare himself.

55

Only a person who can behave as if the entire social and economic matrix which shapes his social and economic life, can find its most exhaustive expression in a pantry stocked up for him with readily consumable products or a warehouse filled with readily consumable objects which are placed at his disposal, can conceivably calculate the emotional effect which the parting with a marginal good might have on him, according to Wieser's claim.

The emotional reaction of the self-isolated individual to his anticipated parting with what he regards as a marginal good, Wieser makes subject to a specific rating in his subsequent argumentation.

The emotional reaction of a self-isolated person to the parting with what he considers to be the least valuable good to him in a readily available stockpile, is to be known as the rate of marginal utility, in accordance with Wieser's instruction.

Marginal utility, Wieser issues a special directive, is to be considered calculable with complete disregard to any hitherto known mathematical device.

Calculations of marginal utility are not even to be required to comply with numerical sequences.

A calculator of marginal utility should consider himself free to count 2, 5, 6, 9, 12, 15, Wieser directs.

A calculator of marginal utility is to consider himself furthermore at liberty to disregard any and all figures which he does not care to enumerate on Wieser's instruction.

A calculator of marginal utility should likewise feel free to honor with his attention only the figures 5-10 and regard any of the respective preceding numbers as nonexistent, with Wieser's permission.

The calculator of marginal utility is for that matter to consider himself privileged to devise a way of counting without figures by claiming that he is conceiving a device with a view of discounting regularities and relying upon irregularities, to follow Wieser's advice.

The individual who becomes engaged in testing his emotional amplitude by way of assaying of a marginal utility is not to be hampered by any known formulation of either space or time, Wieser wants to make it sure.

The personal calculator of marginal utility receives Wieser's permission to make the comprehension of time and space fit the manner in which he is disposed to proceed in testing his emotional reaction.

The impact of subjective quantification, on which Wieser is pleased to dwell, comes to be once more highlighted in his reference to money.

The looseness of the mathematical procedure combined with the looseness of socio-economic methodology which is being propagated by Wieser, is being once more stressed by him when he approaches the subject of monetary exchange.

The monetary form of quantification, Wieser unabashedly protests, is to be considered as being as much devoid of any specifiable economic meaning as the quantification of any other social or economic factor.

Monetary exchange is to be viewed as being as much dependent upon the assaying of personal emotions as other forms of exchange, according to Wieser's directive.

Monetary exchange—Wieser is matching Menger in this instance—is to be regarded as being as much subservient to the calculations of one's feelings as any nonmonetary trading.

Monetary as well as nonmonetary exchange, Wieser restresses the fictitiousness of his proposition, is to be made to appear as if it were conducted in social and economic isolation.

Monetary as well as nonmonetary trading, Wieser advances a historically contradictory proposition, is to be paraded as a phenomenon which forms a major characteristic of self-provisioning.

Anyone who can bring himself to the point of disregarding the run of time, anyone who is capable of ignoring the sequence in which the present follows the past and the future follows the present, can be expected to have a flash in which he will become cognizant of his economic needs, Wieser feels no compunction to assure.

For a fleeting moment an individual to whom time in any

57

specific form does not count, is to be expected to gain a clear and precise feeling of what he wants and what he doesn't want, were one to believe Wieser.

For one instant any person who has all but lost his time sense through his own deliberate efforts to that effect, should be expected to be capable of pointing out to himself the part of a certain good with which he is not prepared to part, if Wieser's argumentation on that point is to be accepted.

At that instant the individual whose time sense has been all but lost should be expected to have a clear realization of the utility he is prepared to attribute to what he considers is the least useful particle to him, if one is to go along with Wieser.

There is no way of telling, Wieser finds it necessary to caution, when that moment of enlightenment will strike a person.

Nor does Wieser offer to explain how it is to come about that an individual who persists in the discounting of timeliness of his feelings is to be able, suddenly, to recognize the pressure of time.

The reader is being asked by Wieser to resign himself to the realization that the gaining of momentary knowledge on the part of the individual whose time sense has been dulled is on his, Wieser's, instruction, to be considered by and large unexplainable.

To the scrutinizer of his thought, Wieser is not willing to offer any other lead for a respective understanding than the pointing to his assertion that the gaining of instantaneous certainty is linkable with a personal intuition.

The cloud enveloping the mind of an individual who persists in disregarding timeliness is being suddenly pierced, Wieser proffers an exclamation, in lieu of an explanation.

Without any forewarning, a ray of clarity comes to fall upon the maze of formless and ambiguous impressions of the individual who, only an instant before the enlightenment came to him, had thought and acted as if he were not in full possession of his mental power.

To his own consternation, Wieser relates something close to a miracle, the person who has continuously insisted that he does not know what he wants and what he does not want, becomes momentarily imbued with the feeling that he is able to calculate the marginal utility which he is disposed to attach to the least useful material particle he senses is within his reach.

The sensing of marginal utility on the part of the individual who becomes graced with that sense, does not refer to a quantitative sense of proportion, Wieser insists.

The sensing of marginal utility can in no way be considered as being in any way conditioned by a feeling which relates the whole to its parts, Wieser finds it opportune to stress.

Marginal utility cannot be sensed in any mathematical terms, Wieser directs.

The feeling a marginal utility bares but the marks of lust and pain in the comprehension proffered by Wieser.

The sense of marginal utility which an individual acquires, is supposed to show scars of a fear which is imbedded in possessiveness, Wieser wants to make sure.

The sensing of marginal utility is to be represented as being fundamentally erratic, according to Wieser's contention.

The sensing of marginal utility is, on the direction of Wieser, to be viewed as being widely subject to either exaggeration or diminution.

The bizarre does not only enter the sensing of marginal utility on Wieser's instruction; the inclination towards the disproportionate is to hold the individual under its sway long after he had ascertained what he is willing to regard as his marginal particle, on Wieser's special advice.

The just stated unrealistic device which is based on the paradoxical proposition which calls for a separate consideration of an unseparated particle, is being, in turn, followed by another unrealistic treatment on the part of Wieser.

Wieser's subsequent device for the sensing of the value of the whole which is to be based on the sensing of the value of its supposedly marginal part, is made to suffer from the same logical and methodological disability as the device for the sensing of the value of the marginal particle itself.

Since the sensing of marginal utility is not supposed to be directly related to any material content, Wieser cannot and does not expect an abatement of sensual aberrations in the individual's mind after that individual had applied Wieser's device of ascertaining,—within the limited range of understanding granted to him as an individual by Wieser—the value which he the individual considers he is willing to ascribe to what appears to him as a marginal particle.

It should therefore not be surprising, Wieser expresses a logically valid assumption, to find the individual evaluator trying to superimpose his highly disproportionate sense of a marginal evaluation of a particle upon what appears to him as a whole.

The degree to which marginal utility can be made subject to ascertainment,—Wieser wants to make sure he has committed himself to nothing definite—does not in any way promise to provide a basis for a comparative evaluation.

Neither the marginal utility of the particles which are considered as being detached from nonidentical wholes by identical persons nor the marginal utility of particles which are considered to be detached from the same whole by nonidentical persons form any basis for a comparative appraisal, Wieser makes a rather odd observation.

He could have phrased the just stated citation in a simpler form by relating that the marginal utility which he espouses is so elusive a factor as to make it well nigh impossible to determine its quantity in any singular case.

The attempt to compare something which is well nigh indeterminable with something other which is well nigh indeterminable, is obviously a hopeless undertaking, Wieser could have stated it in this less involved form.

The indefiniteness of what he terms marginal utility, is being amply demonstrated by Wieser's subsequent insistence that the quantification of marginal utility is not supposed to extend beyond the cognitive range of a reflection which is brought forth by the sensing of the utility of a particle which, in the imagination of the evaluating individual, becomes detached from an identical product or good.

The cognitive relevance of such quantification does obviously not extend beyond the range of the calculating experience of a single person, it can be realized by anybody, even without being told about it by Wieser.

It should not be inferred—Wieser somehow apologizes for his proffering of an ultra subjective marginal utility evaluation, as a principal economic factor—that the human being is generally incapable of assaying a whole before first dividing it into parts.

Nor should it be concluded that it is inconceivable for a person to form an attitude and express an opinion in regard to an agglomeration of goods without first separating one good from another.

Nor should it be construed that an individual cannot consider himself as being placed in a position in which he could appraise an undivided good.

Neither should the methodological strictures, which he, Wieser, imposes upon the procedure of marginal utility evaluation be cited as a proof that comparative judgments do not lie within an individual's province, the author of the "Genesis and the Principal Laws of Value" wants it to be known.

The restrictions which he, Wieser imposes upon the application of the term marginal utility, the author of the "Genesis and the Principal Laws," finds it opportune to stress, are but to provide an assurance that subjective microcosmic evaluations remain confined to the intimate sphere of the individual out of the depths of which such value judgments arise.

One should not deny, Wieser continues, in his own defense, that any person can come to know that one thousand bushels constitutes a larger figure than one hundred dollars.

It should not be disputed that anybody can come to learn that ten thousand bushels represents a larger weight than one thousand bushels.

Such knowledge, however, is to be considered as being of little significance, Wieser becomes assertive again.

Figures are to be viewed as having little meaning, unless they are made to express personal desires and individual wishes, Wieser insists.

In the mind of a single person, each of a given hundred dollars could come to rate higher than each of a given thousand dollars,

Wieser proffers an examplification of his just cited apodictive statement.

An individual should well attach a greater utility to each of a given thousand bushels and a comparatively smaller utility to each of a given hundred thousand bushels, Wieser is ready with a corollary demonstration.

That the individual evaluator whom Wieser cites in his exemplification is required to presume that the hundred dollars and the thousand dollars constitute hoarded treasures, to render the example probable, is not mentioned by the author of the "Genesis and the Principal Laws," in connection with his stated example.

Nor is there any mention in the corollary demonstration which Wieser offers, that the individual evaluation of the thousand and ten thousand bushels is supposed to be undertaken in the presumptuous assumption that the respective amounts refer to hoarded stockpiles, to make the demonstration plausible.

Wieser does not care to make any specific reference to the factor of social and economic isolation in which his evaluating individual is supposed to operate.

By having the individual evaluator in the first example presume that the hundred dollars and the correlated thousand dollars cannot be exchanged with each other, by making it, in turn, appear to the evaluating person in the corollary example that none of the hundred bushels can be traded for any of the thousand bushels and vice versa, Wieser but inadvertently admits that he, Wieser, suggests the staging of the respective demonstration of individualistic evaluation in an exchangeless nexus.

Wieser is, moreover, not able to hide that in a more general way he expects the kind of individual he is espousing to operate in a social and economic vacuum.

His fundamental formulation in which he states that any marginal utility evaluation depends upon nothing else but the person's disposition, is certainly asocial and aeconomic in character.

Nor is there to be any doubt that he presupposes a social and economic vacuum in his followup formulation which states that the ascertainment of marginal utility depends fully upon the emotional makeup of the individual who becomes engaged in calculating his feelings.

Wieser is proud to underscore the social and economic emptiness of his major proposition by declaring that in his attempt to determine a marginal utility any person comes to reflect the emotional tension which he experiences and the mood in which he happens to be.

It might at first glance appear that the author of the "Genesis and the Principal Laws" deviates to some extent from his presupposition of a social and economic vacuum when he proclaims that the utility which an individual is prepared to attach to a particle depends upon that person's sense for the fashionable, as well as the taste which that person has come to develop.

The assessing of marginal utility depends to some degree, Wieser is apparently acknowledging a social angle, upon the educational background, the moral position of the evaluating person and the kind of preferences such particularities evoke in the respective individual.

His excursion into the realm of social factors, Wieser makes it sure, however, is not to provide a clue for anything remotely conclusive.

As if the social qualifications which he introduces in the just cited statement are not vague enough to prevent them from acquiring any specific meaning, Wieser busies himself to make the vague social notions he has just introduced even vaguer.

By piling up qualifications upon qualifications, he renders his social notions about marginal utility procedure completely meaningless.

The assessment of marginal utility depends to a certain degree, Wieser qualifies his highly qualified social notion, upon the variety of choices offered for the satisfaction of varied desires and wants and the kind of appreciation such versatility elicits on the part of any person.

With this qualification, Wieser can well be satisfied, he has restored fully the presupposition of the social and economic vacuum in which his kind of evaluating person is made to operate.

As if the qualification of his social notions which was just stated does not refer to a sufficiently great number of items to rate as disqualification, Wieser adds a disqualifying note of a more general character.

He prohibits the reading of any meaning into unpersonalized data, he specifically forbids the ascribing of any significance to a quantification which does not refer to an individualistic choice.

He proscribes, moreover, any expectation of an individual experience to have itself repeated by branding it as misleading.

Should he grant nonpersonalized data signification, Wieser has reason to conclude, he would by the same token admit the cognitive feasibility of contesting his proposition of the unpredictability of individual sense reaction.

Were he to give up his insistence on the unmatchable uniqueness of individual impressions, Wieser has, moreover, reason to infer, such reversal would make it cognitively unfeasible for him to take a stand against any uniformity in social and economic comprehension.

By insisting on an unqualified acceptance of his proposition that it is unquestionably fallacious to assume that individual experiences can ever reoccur, Wieser, as he doubtlessly realizes, reaffirms a cognitive framework within which he can launch an attack on logical grounds against the very conceptual core which lies at the root of any social and economic law.

Should he concede the possibility of a cognition of the aspect of reoccurrence in regard to personal experience, Wieser has reason to assume, as he doubtlessly does, he would invalidate by the same token his imputation of irregularity of any and all individual sense reactions to which he cares to subscribe.

It is, therefore, understandable that Wieser decries a nonsubjectified evaluation of economic data.

It is, therefore, logical for Wieser to proclaim, as he does, that he considers it impermissible to correlate variations in economic quantification in a manner in which due allowance is made for nonpersonal factors in the quantification results.

The crediting of a common attribute to a number of persons, the crediting, moreover, of a collective body of persons with any specific attribute, Wieser makes it explicit, is barred from his comprehension.

In further committing himself to a wholly subjectivistic cognitive fold, Wieser takes it upon himself to declare that the conducting of an economic investigation with reference to a time sequence is to be held as being out of bounds.

He is but reaffirming the cognitive indistinctiveness of his subjectivistic approach, when he denounces as intolerable the presentation of economic quantities in a form in which the mark of consecutive changes is not removed.

Since he cannot help realizing that the subjectivistic proscriptions and prescriptions, should they be followed, can but lead to a piling up of meaningless wordage, Wieser maks an effort to remove the onus of meaningless verbosity from his exposition by placing the onus on those whom he has set out to defy.

Not he who is consistently pursuing the course of atomization in the recording of social and economic life, but those who insist on viewing economic data within a socially meaningful historical pattern, are warned by the author of the "Genesis and the Principal Laws," that such nonsubjective validation can lead but to a play with words.

The making of a wholly unwarranted accusation constitutes, as Wieser himself could not be unaware, a way for further obscuring the comprehension of relevant social and economic issues.

The realization of marginal utility, Wieser declares without any compunction, is wholly unrelated to what could generally be considered a legitimate want and a justified desire.

Subjective likes and dislikes, personal tastes and individual lusts, Wieser unhesitantly proclaims, are to be rated as varied in their capriciousness as the number of individuals concerned.

The variations of choices on the part of any single individual, are to be noted for their elusiveness, Wieser wants it stressed.

The modification of the preference as it comes to express itself in any given person, Wieser insists, is to be rated as being conspicuous for any absence of generalizing factors.

Marginal utility according to Wieser reflects but a singular emotional vibration.

Marginal utility, Wieser holds, is expressive of the intensity of a feeling which a person is inclined to attach to what he imagines is his most personal want.

Marginal utility is, in Wieser's formulation, but indicative of the degree of the person's emotional tension which that person considers as being imputable to what he as an individual is inclined to view as his most personal desire.

The vagueness to which Wieser becomes addicted, makes a distinction between what in his view is marginal utility and what is not, all but impossible.

Were it not for his subsequent indication that marginal utility is supposed to be incessantly geared to a prevailing mood, one would have to despair of even approaching the subject of how to distinguish marginal utility from what it is not supposed to be.

Were it not for a suggestive linking of marginal utility to a prevailing apprehension under which all individuals are expected to labor, the term marginal utility could hardly come to mean anything.

His procedural device, the progressive decimation of the marginal particles, could well be regarded as but a patent form of equivocation, Wieser realizes, were the spectre of universal scarcity not to be made to grip any individual who is trying to ascertain the degree of his emotional tension.

It is only by having marginal utility express an all permeating fear, Wieser is aware, that he is able to lend some social significance to his highly advertised terminological innovation.

Only if the mirage of a general want can be impressed upon the assaying individual, Wieser is cognizant, can marginal utility come to acquire some economic meaning.

Only if the prospect of an everlasting deficiency in the satisfaction of personal needs can be made to effect the psychophysical balance of the evaluating person, Wieser resolves, can the emotional score which the person attaches to what he considers to be his marginal particle of an economic good become of any social and economic import.

The fear of scarcity, Wieser considers it opportune to forewarn, should not be allowed to recede in the assaying individual's mind in the wake of what is generally conceded to be an advance in civilization.

Neither should an unfolding of what is generally recognized as technological progress be permitted to have a soothing effect on the disturbed emotions of an individual who tries to ascertain what is a marginal utility to him.

The material abundance of goods is not to be viewed as a condition which becomes necessarily reflected in the impressions which any single individual is apt to get.

The anxiety of a person over his inability to satisfy what he considers to be his most personal wants is not to be looked upon as a state of mind which is subject to relief by way of providing a generally more abundant supply of goods.

The sensibility of an individual about what he is inclined to regard as his innermost unsatisfied desire, is not to be regarded as being subject to moderation through a greater abundance of products.

It should be presumed that goods, no matter how large their amount, will never cease to appear scarce to the individual who tries to ascertain a marginal utility.

The wants of an individual who is set upon the determination of a marginal utility are to be seen as being sheer limitless.

An increasing general abundance is, in turn, to be regarded as bringing an intensification of the individual's zest for wanting goods from his fellows to satisfy his own mounting desires.

Neither is an individual who becomes involved in the task of marginal utility determination ever to be expected to free himself from the fear of being deprived of what he is disposed to call his own.

No social and economic road, it is to be held, has been left open for a dispelling of the threat of a criminal attack.

No social means, it is to be presumed, could ever be devised which could dispel in any individual who evaluates his goods according to the marginal utility procedure, the fear of either being murdered or robbed.

Under no conceivable circumstances, it should be presumed, could any human who evaluates his material possessions under a marginal utility angle, ever expect to free himself from the fear of the rule of the claw under which he lives.

The constant apprehension, the continuous stress and strain, under which any individual who tries to apply the marginal utility rules, is made to labor, Wieser does not attempt to deny it, cannot but have the effect of precluding any calm deliberation of the individual with his inner self.

The pervasive fear, Wieser is prepared to admit, cannot but make a dispassionate reasoning on the part of the affected person all but impossible.

Once an individual is seized by the fear of being unable to satisfy his wants, Wieser is willing to accept the consequence, a wholly rational attitude of that fear-ridden individual towards the acquisition and defense of his possessions rules itself out.

Ergo, Wieser concedes, the assaying of an economic good on the part of a fear ridden individual cannot be regarded as proceeding in a reasoned manner.

Whether an individual comes to regard a personal satisfaction threatened or not, becomes in the case of the fear-ridden person fully dependent upon the extent to which that person's emotions come to be charged.

Any individual whose emotions become supercharged when he is trying to evaluate a certain good, Wieser argues in the negative, can well be expected to admit to himself that there exist goods which do not arouse any emotion in him.

Any individual, no matter how emotionally disturbed, should be able to notice that there are products in existence over the disposal of which he does not find himself getting excited, Wieser observes.

Any person, no matter how emotionally unbalanced, can be trusted to become sufficiently disenchanted to abstain from claiming that a certain product or products have economic value to him, Wieser states.

It is this feeling of detachment of the emotionally disturbed individual which Wieser wants to have recognized as the decisive factor in the determination of what product or products fall and which do not fall within the range of economic goods.

Admittedly, Wieser apologizes, the extent of individual wants and desires is extremely varied.

Admittedly, moreover, emotional sensitivity differs from one person to another.

Hence, Wieser preaches resignation; any attempt to ascertain at what emotional altitude economic goods come to be generally separated from noneconomic goods by evaluating individuals, is to be considered as being doomed to futility.

Any single individual, whether he is emotionally disturbed or not, is nonetheless granted freedom by Wieser to manipulate the conceptualization of economic value in accordance with his, the individual's, most personal wishes.

Each person whether he is fear-ridden or not, is left wholly unrestrained by Wieser in his, the individual's, endeavor to grant and deny the attributes of economic value to a good in a manner which satisfies his, the individual's, innermost desires.

Any individual, whether he is emotionally balanced or not, is with Wieser's permission, to consider himself entitled to regard the immediacy of a personal urge or the lack of such an immediacy, in regard to the satisfaction of his wants, as the sole factor which accounts for a differentiation between an economic and a noneconomic good.

It should not be expected, Wieser enters another note of resignation, that any single person whether he is emotionally stable or not will maintain an identical attitude for any length of time.

In his zeal to eschew any specification of the subjective evaluation which he is eager to promote, Wieser wants any evaluating individual to feel at liberty to give his emotions a free and unrestrained play.

Any person who is engaged in the evaluation of a good is to be at liberty to supersede his emotional enchantment with an emotional disenchantment, without giving any advance notice.

Hence, Wieser cautions, no surprise shall be evoked when an individual evaluator instantaneously reverses his value judgment.

At any instant a good or goods which had been granted economic value by an evaluating person, can be expected to be denied any economic worth by the same person, Wieser finds it opportune to forewarn.

The redesignation of a good, the reassigning of an economic good to a noneconomic fold or vice versa, Wieser wants it stressed, does not place the person who undertakes the redesignation under any obligation to give any reason for his action.

Since the subject of economic evaluation is not supposed to pertain to any objective factors, Wieser wants to make sure, the evaluating person is to consider himself absolved from delving into any objective reason for his value judgments and their respective change.

In view of the subjectivistic character of economic values the evaluating individual is supposed to refrain from linking his value judgment to anything else but his personal emotional vacillations.

The evaluating person is to be entitled, in relying on Wieser's scheme, to invoke the unscrutinizability and fluidity of his emotional reverberations in order to gloss over the material constancy of a product which becomes subject to a value judgment.

Emotional gyrations involved in value judgments, Wieser wants to see to it, are not to be considered as being explainable in any other form or manner than by having them presented as an unaccountable changeover from personal enchantment to disenchantment and vice versa.

To block any cognitive penetration which goes beyond the surface of value judgments, Wieser issues a warning to the effect, that any evaluator who shall be trying to account for his emotional ups and downs in regard to what he wants and what he does not want, is to be considered as having no more chance to arrive at any certainty about his economic preferences than the chance he could possibly have in making certain what distinguishes his dreams from his daydreams.

At this stage Wieser has arrived at the point of no return, he can well pride himself of having placed the issue of a realistic presentation of social and economic values beyond the confines of consciousness.

Wieser can well note with satisfaction that he has stated it with an admirable gusto that he is not prepared to tolerate any challenge to the kind of emotionalism which he propounds which can be based on the differentiation of the conscious and the subconscious.

He can well claim that he has made it abundantly clear that he has no scruples whatsoever against overlooking any consciously arrived objection to any subsequent assertion he might be inclined to make.

The author of the "Genesis and the Principal Laws" can well claim credit for himself for showing determination to keep the scope and method of economic thought within a range in which consciousness is blocked.

Wieser can well consider himself as deserving a certificate of merit for having placed the formulation of social and economic concepts into a fold in which they could come to express nothing more than subconscious impressions.

By having the economic evaluator reduced to the status of a sleepwalker, by having the conceptual range of economic values confined to dream and daydreams, Wieser has flung the door wide open for the introduction of unadulterated fictions.

To reinforce the basis for the fictitiousness of his presentation, Wieser makes sure that the submersion of the entire range of economic thinking in a maze of emotionalism is followed through.

It should be considered selfevident, Wieser directs, that all economic activity is due to an emotional imbalance in individuals from which no person can claim exemption.

It should be considered as lying beyond any reasonable doubt, it follows from Wieser's conception, that all economic comprehension is rooted in fear.

No specific proof should be held necessary, in pursuance of Wieser's instruction, to validate the assumption that *value as well as utility* are but expressions of personal anxiety.

No further elaboration is to be required in accordance with Wieser's direction, to ascertain that *value as well as utility* are but indicative of an individual's emotional tenseness.

Value whether economic or non-economic, Wieser takes pains to

71

emphasize, is to be considered as being emotive in character.

Value is to be taken as representing nothing else but a confounded emotional reaction.

A value judgment is not to be viewed, however, as being wholly unspecifiable, Wieser finds it opportune to caution.

Valuation should not be ruled as lying beyond the range of quantification.

The quantification of value judgments should not even present any great difficulties, Wieser sounds an optimistic note.

All that is involved in the quantification of valuation, pertains to the counting of emotional vibrations, Wieser asserts in a rather patronizing manner.

To arrive at a quantification of a value judgment—Wieser tries to keep a straight face—one has to use the simple device of adding up any number of single emotional reactions one might have.

A value judgment can be ascertained in a quantitative form by any individual—Wieser obviously plays on the naivete of his listeners with this insistence—who commits himself to using the device of multiplying the sense of his marginal satisfaction by the number of marginal particles he considers are at his disposal.

How a quantification of a value judgment can actually be arrived at by using a device for a summation of those indefinite and largely unspecifiable feelings which pertain to marginal utility, Wieser does not state in any direct form.

How, as Wieser asserts, an indefinite sensing of marginal utility plus another indefinite sensing of marginal utility plus still another indefinite sensing of marginal utility and so on as many times as there are particles which the individual considers are within his reach, can lead to a definite sensing of value, leaves everybody guessing.

What exactly does Wieser mean by his suggestion that the counting of an indeterminable number of indeterminable impressions of marginal utility is to be accepted without any qualification as a quantitative expression of a respected value, he does not at once disclose.

Only after Wieser gives to understand that in his linking of utility and value he refers but to a *correlation of marginal utility* to marginal value, it dawns upon one what kind of utility and value correlation the author of the "Genesis and the Principal Laws" has in mind.

The correlation of utility to value is supposed to be preconditioned by a marginal assessment of a consumer's stockpile.

A correlation of utility and value, Wieser brings it out, cannot be properly undertaken unless the assessing person becomes obsessed with hoarding a given supply.

The assessor of utility and value is supposed to impose upon himself a complete social and economic isolation on Wieser's direction.

The assessor of utility and value is to isolate himself to such extent as to become unaware of the factor of restocking.

The appraiser of utility and value is supposed to conduct himself as if he were operating within the restricted scope of a household production in which there is no room for a replenishment of a wider range.

In forcing himself to ignore the factor of exchange, the appraiser of utility and value is furthermore to act as if an ever present threat of short supply hangs over him.

In compelling himself to disregard the aspect of production for the market, the assessor of utility and value is supposed to behave, as if he has assured himself that a perpetuation of scarcity cannot be avoided.

Imaginary present shortages, Wieser wants to make sure, are to appear to the assessor of marginal utility and marginal value as signs of increasing future shortages.

Imaginary current scarcities are to be considered by the appraiser of marginal utility and marginal value as presaging a further dwindling of supplies in times to come.

Imaginary present privations are therefore to be taken by the appraiser of marginal utility and marginal value as indications of increasing privations in the future.

Hence, imaginary present privations are to make the assessor of marginal utility and marginal value succumb to an ever increasing fear of not being able to provide for himself in the future.

An attempted ascertainment of a marginal utility under the just stated supposition, Wieser is willing to admit, cannot be credited with a greater exactness than the one attributable to a guess.

Neither, conversely, can an attempt of calculation of marginal value under the cited supposition can ever be rated as being more precise than a compounding of a fleeting notion.

Wieser but offers a procedure to arrive at something which he expects to turn out as bringing out next to nothing.

The terminological runaround which accompanies Wieser's device for the catching of a glimpse of marginal utility and marginal value, is hardly conducive for the maintenance of any cognitive distinctiveness.

There is hardly anything left in a cognitive sense which would permit a differentiation of marginal utility and marginal value, when Wieser is through with devising the procedure by which those two factors are to be ascertained.

The depriving of marginal utility and marginal value of any specifiable meaning, one can assume, does not constitute for Wieser an end in itself.

The indefiniteness to which he condemns marginal utility and marginal value, makes it feasible for Wieser to have utility and value utilized as terminological instrumentalities for the promotion of an unrestrained social and economic manipulation.

A person who tries to apply the procedure for the appraisal of marginal utility and marginal value as it is suggested by Wieser, —to get its real impact—can hardly avoid giving an unbalanced account of what is taking place in as well as about him.

A selfisolated individual will hardly be in a position to balance inner and outer factors in accounting for his social and economic position, Wieser is well aware.

A person who is supposed to consider nothing but his subjective feeling as a proper factor in a social and economic accounting, in an attempt to account for his attainments and failures, Wieser rationalizes, will logically rule out any outside social and economic conditions as legitimate factors in his economic failures.

A person who is supposed to reason by way of subjective imputation can hardly be expected to recognize the propriety of objectified causation.

An individual who is committed to operating in a subjectivistic fold, Wieser enters a piece of sophistry, is likely to attempt to explain away his own economic failings by placing the blame on an uncalled for intrusion of either social forces or the force of nature or both which according to his, the individual's subjectivistic preconception, was not supposed to occur.

A person who presumes that nothing but his inner self is of any relevance, to reverse the just stated sophistry, can, in turn, be expected to impute his economic gains to the factor that the social forces or the force of nature or both have been prevented from interfering with his the individual's, subjectivistic notion.

A person who is bent on enforcing a no trespassing order against the entering of social forces or the force of nature or both into a social and economic accounting, will be inclined to attribute his economic gains to the honoring of this ordinance of his, according to Wieser's rationalization.

Instances can be cited, Wieser considers it appropriate to apologize, in which the subjectivistic character of marginal utility and marginal value, do not meet the situation.

Marginal utility ascribed to a part, Wieser cautions, cannot be said as necessarily providing the basis for the assessment of either utility or value of the respective whole.

It should be granted, Wieser is prepared to state an example, that the utility or value of a forest cannot be arrived at by way of using the device of simple multiplication of the marginal utility which is being accorded to a single tree in that forest.

Extraneous conditions cannot always be ignored, Wieser considers it opportune to remark at this instance.

The fertility of the soil as well as the climatic conditions, to relate the stated example, might have to be acknowledged by a person who undertakes the evaluation of the forest, the author of the "Genesis and the Principal Laws" finds it appropriate to concede.

If such a situation arises, the evaluating person is, on the advice of Wieser, to consider it incumbent upon himself to come forward with a solemn declaration that he finds himself confronted with something unrealizable.

Should an individual who attempts to ascertain marginal utility or marginal value come to admit as in the stated case of the forest, that he could not possibly disregard the presence of objective factors, he is being given a followup advice by Wieser, to voice a protest against being placed in a position in which he faces the all but impossible task of expressing something imponderable, as strange as such a protest might appear coming on the advice of one like Wieser, whose whole exposition is devoted to turning ponderables into imponderables, let us add.

Should an individual who attempts to ascertain marginal utility and marginal value find himself in circumstances in which it were to become patently absurd not to recognize certain objective factors, he is to feel constrained to proclaim that against his free will he has been forced to amend the subjectivistic evaluation procedure to which he had voluntarily subscribed, by an inclusion of an "unknown factor" in accordance with the perverted cognitive advice given by Wieser.

The permeating vagueness which presents a sine qua non of his subjective evaluation procedure, Wieser undertakes to emphasize when he advises to present extraneous circumstances as imponderables.

The utter indeterminableness of a subjectivistic form of marginal utility or for that matter the indefiniteness of a subjective marginal value, Wieser would like to have stressed when he takes it upon himself to counsel, to refer to plainly recognizable objective factors as the unknown and by implication the unknowable or for that matter the unrealizable, the term Wieser himself, chooses.

In his left handed acknowledgement of other but subjective conditioning with regard to the evaluation of the forest to which Wieser refers as an example, he does not deem it necessary to maintain any meaningful link between the subsequent and the antecedent in his presentation.

He comes to make any of his statements in the form of but casual remarks.

He is, moreover, willing to rely on the immediate impression of his utterance of single words.

He does not even care to acknowledge any sense to the rules of syntax.

He does not proceed to evolve a stricter cognitive procedure for the evaluation of the forest as a whole after he disavows the marginal utility and marginal value device in respect to that case.

He ends up without any further argumentation by disowning any conceivable rules for the evaluation of the forest as a whole regardless of whether such rules are economic or a-economic or for that matter whether they refer to a common usage of language or not.

The evaluation procedure which he suggests for the whole in the case of the forest, comes to amount to a compounded negation of cognitive means for the fathoming of the object.

From the kind of evaluation which is being indicated for the whole of the forest by Wieser, only a chaotic impression can be gained as far as the comprehension of the forest is concerned.

How any signification of the forest as a whole is to be attained by the haphazard evaluation procedure, which Wieser suggests, remains and is no doubt supposed to remain, everybody's guess.

Wieser himself does not care to spell out the utter consequences of the disruptive stand which he advises to take to counter objective analytical factors.

He is nonchalantly moving on to what he wants to be regarded as another exemplary case for which he does not expect the marginal evaluation procedure to take effect.

Were for instance, Wieser cites, arable land to be threatened with flooding, nobody should be expected to think of the factor of marginal cultivation.

Were, to state a similar instance, a house to be set on fire, nobody should be expected to ponder about the marginal occupancy of the house.

In such cases in which the imaginary fear of increasing scarcity which underlies the conception of marginalism is being replaced by a real fear, a compliance with the rules of an attempted assessment of marginal utility and marginal value, could hardly be enforced, Wieser inadvertently admits in the two just stated examples.

In cases in which the whole of a possession is threatened, as in the case of a flood or a fire, to which Wieser refers, the imposition of blinds intended to narrow the individual's evaluation capacity, to the extent that he, the individual, is forced to attach an increasing value to progressively decimated particles at the exclusion of any other of his value judgments, can hardly prove effective, Wieser is implicitly conceding in bringing up the last cited two examples.

While he acknowledges that in the cases where the whole of the possession is threatened with actual destruction, it becomes unfeasible to keep a marginal evaluation procedure from being superseded by the evaluation of the whole, Wieser is in no way prepared to admit that a nonmarginal evaluation shall prove more realistic and precise.

Just the opposite is to be inferred.

Neither in the case of the forest in which allowance for nonmarginal evaluation is made without the implication that the imaginary threat of scarcity becomes superseded by a real threat, nor in the case of the land and house for which an allowance for nonmarginal evaluation is made with the implication that the imaginary fear is subject to replacement by a real fear, are any evaluation standards offered for the actual evaluation of the whole.

Since no rules for evaluation are offered, it can be well inferred that in the cases where real fear comes to overtake an imaginary fear as in the examples of the flood threatened soil and the fire threatened house, the comprehension of the object to which that real fear is made to refer is supposed to assume an even more chaotic form, if that were possible than in the example of the forest the existence of which is not subjected to a real threat.

Wieser is but trying, to conclude the just stated observation, to make nonmarginal evaluation as incomprehensible as marginal evaluation.

Wieser does not care to enter a denial that a nonmarginal evaluation which is predicated upon the specific consideration of material production factors can be carried out.

He does not attempt to negate the feasibility of what he acknowledges to be a common or a commonly accepted evaluation to which material costs of production and reproduction are relevant.

He is but eager to convey the impression that no particular advantages can be ascribed to a nonsubjective evaluation procedure.

He is but concerned with having the usual evaluation procedure branded as the most inexact evaluation device.

On the strength of his assertion that all objective factors are unfathomable, Wieser expects the inference to be drawn that any nonsubjective evaluation is of necessity leading to a lack of precision.

On the basis of his presumption that objective factors are beyond the range of the knowable, he would like a wholesale readmission of objective evaluation to be viewed as being of such momentous cognitive consequence as to foredoom that kind of evaluation to complete unreliability.

Those who are inclined to maintain a critical attitude in regard to Wieser's inferential claim that marginal utility evaluation is the more precise, the more exact and the more reliable, are being told off by Wieser in a rather unceremonious manner.

Those who are prepared to demonstrate to Wieser that anyone who becomes engaged in the calculation of marginal utility, cannot but help to become engrossed in a ceaseless effort of endless decimation, are made to hear some harsh words.

Those who in particular are determined to prove to Wieser that anyone who tries to assess a value on the basis of a marginal utility, is apt to find himself lost in an effort to multiply something unmultipliable, are being forewarned by the self-designated reformulator of economic value that such proof can mean nothing else but that the person who is providing such a test has fallen victim to his, the person's, misconception.

Those who are able to marshal evidence to indict the entire case made for subjective evaluation as a move to substitute a manipulation of indeterminable factors for systematic economic reasoning, are treated to Wieser's high sounding pronunciamento which contends that such indictment reflects preconceptions which have been dispensed with.

Subjectivistic evaluation, Wieser does not mind revealing the preconception on the basis of which he operates, is predicated on a deliberate disregard of any social and economic issues which do not directly refer to a presumably isolated consumption.

Wieser discloses the source of his own misconception by making it clear that he has so devised the scope of marginal utility evaluation as to prevent the aspects of distribution, production, and exchange from gaining any respective social and economic relevance.

Wieser gives away his own misconceived projection when he declares that marginal utility and marginal value have been framed by him with a view of steering clear of social and economic problems which arise out of the appropriation of means of production and avoiding any questions which pertain to the societal relevance of economic division.

His nonobjective evaluation, Wieser defends his stand, is assured of a smooth operation since it has been evolved under a preconception which calls for a vacation of all social and economic factors which could possibly interfere with the granting of an exclusive relevance to a secluded consumption.

In furthering his stand, Wieser undertakes to leave no human expression unscathed which is based on a preconception which is not his own.

Words, Wieser registers a major complaint in his essay on "Natural Value" have not ceased to express a common experience.

Words, the designator of what he calls "natural value" objects, have not ceased to be formulations commonly arrived at.

Words, Wieser laments, continue to represent socially significant generalizations.

The time has come Wieser insists, to restrain those to whom words continue to have a social relevance.

The time has come Wieser is adamant, for those who are using words to refrain from reading any generally accepted meaning into a wording.

It is about time Wieser becomes impatient, to narrow linguistic interpretations.

It is about time, Wieser is in a hurry, to proscribe any linguistic explanation which goes beyond a subjective intimation.

Only if words were to be made to account for no more than an indication of a personal feeling, Wieser is eager to direct, they can come to be regarded as meriting real significance.

Only if words were to be made to register nothing but sensual reactions, human expressions should be expected to assume a depth of meaning.

If words were to be ascribed to nothing more but an urge to make vent of individual emotions, if words were to be regarded as nothing else but reflections of emotional fluctuations, Wieser has no hesitation to predict, linguistic formulations will invariably become a model of exactitude.

To exemplify his scheme for a new kind of linguistics, Wieser cites what he cares to identify as a much abused word.

In his exemplification, Wieser relates the attempt to explain value in a commonly accepted fashion.

As one instance of the attempt to explain value in a commonly accepted fashion, Wieser brings up the presentation of value as a social manifestation of material conditions; he means by that the according of value to production factors.

As another instance of the attempt to explain value in a commonly accepted manner, Wieser cites the presentation of exchange value as a price factor.

With reference to the last cited instance, Wieser wants it understood, that he has the commonly accepted view in mind which sees in prices a reflection of existing social relations.

All the cited attempts to interpret value, Wieser feels no scruples to declare, are intended to mislead.

All the stated citations of the attempt to interpret value which have in common that they place value within a specific social context and a definite economic frame are being denounced by Wieser as the kind of explanations which are most likely to lead astray.

In making a bid for the acceptance of his own interpretation, Wieser advances a contention that value cannot be held as being expressive of more than fleeting wants and passing desires.

Value, Wieser amplifies his contention, cannot be considered as representing anything but a mental chain reaction.

Value, Wieser is insistent, cannot be permitted to be referable to anything else but to personal intimations of appreciation and individual indications of satisfactions.

81

In trying to show how he intends to apply his kind of interpretation of value, Wieser wants to have it noted, that what one individual might consider he is desirous of, another individual might not desire for himself.

What one person might, in turn, view as providing satisfaction for himself, another person might regard as not offering him any satisfaction.

Hence, Wieser has finally arrived at the subjectivistic maxim he was after, that what one man might consider to be of value to him, another man might well consider valueless.

Within the range of the subjectivistic maxim of evaluation—Wieser is at pains to stress—it is not to be requisite to ask any socially relevant question when it becomes apparent that what one single person considers worthwhile to exchange, another can well come to consider worthwhile to hold on to.

Within the range of the subjectivistic maxim of evaluation, it should be superfluous to investigate, any respective social ramifications—Wieser is eager to emphasize—when it appears that what one individual regards as a fair price, another individual can come to view as a wholly unfair price.

Since nothing else but individual notions are to be given consideration, since no other than highly personal feelings are to be recorded, no two persons could ever come to agree among themselves about what constitutes value to them, in a proper application of the subjectivistic evaluation maxim, Wieser is sure.

No individual, Wieser proceeds to expand the subjectivistic maxim of evaluation to the range of a solipsist dictum, can ever come to know what takes place in the mind of another individual.

No one, Wieser decrees, can ever come to ascertain the sense reaction and the feelings of somebody else.

Human wants and desires, Wieser would like to have inferred, are therefore to be considered as lying beyond the range of generalizability.

Neither is it to be considered conceivable to arrive at a generalization of human satisfactions.

Wieser would like to have it concluded that through his anti-cognitive efforts have not only all approaches to the formation of concepts been invalidated, but that all procedures for the generalization of perceptions have been found wanting as well.

In a perfectly Nietzschean manner Wieser is prepared to claim that he has destroyed any and all conceptual and perceptual prerequisites which could conceivably be used for the ascertaining of a common denominator of social values.

In presenting words which are uttered by one person as being incomprehensible to any other person, Wieser cancels out the unity and coherence of the spoken language.

All linguistic formulations are to be deprived of any consequence, if Wieser is to have his way.

No two persons could ever come to agree in regard to the meaning of the expressions they use.

UNDERLYING FICTIONS

With social sequence and economic uniformity denied validation, means of identification of a sustained human effort have come to be lacking at the time of departure of Wieser.

A standing invitation had been extended to gloss over the distinctions between the effort and the effortless.

With social division committed to the fold of the incomprehensible, the door had been wide opened for the advancement of fictitious claims.

Thuenen started out on a note of challenge to emerging industry, to retrace the rise of fictitiousness.

He invokes the shadow of self-sufficiency to advance in his "Der Isolierte Staat" a scheme for the recapture of social and economic supremacy of the self-sustaining agriculturist.

Thuenen was followed by Menger who devoted his literary labors to a subsequent defiance of the spread of industrial domination.

Menger introduces the ghost of exchange in kind in his "Principles", to evolve a device for the apparent reassertion of the preeminence of the barter trader.

Menger, in turn, is followed by Wieser, who launched still another attack on the evolving industrial pattern.

Wieser resurrects the spectre of self-provisioning in his "Genesis and the Principal Laws of Economic Value," in an apparent effort to bring back the prevalence of the producer who produces for self use.

Part 2

The Climax of Economic Subjectivism

CHAPTER 4

ENDING UP IN PARADOXES

WITH images turned into empty symbols, with frames of historical reference made to play the role of fictions, the dissolution of objectivistic economic thought was well on its way.

Major concepts having been redesigned as disjointed notions, basic economic categories having been redesignated as reverbera-tions of inner voices, a further addiction to personal improvisation became imminent.

To avoid answering any embarrassing questions pertaining to pressing economic problems, a would-be theoretician had but to retreat into the comforting know-nothing of an artificial primi-tivism.

In musing upon the dimming of social insight brought about by the dismantling of the methodological tools, a friend and collaborator of Wieser had come to realize that the social and economic sights have been sufficiently lowered to insure a success-ful implementation of the sterilization effort.

In pondering upon the beclouding of the conceptual economic outlook due to the introduction of a fictitious framework, Boehm-Bawerk had come to sense unexplored possibilities.

Boehm-Bawerk was in no way troubled by a feeling of anxiety that economic reasoning might regain its vitality at an early date.

The havoc wrought by Menger and Wieser in their frontal assault on the constitutional elements of conceptualization, Boehm-Bawerk was keen to observe, made an early resubstitution of con-cepts for notions appear very unlikely.

The concerted drive to wreck the very approach to the hitherto recognized economic categories appeared to have been so effective as to make an early resumption of conceptual construction look highly improbable to Wieser's great admirer.

Boehm-Bawerk does not intend to conceal that he is well pleased to notice that the successive mutilation attempts of the focal concepts of profit and rent by Thuenen, Menger and Wieser have left those concepts in a condition in which they could hardly be identified as economic categories.

Boehm-Bawerk does not hide that he is highly gratified by the undermining ventures of the inaugurators of economic subjectivism which have rendered the concepts of interest and wages economically meaningless.

Nor is Boehm-Bawerk willing to deny that he is particularly delighted by the thoroughness with which Wieser had proceeded in the disqualification of production costs.

The disassembling of that controlling concept by his friend and collaborator became a source of particular inspiration to Boehm-Bawerk.

Boehm-Bawerk senses that he can well seize the opportunity and exploit those extraordinary feasts of conceptual dissolution.

Wieser's friend and collaborator shows all signs of being delighted by the prospect of having a chance to partake in the fame which the initiators of economic subjectivism had come to claim.

Were he to add a note of dissolution, Boehm-Bawerk appears confident, he'll be entitled to full membership in the select group which had unleashed a fury of detraction upon objectified thought.

Were he to concentrate on an attack on a hitherto neglected aspect, were he to try his wits in the dissolution of a composite comprehension, Boehm-Bawerk appears to be sure, he could put himself into the limelight.

Were he to engage his talents of piling words upon words in an effort to decompose a major conceptual integration, he himself would be able to rise to fame, Boehm-Bawerk shows little doubt.

Were he to be successful in undermining the significance and meaning which had hitherto been attached to the conceptualization of capital, Boehm-Bawerk is hopeful, he could lay claim to a leading role among the ascending coterie which had been launched on its career by Thuenen, Menger and Wieser.

In proceeding to realize his high ambition, in making his bid for membership in the select literary club, Boehm-Bawerk first undertakes to secure for himself a foothold on the ground which had hitherto been claimed by recognized definers of capital.

Capital, its decomposer observes, capital Boehm-Bawerk relates in the opening chapters of his "Positive Theory of Capital and Interest" has been variously defined.

Capital, its detractor recalls, had started out on its conceptual career as a monetary source of money income.

Capital qualified as money capital, Boehm-Bawerk recounts. had been first brought into conceptual prominence by Aristotle.

The distinction between the fixed amount of a monetary loan and the varied amount of due interest—the distinctive feature of the definition of the Saugerite—had implanted itself in the minds of social thinkers through the ages, Boehm-Bawerk reminisces.

The Aristotelian conception of capital, Boehm-Bawerk observes, ruled over European thought from the close of the slavery period of antiquity up to the early period of feudalism.

It was not until the trade routes had made distinct inroads on the European continent that scholastic thinkers had come to attribute interest bearing to other than monetary factors, Boehm-Bawerk rounds out this historical reference note.

Money interest when feudalism was on its way out, had come to be regarded as being but outwardly a monetary increment, to implement Boehm-Bawerk's reference material.

When David Hume became the spokesman for the princely trader, he made it plain he had disposed of the definition of interest which had presented the interest rate as a direct correlate of the amount of money in circulation.

The interest rate in Hume's own definition, as Boehm-Bawerk records it, is being related to the amount of products in the amassment of which money plays but a transitory role.

Hume's definition presented the social insight gained at the time when trade capitalism had reached its apex, when the trade economy was on its part, on its way out, to place Boehm-Bawerk's conceptual chronology in a socio-historical perspective.

The time had ripened for a new formulation, the one which was advanced by Turgot.

Turgot, Boehm-Bawerk notices, sees a major relevance in the surplus of goods.

Turgot, Boehm-Bawerk records, ascribes major importance to those amassed goods which could be laid aside.

The author of "Les réflexions sur la formation de richesse" accords special significance to that part of the stockpile of goods which is known to exceed the required income in terms of current consumption needs and which can thus come to form capital.

Turgot, Boehm-Bawerk tries to show, removes the definition of capital as well as income from the strictly monetary range.

In Turgot's understanding, capital presents an identification of a pile of goods.

The monetary and nonmonetary embodiment of a good are presented by Turgot as interchangeable aspects.

Turgot, to place Boehm-Bawerk's reference to the conceptual innovation of the author of "Les réflexions sur la formation de richesse" within a socio-historical framework, has written the closing chapter of the pre-manufacturing period with his definition.

The opening chapter of definitions of capital which pertain to the period of manufactories has been composed by Adam Smith, —to place Boehm-Bawerk's references once more within a socio-historical perspective.

Turgot's formulation of capital as a surplus of goods presents to Smith a step in the right direction, to preface Boehm-Bawerk's observations on Smith.

In Smith's candid observation Turgot's conceptualization of capital stops short, however, of dealing with a fundamental question.

Smith is critical of Turgot for his having considered the task of defining capital completed before making any statement about the designation of what he calls capital.

Smith criticizes Turgot for having failed to point out in his presentation of surplus goods as capital that capital can be designated for productive assignments. Turgot has in particular neglected to distinguish goods designated as instruments of future production from goods diverted to future consumption in the criticism advanced by Smith.

Smith finds Turgot's formulation of capital wanting in another respect. Turgot's definition is regarded as incomplete by the author of the "Wealth of Nations" since it does not provide for a distinction between capital as a national economic category and capital as a source of personal income.

In his own formulation Smith is careful to differentiate between capital of national economic range which he considers can be effected only by way of production and capital as a source of personal income which in his view can be attributed to other than production factors.

Income in the form of personal income can for instance be secured by making goods available, Smith stresses.

Income, to state an example, can be derived from renting houses and furniture, Smith is at pains to point out, as Boehm-Bawerk should have informed himself.

Boehm-Bawerk on his part does not find it requisite to begin his reference to the conceptualization of Smith by citing Smith. Instead he proceeds to cite interpreters of Smith.

Basing himself on what he regards as authentic interpretation of Smith, Boehm-Bawerk proceeds to attack Smith's own formulations.

In his conceptualization, Boehm-Bawerk protests, Smith has not sufficiently guarded himself against subsequent misrepresentations of his formulations.

The twofold meaning which Smith had attached to capital, Boehm-Bawerk complains, has not been properly understood.

The double projection of capital which has been advanced by Smith has subsequently come to be lost sight of, Boehm-Bawerk draws up his indictment.

Without Smith's explicit authorization, Boehm-Bawerk charges, capital in the national economic sense and capital as a source of income have come to be causally related to each other, Boehm-Bawerk complains.

Capital as a source of income in Smith's conceptualization,—and this Boehm-Bawerk finds particularly objectionable, has come to be imputed to capital as an instrument of production.

Capital income has in short come to be regarded as being identical with produced income, Boehm-Bawerk expresses regret.

The discounting of a distinction between capital in the national economic sense and capital as a source of income which Smith had preserved, have led to an unwarranted oversimplification, Boehm-Bawerk contends.

The disregard for the differentiation between capital income and produced income which is implicit in Smith's formulation, Boehm-Bawerk claims, has paved the way for a gross error.

The placing of a spotlight on income in the form of productive income and capital in the form of productive capital have led to an intolerable integration in the subsequent history of economic thought, according to the charge advanced by Boehm-Bawerk.

The disregard for the duality of Smith's formulation of income and capital, Boehm-Bawerk reemphasizes his charge, has in the subsequent path of conceptualization resulted in the monstrous integration which had been given expression in the term productivity of capital.

In giving vent to his bitter resentment of those wro profess to be following Smith and have failed to sustain Smith's formulations in all their purity, Boehm-Bawerk fails once more to place his argumentation into any kind of socio-historical perspective.

Boehm-Bawerk treats Smith's definitions as a logical non plus ultra.

He rejects any subsequent formulations which present a variation of Smith's conceptualization without inquiring whether those variations do not reflect changes in the social and economic situations which have occurred since the time in which Smith had given expression to his thought.

Boehm-Bawerk withholds the information that Smith had conceptualized at a time when he, Smith as a promoter of the cause of the manufacturer had no reason to shy away from complete social and economic identification.

The new way of production promised to be beneficial to all social and economic strata.

The redivision of existing wealth which constitutes the socio-historical framework within which Turgot labored had ceased to be the exclusive source for a reapportionment of social shares.

Due to the prospect of a general rise in productive wealth, each social group could expect to receive a greater amount of goods.

The division of labor, as Smith was keen to observe, pointed in the direction of a general increase of productivity of work for the benefit of all concerned.

In the view of an expected increase in the general welfare, Smith could afford to offer a definition of capital and income with very little disguise.

In view of the bright social prospects which loomed on the economic horizon at his time, Smith could see no reason to avoid a straightforward conceptualization.

There was little Smith had reason to hide in his making the case for the rising manufacturer.

Were any social abuses which existed at the time of Smith to require disclosure, they could easily have been attributed to those in the seats of economic power and those subservient to them who were overdue for retirement and were on their way out from the forefront of the social and economic scene, as Smith himself had made it clear though, obviously, not to Boehm-Bawerk.

Subsequently economic conditions changed, the manufacturer and the industrialist who followed in the footsteps of the former, found themselves in a position of almost uncontested economic prominence.

Subsequently the manufacturer and his techno-economic heir had succeeded in entrenching themselves to the extent that they, as the princely merchants before them, have come to be able to misuse their economic power.

Subsequently the producing enterpriser and those who had taken over the task of defending his aspirations could not afford to be as outspoken as Smith had been in his conceptualization.

93

Subsequently the economic theorists felt themselves compelled to evade a straightforward social signification of capital.

Say, in consequence, came to characterize capital as one of three socially unidentifiable production factors, to place Boehm-Bawerk's complaint about the misreading of Smith in its proper place in the history of economic concepts.

The social designification of capital has, in turn, cleared the road for the social designification of income, Boehm-Bawerk ought to be instructed.

The designation of capital as mechanical production factor, a delineation which pictures capital as a selfpropelled generator of income, the reduction of capital to a role of a mechanical implement is fully in line with the notion of productivity of capital in which capital appears as a kind of automaton which spits interest along with other income ingredients, Boehm-Bawerk is to be made to realize.

That monstrous integration about which Boehm-Bawerk complains can be well traced to Say.

Boehm-Bawerk instead prefers to go all the way back to Smith in trying to assess the blame.

Smith's conceptual delineations, Boehm-Bawerk directs, are to be treated as inviolable under any and all circumstances.

The author of the "Positive Theory" does not care to inquire into the historical evolution of concepts.

The question of the historical evolution undergone by Smith's concepts in the course of changing social and economic conditions does not lie within the purview of Boehm-Bawerk's exposition.

A comparative evaluation of the respective conceptual delineation of Smith and those who came after him with particular reference to the social and economic background which has come to be reflected in the respective conceptualizations is far removed from the task which Boehm-Bawerk has set for himself.

Boehm-Bawerk inquires into the conceptualization of capital and income in the post-Smithian period with a view of ascertaining whether Smith has been properly or improperly quoted by those who had advanced their formulations after the time when the "Wealth of Nations" was written.

In proceeding to conduct an investigation whether Smith's text has been exactly quoted, Boehm-Bawerk is at pains to emphasize that the exact wording of the "Wealth of Nations" does not contain a formulation which specifically refers to income as a factor derived from production.

Capital as production factor and capital as income source do have some verbal kinship in Smith's formulation, Boehm-Bawerk is constrained to admit.

But those who have used Smiths' text, Boehm-Bawerk argues, have mistakenly assumed that the formulations in which Smith refers to capital as production factor and capital as a source of income have a common core.

An authentic interpretation of the "Wealth of Nations," Boehm-Bawerk insists, calls for the acceptance of a conceptual incongruity in Smith's formulation of capital in its relation to production and capital in its reference to income.

Smith though, did not make a complete conceptual break between capital as production factor and capital as a source of income, Boehm-Bawerk hastens to admit.

The sounds which accompany the use of the word capital by Smith in either reference to production or income may even have a similar ring, Boehm-Bawerk wanders away into literary impressionism.

Smith's use of the word capital as an adjective in conjunction with his use of various substantives, Boehm-Bawerk continues in an impressionistic vein, does however provide a sufficient ground for distinguishing *nuances* (p. 27 *Positive Theory*) in the formulations of capital which he, Smith, advances.

The nuances in the varying formulations of capital offered by Smith are to prove, Boehm-Bawerk insists, that the author of the "Wealth of Nations" was more concerned with pointing to dissimilarities than to similarities in employing the concept of capital in conjunction with either production or income.

Smith, Boehm-Bawerk implies, is so indistinct in his formulation as to make it incumbent upon the reader of the "Wealth of Nations" to depend on reverberations of sound effects which are expected to result by reading Smith's exposition aloud for a proper interpretation of his text.

Boehm-Bawerk does not care to acknowledge that Smith conceptualized within a distinct social context.

The author of the "Wealth of Nations," as Boehm-Bawerk should have known, was not at all reluctant to disclose the social implications of his terms in a quite unmistakable form.

To know what Smith wanted to point out when he formulated capital as national production factor and what he wanted to bring out when he formulated capital as a source of income, one does not have to attempt to guess as Boehm-Bawerk would have it, what emotional undertones or overtones could be ascribed to the respective formulations when they are being recited.

By having committed himself to an evolvement of concepts in close proximity with social and economic conditions which he had come to witness, Smith had amply demonstrated that he did not care to depend upon the emotional impact of words for an interpretation of his text.

Even Boehm-Bawerk is willing to admit that Smith looked askance at a mode of textual interpretation in which personal introspection plays a major role.

Why then does Boehm-Bawerk consider himself entitled to conclude that Smith's formulations of capital and income are characteristic of a primitive undeveloped form of conceptualization.

Why then does Boehm-Bawerk feel free to charge that Smith's formulations are not sufficiently advanced in their form.

Is it because Smith was concerned with using cognitive instruments to prevent verbosity?

Is it because Smith did not conform to a looseness in conceptualization which Menger and Wieser had set out to promote?

The answer though in an indirect form is slowly forthcoming.

To overcome what he regards as infantile conceptualization, Boehm-Bawerk proffers an improvement of the techniques which Smith and his followers had used in their formulations.

To overcome what he regards as undeserving influence of Smith's conceptualization, Boehm-Bawerk advances a strictly formalistic approach.

He is in a position, so Boehm-Bawerk boasts, to silence the whole controversy on the conceptualization of capital and income which had been raging from Smith's time on, by depriving it of any significance.

By depriving the dual conceptualization of capital and income as it had been performed by Smith as well as the conceptual symbiosis of capital and income which had been advanced by those who professed to follow Smith of any socially relevant content, Boehm-Bawerk is proud to announce, he is able to render the whole argumentation on that subject meaningless.

In carrying out his design of disowning the conceptualization of capital and income by Smith and those who professed to follow him, Boehm-Bawerk does not hesitate to assert the conception of production as means of multiplication of products is of no real import.

Production conceived in particular as a means of utilization of mechanical implements, Boehm-Bawerk insists, can be granted only apparent relevance.

The conception of income, Boehm-Bawerk would have it, is, in turn, not to be permitted to have any real connection with either the productive effort or the social division of the affected product.

The meaning of production and income can be fully exhausted, Boehm-Bawerk would like to show, by having those two concepts presented as nothing more than formulations of varying modulations in administrative procedures, which are involved in an allocation of consumer's goods as between immediate or deferred consumption.

To bolster his claim that production and income are but manifestations of shifting consumption, Boehm-Bawerk advances the contention that only those material aspects which have the qualifications of consumer's goods are really extant.

Non-consumer's goods do not really exist according to the proclamation of Boehm-Bawerk.

Producer's goods do not have any distinctive features, Boehm-Bawerk has no hesitancy to insist.

Producer's goods are in reality undistinguishable from consumer's goods, in the asseveration of Boehm-Bawerk.

Money, in turn, is presented as lacking any specific attributes in the formulation offered in the "Positive Theory."

Boehm-Bawerk is prepared to stake his own peace of mind on the notion that those who are not prepared to accept his verdict that only consumer's goods have distinct qualities are laboring under a self-deception.

He wants his contention that the delineation of producer's goods does not refer to any qualitative specification to be regarded as unchallengeable.

Only quantitative variations can be detected in non-consumer's products, Boehm-Bawerk insists and proffers his contention as a heuristic device.

How something can be quantified which is not supposed to exist, Boehm-Bawerk does not confide.

The author of the "Positive Theory" is obviously misusing the term heuristic, since he continues to be determined not to have anything ascertained which could rate as a particular characteristic of a producer's good.

He is thus using the term heuristic in the opposite of its commonly accepted meaning.

Heuristic in the sense in which Boehm-Bawerk is set to applying the device is not intended to lead to the uncovering or discovering of anything.

Heuristic in the manner in which Boehm-Bawerk uses that device becomes but a misleading word, which he uses in order to mislead those who judge words merely by their sound.

"Heuristic" in the context in which Boehm-Bawerk places it, can but throw an added veil around what might become known.

"Heuristic" in the context in which Boehm-Bawerk refers to it, serves more specifically as a device for the prevention of a rediscovery that producer's goods have a significance of their own.

Boehm-Bawerk is committed to the stated misapplication of what is generally known as a heuristic device, since he wants to be left free to refer to production and income as socially and economically unqualified variations.

By underwriting through a supposedly heuristic procedure, the notion that producer's goods are lacking any social and economic significance, Boehm-Bawerk reasons, he has removed the methodological obstacles to have consumer's goods imbued with an all embracing social and economic meaning.

If producer's goods, i.e. production results, are denied any qualitative distinction, Boehm-Bawerk sees himself entitled to argue, it should be terminologically permissible to have all of production and all income from production labeled as a form of consumption.

If producer's goods remain socially and economically disqualified, Boehm-Bawerk is confident, he can proceed to present production and income as but a secondary characteristic of something which by its very definition constitutes the antidote of either production or income.

With production and income made to refer to factors in contradistinction to which those two concepts have been formulated, a precedent is being created, in the inference of Boehm-Bawerk, by which another concept would be made to refer to a factor in contradistinction to which that concept has, in turn, been devised.

With production and income labeled as something they are not, Boehm-Bawerk is led to assume, capital can as well be called as something it is not.

By having eliminated any specific social content from either the denotation of production and income, Boehm-Bawerk realizes, he is precluding the delineation of capital from assuming any specific meaning.

By having production and income consigned to a non-acquisitive sphere, Boehm-Bawerk is aware, he is preparing the ground for the removal of capital—the conceptual correlator of production and income—from the acquisitive nexus.

By having production and income refer to nothing more than to a manipulation of consumption, Boehm-Bawerk is fully conscious, he has furnished himself with a terminological lever by means of which he can have capital as the conceptual correlator of production and income fall to the level at which that focal concept comes to signify nothing else but a form of reference to the modes of immediate and deferred consumption.

Production and income as well as capital as their conceptual counterpart, Boehm-Bawerk expresses confidence, can in their ultimate reference be safely presented in view of his, Boehm-Bawerk's terminological strictures, as nothing but reflections which come to a secluded individual in the sight of an isolated consumer's stockpile.

The designification of the concept of capital which Boehm-Bawerk is sure he can accomplish by going through with the reduction of that focal category to but an indication of something which has nothing to do with any social and economic nexus, is, in turn, being regarded by the author of the "Positive Theory" as providing a basis for further disqualifications of objectivistic social and economic thought.

Once, the once potent category of capital is mutilated beyond recognition an effort to split the concept will hardly be noticed, Boehm-Bawerk could well reason with himself.

Once the category of capital is deprived of any specific meaning an opposition to a proposal to cut that concept into two but loosely connected parts would make little cognitive difference, Boehm-Bawerk has reason to maintain.

Hence, after he is satisfied he has effectively barred the word capital from touching upon the sphere of social and economic appropriation in the acquisitive sense, Boehm-Bawerk goes ahead with a terminological division of capital into what he terms social capital and private capital.

Without offering any definition, Boehm-Bawerk proceeds with a listing.

Under the heading of social capital, he chooses to list

1) soil improvements
or 2) buildings for shops
or 3) production instruments
or 4) production implements (Arbeits und Nutztiere)
or 5) raw materials
or 6) consumer's goods stored for delivery
or 7) money

Plus

such passing instances as buildings and materials designed either for rent, lending or exchange.

By this listing in particular by his indiscriminate citing under the heading of social capital of means of production under 1-6, means of circulation listed under 7 and nonproductive means of deriving income listed under the sign of plus, he markedly contradicts Smith whose concepts he professes to be purifying.

Smith, it should be noted in this context, distinguishes capital in the national economic sense and capital as a private source of income, a distinction which Boehm-Bawerk disregards in his listing.

The listings which are offered by Boehm-Bawerk under the heading of social capital, bear testimony to a cognitive undifferentiation of social and nonsocial capital or for that matter private and nonprivate capital, on the part of Boehm-Bawerk.

When he then proceeds to list under the heading of private capital the same heterogeneous items which are listed by him under social capital, plus consumer's products which are set aside 1) either (a) for immediate consumption of the owner (b) or for the consumption of producing laborers, he but reemphasizes that he does not recognize a cognitive distinction between private and nonprivate capital in any acquisitive sense of the term.

In listing means of production (1-6) means of circulation (7) non-productive means of income and means of consumption within a single social and economic range labeled by him as social capital, Boehm-Bawerk moreover reiterates his refusal to contrast production and consumption.

In listing, in turn, under private capital consumer's products, regardless of whether they are designated for immediate consumption by the owner or for consumption of producing laborers, Boehm-Bawerk but reemphasizes his nonrecognition of any distinction between acquisitive and nonacquisitive factors in regard to ownership.

Boehm-Bawerk withholds, it should be noted, a definition of either social capital or private capital, he does not care to go beyond a listing and thus relieves himself of the task of making an outright statement on what he regards as social and private capital.

By having denied his general category of capital access to the acquisitive nexus, Boehm-Bawerk obviously realizes that he is bound to avoid a formulation of a sub-division of capital in which he could conceivably have to make an allowance for acquisitiveness.

After having denied that social appropriation in the acquisitive sense plays any role in the general conception of capital, he could hardly proceed to allow the subject of social appropriation to enter into the formulation of a divided category.

Since in particular the banning of the subject of social appropriation and economic acquisitiveness precludes a cogent explanation of how social capital comes into private ownership and how, by virtue of what factor private capital is turned into social capital, Boehm-Bawerk considers it the better part of wisdom to abstain from even attempting a conceptualization of either social or private capital.

Boehm-Bawerk's insistence that what he lists under private capital is more real than what he lists under the heading of (real) social capital is not helping to draw a clear line between the two subdivisions.

Boehm-Bawerk's assertion that the individual's concern for private capital is of more real importance than the individual's concern for social capital presents but a reemphasis on the part of the author of the "Positive Theory" that subjectivistic notions are more real to him than any conceivable objective factors.

In implementing his deconceptualization efforts of the most potent economic category, Boehm-Bawerk undertakes to block reasoned validation.

Quite a few devices for breaking loose from coherence and sequence, Boehm-Bawerk is well aware, are contained in the writings of Menger and Wieser.

Menger and Wieser, Boehm-Bawerk is fully conscious, have spared no effort to unburden themselves of the categories of causation and time.

It remained for him, the aspiring author of "Positive Theory of Capital" to add some force to the drive which was intended to disrupt the power of reason in social and economic thought.

Boehm-Bawerk finds it opportune to desist from a head-on attack on the prerequisites of thought.

The emasculation of time and causation had progressed to a point, Boehm-Bawerk came to realize, at which the powerlessness of those two categories in providing either direction for social and economic thought or in bringing order into social and economic thinking could be taken for granted.

At the stage at which deconceptualization of time and causation had arrived, at the period in which he had his say, a social and economic theorist like Boehm-Bawerk could start out with applying the deconceptualized forms of time and causation by demonstrating that they have no bearing on specific social and economic factors.

As far as the social factor in production is concerned, Boehm-Bawerk wants it to be considered as self-evident, time is of no essence.

Time is of no relevance in regard to an ascertaining of the social course which production takes, Boehm-Bawerk would like to have it considered as self-understood.

A reference to time Boehm-Bawerk insists without further explanation, can serve but to underly the nonhuman course of production.

The time aspect, Boehm-Bawerk asseverates, can only be brought in to underscore the social insensitiveness of production.

Time, should it be related to production, can only result in the calling of attention to the inanimate nature of the production process, Boehm-Bawerk wants to have it accepted as a preconception.

Hence in any production analysis the factor of time is but to reiterate that all production presents nothing more than an indeterminable force.

In any interpretation of production data the entering of the time factor is to bring about nothing more than a restatement of the ceaselessness of all production activity.

Any attempt to ascertain a production time is to end up in an admission that production has neither a beginning nor an end.

Any effort to establish a timing in production is to result in an acknowledgement that the production process is timeless.

Within the social and economic vacuum in which Boehm-Bawerk places the production process, he can safely assume, time cannot be made to count.

The playing up of the unspecifiability of time as a way of underwriting the social and economic designification of the production process, Boehm-Bawerk is not unaware, can be applied with equal success in the wresting of any social and economic meaning from production instruments.

If one is to accept the notion that production time is unspecifiable, one is enabled to deny with impunity, Boehm-Bawerk assumes, that production instruments are time saving devices.

In the absence of any specifiable production time even such a paradoxical assertion that machines are time wasters can go unchallenged, Boehm-Bawerk is not unaware.

The adherence to the view that time is a factor which defies a consecutive accounting goes well with the assertion that a delineation of production in terms of a specific output is unfeasible, Boehm-Bawerk is not unmindful.

Within the aspect of timelessness the question in what particular production period a particular means of production is or was effected, is unanswerable, as Boehm-Bawerk undoubtedly knew.

Under the stricture of timelessness all existing production instruments can be logically refused any other identification than the one which describes any given mechanical implements as implements which have been reproduced from other implements and so on and so forth ad infinitum, Boehm-Bawerk provides a syllogistic argumentation.

Through the invocation of the stricture of timelessness the reference to any single presently available production instrument is thus being predetermined by Boehm-Bawerk to lose itself in a reference to an endless chain reaction.

Since he rules out the consecutive recording of present and past production, Boehm-Bawerk has reason to expect that any attempt to collect production data with a view of determining a respective social and economic sequence will come to naught.

Since he rules that timing is epistemologically and methodologically unfeasible, Boehm-Bawerk has reason to anticipate, the recording of production can have no other result than the confrontation of the recorder with a fleeting mass of infinitesimal particles.

With time required for any given production held to be unascertainable, Boehm-Bawerk moves on with his syllogistic exercises, it becomes logically and methodologically impossible to distinguish between the actualization and realization of production, i.e. between production in process and effected production.

When the generation of a product is regarded as indeterminable in any specific form, can it ever be established whether or not there exists any real causal connection between the factor of producing termed as process of production and the effected product termed output, Boehm-Bawerk asks an empty question.

The negation of the feasibility of giving a consecutive account of what brings a product about, Boehm-Bawerk can have little doubt, makes the sustaining of a causative linkage between production and product a highly problematic proposition.

Not much more can be determined in regard to a possible causal connection between production in process and effected output under the stated conceptual disabilities, Boehm-Bawerk argues, than the ascertainment that products are but outward expressions of productive activity.

As far as the causal link between products and production is concerned, Boehm-Bawerk points out, that in view of the cognitive restrictions he has imposed upon himself he can refuse to acknowledge anything more than the recognition that products are but remote signs which indicate a somewhere and a sometime of production.

It should not be considered permissible, Boehm-Bawerk draws upon his own disqualification of causative interpretations, to ascribe any real causal efficacy to production instruments.

It should be viewed as being even more strictly prohibited, Boehm-Bawerk emphasizes, to attribute a primary cause to production implements.

In order to sustain the substitution of an apparent causal linkage between products and production for a real causal connection, Boehm-Bawerk plays with the aspect of sequence; it is to be appropriate to suggest the placing of such products which are not production instruments at the head of the causal chain.

Since it is to be regarded as socially and economically irrelevant whether products are being effected by production or not, Boehm-Bawerk rationalizes, no real distinction can ever be established between manufactured and non-manufactured products.

An added impetus to his methodological fence riding is provided on the part of Boehm-Bawerk by an indulgence in sweeping historical generalizations.

It is well known, Boehm-Bawerk nonchalantly declares, that products have in times long past preceded the most primitive of tools.

Hence he argues the viewing of any production instrument as the efficient cause in bringing about products can well be considered as violation of historical truth and an unwarranted overriding of methodological requirements.

Technological changes, Boehm-Bawerk feels no hesitation to assert in the stated connection, cannot be considered as having had any telling social and economic impact.

Even the change from the Stone Age to the Iron Age, Boehm-Bawerk does not have any scruples to insist, is to be held as being of no great social or economic import.

Neither is the transformation which accompanied the change-over to hand tools and from hand tools to mechanical equipment—which has come to be named machine—to be viewed on Boehm-Bawerk's direction as having had any outstanding social and economic significance.

Drawing upon the just stated dictum as a proven thesis, Boehm-Bawerk arrives at the desired conclusion.

In support of his assertion that production implements have since time immemorial failed to exercise any marked social and economic influence, Boehm-Bawerk wants to have it inferred, that it is historically incorrect and methodologically erroneous to attribute a primary and efficient cause to instruments of production.

Changes of social and economic systems, Boehm-Bawerk continues in a self-assertive mood, are to be granted as little social and economic significance as changes in technology.

Neither the change from the tribal economy to the artisan economy, nor the change from the artisan economy to the market economy are to be rated as having any particular social and economic meaning.

Productive activity, Boehm-Bawerk overgeneralizes, is to be considered as having at all times been directed at a single goal.

Productive activity, Boehm-Bawerk insists, was at all times aimed at the disposition of consumer's surpluses.

Taking his bare assertion as a proven thesis, Boehm-Bawerk proceeds to maintain that it is entirely out of place to link means of production with the social and economic role which pertains to the effecting of added products.

Production instruments would never have been introduced nor would any mechanical production implements ever have been applied, Boehm-Bawerk feels no compunction to assert, were it not for the need of husbanding given consumer's stockpiles.

It is not to be considered, Boehm-Bawerk appears to be ready with qualification, that means of production have no part at all in causation.

It is not to be concluded, Boehm-Bawerk warns, that means of production are fully barred from assuming causative effectiveness.

It should be regarded as conceivable for means of production to qualify as the cause of some passing effect, Boehm-Bawerk offers a mild concession.

As far as the technological range of causation is concerned, it is to be held that means of production cannot cause anything determinable and definite.

As far as the technological range of causation is concerned, Boehm-Bawerk is ready to rate means of production as a kind of intermediary in the indeterminable interplay of the forces of nature.

Only the specification of social and economic causation is to be considered barred from any reference which is made to production instruments, Boehm-Bawerk wants to make it sure.

Only the distinguishing marks of social and economic causality are to be regarded as having no traceable relation with production instruments.

Means of production, Boehm-Bawerk spells out his concession, can be regarded as having some roundabout causal effect on one or the other phase of an unspecifiable interaction.

After having denied that causation can play any meaningful role in the signification of production instruments, Boehm-Bawerk proceeds towards the revocation of any meaningful imputation from the consideration of mechanical implements.

Imputation, Boehm-Bawerk delivers a blast, has been miscast in the way it had been applied to the income category.

The imputation of income has been particularly misconstrued, Boehm-Bawerk would have it, when such imputation contains a direct reference to specific production factors.

The imputation of income to production instruments, Boehm-Bawerk insists, deserves to be branded as the most blatant misapplication of the rules of reasoning.

The gross error as which Boehm-Bawerk parades the imputation of income to mechanical instruments, he cares to attribute to what he terms as a misleading reference to a production factor.

It is wholly illogical, Boehm-Bawerk protests, to impute any specific income form to a concretized production factor.

All rules of formal reasoning are to be considered violated, Boehm-Bawerk rages, when income in the form of interest is being found imputed to a factor of production which has taken the concrete form of a production instrument.

In an effort to provide some justification for his protestation, Boehm-Bawerk delves into what he terms as a special chapter on the history of economic conceptualization.

He relates the history of conceptualization as if it were a history of logical exercises.

After income in the form of rent had been imputed to a production factor which was positively identifiable as land, Boehm-Bawerk recites, after, in turn, income in the form of wages has been imputed to a production factor which was positively identifiable as labor, Boehm-Bawerk proffers an exercise in the assaying of logical equilibristics, there was one income form left which had not been attached to anything specific.

Subsequently somebody had come to observe—Boehm-Bawerk tells a story about a subjectively conceived imbalance in logical propositions—that a production factor is available to which no income form has yet been imputed.

It had suddenly dawned upon somebody—Boehm-Bawerk tells about the subjective way which promises the regaining of a balance in logical propositions—that no income has yet been made referable to that production factor which had come to be known by the name of production instruments.

In consequence—Boehm-Bawerk relates a subjective form which makes logical propositions regain their balance—a decision has been made to close a gap in the array of economic formulations.

For the sole reason, Boehm-Bawerk would have it, that interest had not been imputed to anything while one particular production factor was left without any attachment, it had been decided to bring the two together by having interest imputed to production instruments.

In the imputation of income in the form of interest to a production factor represented as production instruments, although it was logically called for—Boehm-Bawerk turns around to charge—has been made under the false assumption that production instruments can be credited with a social and economic role of their own.

The imputation of income in the form of interest to a production factor in the form of production instruments, though Boehm-Bawerk admits that it was logically justified, is not however to be considered socially and economically warranted.

The imputation of interest to production instruments, Boehm-Bawerk objects, is based on the untenable proposition that production instruments do merit a social and economic signification of their own.

In invoking his own allegation as proof, Boehm-Bawerk reiterates his insistence, that production instruments have no specific relevance.

Boehm-Bawerk assumes an injured pose to ask the question of whether he has not been convincing in showing that production instruments play but an incidental role in production.

He shows signs of distemper in asking whether he has not proven to everybody's satisfaction that production instruments present but indistinct manifestations of a ceaseless process.

Production instruments, Boehm-Bawerk leaves no doubt about his resolution, are not to be found as expressing anything else but undistinguishable reverberations of either animate or inanimate nature.

Production instruments, Boehm-Bawerk is very definite about it, are never to be credited with any distinct efficacy.

Production instruments, Boehm-Bawerk would not permit it to be questioned, have no specifiable function.

Production instruments, Boehm-Bawerk does not want to permit any doubt about it, can have no other function than the one which is imputable to either land or labor.

On the strength of his terminological taboo with which he surrounds the factor of production instruments, Boehm-Bawerk wants to have it inferred that the formulation which presents production instruments as a factor of production to which a specific form of income is held imputable constitutes a patent example of misrepresentation.

Above anything else, Boehm-Bawerk is out to condemn the presentation of production instruments as a production factor to which interest can be imputed, by leveling against such comprehension the charge of "grossly misleading."

Production instruments—Boehm-Bawerk considers it does not require any further proof—are not qualified to play any specific role.

Production instruments are not qualified, there should be no further doubt, to function as a socially signified factor of production.

Nor are production instruments for that matter, there shouldn't be any question about it to be qualified to serve as a socially designified production factor.

Production instruments, moreover, it should not be doubted, are not qualified to account for a socially signified income, Boehm-Bawerk is eager to stress.

Nor for that matter, there should not be any uncertainty about it, are production instruments to be accountable for a socially designified income, Boehm-Bawerk wants to make it sure.

He is purposely assigning an unspecifiable role to production instruments in order to keep mechanical implements from forming a distinct causal link between production and income.

He is deliberately supplying production instruments with indistinct characteristics to prevent production instruments from serving as a distinct basis for the imputation of income to production.

Boehm-Bawerk should, in turn, not be unwilling to confess that *his misrepresentation* of the conceptualization of production and income by the economic classicists which he at first presents as a mere logical exercise and then attacks on allegedly social and economic grounds, has been devised by him in order to furnish himself with a terminological justification for an alogical formulation of production instruments and income.

The way Boehm-Bawerk approaches the formulations of production and income, there can hardly be any doubt, that he is concerned with nothing else but the offering of contrived schemes.

His disqualification of production and production instruments as causal factors in the generation of income, Boehm-Bawerk cannot hide it, constitutes the first step in the evolvement of his fanciful projection.

His barring of production and production instruments from any connection with the allocation of income, Boehm-Bawerk cannot conceal it, brings him a step further in the advancement of his arbitrary scheming.

His disqualification of production and production instruments as a factor to which income could be imputed—Boehm-Bawerk looks for a logical basis for his scheming—has left one income form floating in the air.

In pondering upon the possible factors to which he could attach the unattached form of income, Boehm-Bawerk confesses, that he finds himself greatly attracted by the prospect of imputing the unimputed income form to consumption.

The reason why an imputation to consumption presents a particular attraction to Boehm-Bawerk is not difficult to find.

The category of consumption, Boehm-Bawerk can hardly be unmindful of it, has been shorn by him of any objectifiable social and economic meaning.

Due to the deconceptualization efforts of Menger and Wieser, Boehm-Bawerk can hardly be unaware of it, consumption had come to express nothing more than a psychophysical preconditioning.

The material aspect of consumption and its embodiment in consumer's goods, Boehm-Bawerk should cite it with approval, has been relegated to the role of the incidental.

Under the impact of the wave of conceptual dissolution which had set in with Thuenen, Boehm-Bawerk should have noticed with satisfaction, consumption had come to signify no more than a reference to an array of unidentifiable and unmeasurable particles.

At the hands of the framers of the marginal utility, Boehm-Bawerk should acknowledge it with commendation, material factors and objective aspects have come to be submerged in the formulation of consumption.

Pressed into the perceptual range of subjectivism, Boehm-Bawerk should not be at all averse to observe with particular appreciation, the interpretation of consumption came to be committed to an introspective sphere.

On the strength of the restraining order issued by Menger and Wieser, Boehm-Bawerk should see no reason to hide his sense of obligation, the significance of consumption came to be limited to the manifestation of personal emotions.

With as commanding a category as consumption taken out of the objective and material fold of conceptualization—Boehm-Bawerk should not be at all opposed to welcome it—the subjectivization of related categories can well be presented as a logically and methodologically legitimate move.

The inclusion of an income category within the subjective frame into which consumption had been pressed—Boehm-Bawerk could hardly have failed to see it—can be justified on the ground that it is logically and methodologically permissible since it constitutes but an implementation of a drive to reduce all comprehension to a perceptual level.

His confining of the income form named interest to the emotional sphere, Boehm-Bawerk can well claim, falls completely in line with the effective reduction of the category of consumption to an expression of personal feelings.

The presentation of an interest rate in a form of an emotional vexation—Boehm-Bawerk can well consider himself justified to contend—is fully in keeping with the subjective notion of what constitutes a consumer's good.

Boehm-Bawerk can be sure that he is on familiar ground when

he advances a view in which interest comes to represent nothing but a reflection of emotional frustrations and emotional releases.

He can be confident he is traversing well explored territory when he proposes to make the interest rate dependent upon the squaring of conflicting desires.

He is but adjusting a particular concept to the general approach of Menger and Wieser, Boehm-Bawerk can well claim, by demanding that the level of the interest rate come to be regarded as but tangent of an emotionally charged condition in which the individual dispassion of frugality is tending to assert itself over that person's passion for becoming a spendthrift.

The rate of interest comes to play in Boehm-Bawerk's formulation, the role of a testing device for the pitching of individual steadfastness against personal prodigality.

The rate of interest becomes more specifically a vehicle for the testing of the margin by which the personal predilection to defer the emotional experience held out by the prospect of immediate consumption is expected to assert itself over the individual inclination to indulge in the emotional experience which the prospect of immediate consumption promises.

The dispassion of frugality as regards the emotional experience involved in consumption, Boehm-Bawerk finds it opportune to stress, does not refer to any actual foreseeable supply situation.

The dispassion of abstinence, Boehm-Bawerk sees it fit to emphasize, is not to be considered as being referable to any objective supply situation which could really be expected to occur.

The emotional restraint which finds its manifestation in deferred consumption is not supposed to refer to any statistical computations or mathematical calculations of any material or objective factors which could be expected to be realized in the future, Boehm-Bawerk wants to make it sure.

As far as the determination of the interest rate is concerned, the consideration of the future aspect of consumption is not supposed to extend beyond the vaguest of speculations, if Boehm-Bawerk can help it.

As far as the determination of the interest rate is concerned, the future aspect of consumption is not supposed to indicate more than a dim premonition in Boehm-Bawerk's scheming.

As far as the ascertainment of the interest rate is concerned, the future aspects of consumption enter but in the form of an assessment of present consumption in the formulation advanced by Boehm-Bawerk.

As far as the ascertainment of the interest rate is concerned, the future aspects of consumption, Boehm-Bawerk's formulation implies, can only be comprehended in the form of a person's remote emotional reaction to a subjectively conceived exigency of current consumption.

In the assaying of what Boehm-Bawerk wants to be regarded as current consumption, he rules out the present as a factor which influences the future.

He is assiduously trying, however, to have the future bow or, to use an economic term, to have the future mortgaged to the present.

Future consumption is being entered but as a factor which presents itself as a burden to present consumption.

The future consumption is pictured by Boehm-Bawerk as but a factor which calls for a decrease in the share of present consumption.

Marginal utility preconceptions, he could well cite in the stated connection, do not provide for the recognition of production as a source of increasing future abundance.

Marginal utility preconceptions, Boehm-Bawerk could well point out in the stated context, require the future to form a threat of increasing scarcity.

To comply with the tenet of marginal utility, Boehm-Bawerk would have the interest rate reflect the emotional letdown which the individual feels when he subjects himself to what appears to him as a voluntary curtailment of his immediate consumption.

In the determination of the interest rate, Boehm-Bawerk offers a terminological twist, the future aspect of consumption is not supposed to play a part of its own.

In the determination of the interest rate, the future aspects of consumption are supposed to be marked only by a personal emotional reaction to current consumption.

In the determination of the interest rate, Boehm-Bawerk implies, the future consumption is to be rated as but an added stress on present consumption.

Future consumption, Boehm-Bawerk emphasizes, is supposed to form a factor which burdens present consumption.

Future consumption signifies but a phase to Boehm-Bawerk which points in the direction of a decrease of present consumption.

An anticipation of an increased source of consumer's satisfaction cannot be squared with Boehm-Bawerk's scheming.

To have an enlargement of the production base or even an enlargement of output figure in future consumption, is in particular something which is wholly incompatible with the social and economic disqualification of the means of production which lies at the base of Boehm-Bawerk's scheme.

The promise of a greater abundance is, moreover, wholly unacceptable, it should be noted, under the general premise of increasing scarcity.

Within the terminological and methodological straitjacket in which he places himself, Boehm-Bawerk has no alternative than to have the interest rate expounded as an emotional letdown which the individual feels who subjects himself to a voluntary curtailment of his immediate consumption.

The interest rate is specifically referred to by Boehm-Bawerk as an emotional discount rate.

That emotional discount rate, Boehm-Bawerk wants to have determined on the basis of a comparative dissatisfaction which any single individual is likely to feel in anticipation of his deferring for future consumption of what he considers a marginal share, of what appears to him is presently available for his consumption.

The setting of the interest rate is thus to be undertaken through a procedure which provides for a calculation for which compounded subjective notions are supposed to serve as a basis.

The multiplication of his own personal uncertainties about his desires and the means for their satisfaction is to help that person calculate the interest rate which is most adequately to express his feelings, in the perplexing notion proffered by Boehm-Bawerk.

As the setting, so is the maturing of the interest rate made subject by Boehm-Bawerk to an emotional preconditioning.

The dissatisfaction which has come to affect the individual in connection with his deferring of what he regards as his marginal share, comes to make way to a feeling of satisfaction, Boehm-Bawerk assures.

In Boehm-Bawerk's interest maturing scheme, the individual's emotional stress comes to be compensated through the sensing of a gradual emotional relief, as the future becomes the present and the once deferred marginal share comes to be slated for a release for immediate consumption.

What else comes to transpire during the time when the interest rate goes through the process of maturing by way of emotional adjustment, Boehm-Bawerk appears to realize, cannot be altogether ignored.

The question what utilization in particular had been made of the (marginal utility) particles the consumption of which has been deferred, cannot be left entirely unnoticed, Boehm-Bawerk is willing to admit.

The commitment to production of the marginal shares which had come to be withdrawn from current consumption cannot be wholly overlooked, Boehm-Bawerk concedes.

Such admission on his part, Boehm-Bawerk does not want it to be misunderstood, is not to be interpreted as a recognition on his part that any specific techno-economic or socio-economic factors have any bearing on the maturing of interest.

The generation of interest is to be viewed as but a ripening process which takes part in nature.

The realization of interest is to be regarded as a matter of natural growth.

No ingenuity, no personal enterprising, is supposed to be required to have nature effect the increment which is to form interest.

No productive effort is in particular to be involved in bringing about the increment which is to rate as interest.

The natural increment which is to rate as interest is in no sense to be regarded as a reward for labor.

The increment which is supposed to account for interest, is supposed to be treated as a gift of nature.

The interest collecting individual, Boehm-Bawerk goes on record, is but required to display patience.

The interest taking person is but admonished by the author of the "Positive Theory of Capital" to profess he is prepared to wait.

The interest seeker is but to demonstrate he has no design of consuming something which is not yet there.

The person who considers himself entitled to interest is but to make sure that he has sufficient self restraint to withstand the temptation of reaching out for the growing fruit before its ripening time has expired.

The person who views it as his privilege to collect interest is but to convince himself to his own satisfaction that he has frugal habits and is possessed of a high degree of abstinence.

It could hardly appear terminologically objectionable, Boehm-Bawerk rationalizes, to have the maturing of the self-growing capital increment, the socio-economic origin of which has been rendered unknowable by the denial of socio-economic causation, referred to as the major function left to a social capital which has been deprived of its social and economic core via the route of social and economic designification of production.

No terminological obstacles stand in the way, Boehm-Bawerk extends his rationalization, to have the selfgrowing capital increment referred to, in turn, as the basic form in which a private capital is being realized which has been divorced from the sphere of social and economic appropriation through the disqualification of the factor of social and economic imputation.

In continuing to advance empty syllogisms, Boehm-Bawerk wants his socially and economically designified form of interest to be regarded as an overriding income category.

Since he has refused to grant a social and economic signification to any income form, since he has, moreover, denied the generation of income any social and economic signification, Boehm-Bawerk proffers a sophistic argumentation, he is free to infer that all income is a gift of nature.

Since he has confined income allocation within the range of a personal attitude, Boehm-Bawerk amplifies his sophism, he is at liberty to infer that all forms of income appropriation are due to nothing but patient waiting.

Profit postulated as a distinct income form presents a particularly indefensible proposition, Boehm-Bawerk maintains, since the sustaining of profit as a category of its own is wholly incompatible with the notion that capital increments do not require for their generation any kind of productive enterprising.

Neither is the postulation of rent as a separate income category, Boehm-Bawerk continues his formalistic argumentation, compatible with the notion that capital gains accrue without the benefit of cultivation.

Neither is in Boehm-Bawerk's argumentation the appropriation of profit or rent to justify a specific conceptual identification since in his comprehension those appropriations do not reflect any attitude which is dissimilar from the one which he considers is called for in the case of the appropriation of interest.

Profits as well as rent fall within Boehm-Bawerk's formalistic argumentation to those who are willing and able to defer their consumption.

Although the generation of wages does not in any way differ from the generation of profit, rent and interest, in Boehm-Bawerk's comprehension, although he takes it for granted that wages are generated in the same naturalistic manner as profits, rent and interest, he does not consider it proper to assert that wages are being appropriated in the same manner as profits, rent and interest.

Due to his inability to defer his current consumption for any length of time, Boehm-Bawerk argues, the wage-earner excludes himself from directly benefiting from those gifts of nature which fall into the lap of the interest taker, the profit maker and the rent collector.

Due to his incapacity to indulge in a do-nothing attitude, Boehm-Bawerk rationalizes, the wage earner comes to depend for his income share on the good will of the interest taker, the rent collector, and profit maker.

The wage earner stands therefore exposed in Boehm-Bawerk's formulation as the only sharer of private capital who cannot master the proper attitude which is requisite for the laying of a direct claim to a share in the private capital.

The wage earner comes thus to be presented by the author of the "Positive Theory of Capital" as the one who is deriving his income by imposing himself upon those who are not wage earners.

Since toiling in production has no relation to either generation or appropriation of income in Boehm-Bawerk's scheme, he cannot see anything perplexing in his assertion that the wage earner who is incapable of mastering sufficient fortitude to desist to any degree from immediate consumption, thus renders himself unable to earn his income in any other way than by exploiting the gains which are being made either by the interest taker or profit maker or rent collector who come into the possession of their income shares through their emotional predisposition to defer consumption.

Those who have to exert themselves in bringing about means of consumption, Boehm-Bawerk wants to have it inferred, are the ones who are abusing those who do not have to make a direct productive effort.

Those who have to labor to bring forth means of consumption for all income receivers, emerge from Boehm-Bawerk's presentation as the ones who have damned themselves by their anti-social attitude, while those who can afford to sit back when work in production is being performed, are being pictured by the author of the "Positive Theory of Capital" as the ones who grace themselves by socially commendable traits.

In effecting the conceptual decomposition of the most focal economic category, Boehm-Bawerk has availed himself of the most up-to-date deconceptualization methods of his time.

In bringing about the dissolution of the concepts of capital and income, Boehm-Bawerk had come to profit from the general deterioration in the approach to social and economic generalization.

Menger and Wieser on their part invoked the aid of those who had attacked coherence and sequence on the higher levels of reasoning.

Menger and Wieser echoed the epistemological revolt against Kant's "Thing in Itself."

Kant's insistence on the apparent as a symbolic expression of the

119

real has come to be supplanted by the neo-Kantians with a contriving of appearances with regard to which the question of reality was not supposed to be asked.

Boehm-Bawerk as did Menger and Wieser before him, joined the onslaught of the neo-Kantians against Kant by fully complying with the restriction of cognition to subjectified appearances.

In placing personal attitude at the base of his deconceptualization effort, Boehm-Bawerk merits the title of a full fledged neo-Kantian.

Social and economic thinking had, furthermore, come to show a tendency in Boehm-Bawerk's time towards a flattening out.

Social and economic scientists had come to abandon in Boehm-Bawerk's time any probing of what lies under the social and economic surface.

The protestation of Auguste Comte, his insistence that merely such social and economic factors which present an outer manifestation of social and economic life merit any signification, has brought about a form of positivism which restricted itself to the devising of outer contours with complete disregard of any respective social and economic content.

Positivism had come to authorize the withdrawing of any demarcation line between a reasoned generalization and a concocted abstraction.

Positivism, as Boehm-Bawerk had ample opportunity to demonstrate, made it unfeasible to form a distinction between a meaningful debate and a meaningless sophistry.

Since objectified criteria for the generalization of social and economic observations had been disqualified and the factor of relevant social and economic content in social and economic conceptualization had been designified, when Boehm-Bawerk started to write his "Positive Theory of Capital," he had reason to consider himself privileged to imply that no sensible distinction could ever be made between an array of compounded fictions which he set out to devise and a systematic correlation of concepts which are designed to approximate social and economic reality.

CHAPTER 5

APPROACHING MEANINGLESSNESS

THE placing of an ominous category beyond the realm of social scrutiny and economic criticism is too alluring a venture as not to be tried again.

The creating of obstructions to the viewing of a conceptual mainstay in a relevant perspective, the obfuscation of the central position held by a focal concept is too tempting an adventure to be attempted only once.

The reduction of the most vital generalization to the level of a vague intimation presents too promising a prospect not to be repeated.

The subjection of a socially identifiable conceptual delineation to a maze of submerged notions and suppressed desires is too inviting an undertaking to be left without duplication.

The submerging of the comprehension of capital in a muddle of unspecifiable manipulations presents too luring a device to be left without imitation.

The turning of capital and income categories into hollow sounds is too provocative a design not to be readapted.

The paradoxical intimation that concepts are but indications of individual emotional vibrations, the perplexing insinuation that macrocosmic manifestations express themselves exclusively in microcosmic configurations is too inciting a scheme for social and economic disorganization to be applied a single time.

Boehm-Bawerk's subjectivistic superimpositions, the superb conceptual disintegration which had come to be advanced in the "Positive Theory" was not meant to remain and did not remain an isolated case.

The self-professed designifier of capital labored in a climate of conceptual decomposition.

Boehm-Bawerk breathed an intellectual air which was filled with the nauseating odor of artistic and scientific decadence.

There appeared quite a few self-professed guardians of economic thought to whom Boehm-Bawerk could look for sympathy and support.

There emerged quite a number of self-appointed rejuvenators of theoretical thinking who were favorably disposed towards the self-anointed custodian of the designified category of capital.

Among those who were eager to join the forming new group of would-be heirs to economic classicism an American theoretician has come to stand out.

Among those who could well be trusted with the task of performing another act of subversion of classical thought, John Bates Clark has come to be entitled to a prominent place.

Among those who could be fully depended upon for a furthering of the submerging of classical traditions of economic thinking in a wave of anti-intellectualism the author of "Distribution of Wealth" comes to rank high.

Clark to be sure is less pretentious than Boehm-Bawerk.

Boehm-Bawerk, to appraise him correctly, does not just protest, he is a highly subtle subverter.

Clark, on his part, does not care to have implied that his devious scheme of designification bears the stamp of either Kant or Comte.

Clark is satisfied to operate within a cruder epistemological range.

Clark does not mind basing himself on a vulgarized version of the Common Sense philosophy. He does not hesitate to lean on the obscurantist version of the Scotch philosophical school which had a certain influence among Americans in the early days of the Republic.

Clark does not have any scruples against taking recourse to what he calls the self-evident, in an attempt to validate his propositions.

The question of methodological prerequisites does not occupy Clark.

The utter disregard of the author of "Distribution of Wealth" for any and all rules of conceptualization is sheer astounding.

From the very start of his exposition Clark lapses into a kind of epistemological and methodological primitivism.

He is apparently satisfied to have the tedious task of disqualifying the means of conceptualization left to Menger and Wieser.

At some points, it should be noted, the author of the "Distribution of Wealth" appears to be descending to a kind of instrumentalism.

In a roundabout manner Clark makes his favored terms fit into a kind of functional device.

In riding the tidal wave of conceptual dissolution Clark displays a certain attachment to those pragmatistic practices which had come into vogue with William James and John Dewey.

The theme which fascinates Clark, the thematic proposition which attracts the author of the "Distribution of Wealth" does not vary greatly from the one that had attracted Boehm-Bawerk.

The categories to the subjectivistic subversion of which Clark dedicates his literary labor do not in any way differ from the categories to the disintegration of which Boehm-Bawerk had devoted himself.

In some regard it may even appear that Clark and Boehm-Bawerk have entered a contest.

In some way it might even seem that Clark and Boehm-Bawerk are drawn together by the desire to match each other's deconceptualization devices.

In a sense Clark and Boehm-Bawerk are vying with each other for the designification of the conceptual mainstays of classical economic thought.

Clark writes as if he is trying to outdo Boehm-Bawerk in offering his kind of obfuscation.

The author of the "Distribution of Wealth" writes as if he were attempting to wrest the laurels from the author of the "Positive Theory" by proffering his own way of obstruction of a unified view on capital.

The word capital, Clark starts out on his terminological joyride, can be used in a capricious manner in its relation with other words.

The word capital can be used, Clark offers an exemplification, either in the word combination of abstract capital or the word-conglomeration of concrete capital.

The word combination of abstract capital, Clark extends his exemplification, can on its part be referred to as mobile capital, while the word-conglomeration of concrete capital can, in turn, be referred to as immobile capital.

The word-combination of mobile capital as the word-conglomeration of immobile capital, Clark wants to make it sure, is not supposed to have any meaningful link to the conceptual division of circulating and fixed capital.

The word mobile, when it comes to be attached to the word capital, is not supposed to relate anything which has something to do with material changeability and flexibility, Clark insists.

The term mobile used in connection with the word capital is, in turn, not to be taken as providing an indication of material constancy and inflexibility.

The attachment of the word mobility to the word capital, Clark lectures, is but to provide an intimation of the essential flexibility and changeability of some unidentifiable capital substances.

The words constancy and flexibility when referred to—Clark is devising a hide and seek game—are not to be linked with the word combination of immobile capital.

Constancy and flexibility, when referred to, are to be linked with the word combination for which mobile capital is supposed to serve as a terminological substitute, i.e. to the word combination of abstract capital.

When the words changeability and flexibility are referred to, Clark displays the reverse side of his hide and seek game, they are not to be linked to the word-conglomeration of immobile capital but its terminological substitute.

When the words changeability and flexibility are uttered they are, in other words, to be referred back to the word conglomeration of concrete capital.

Concrete capital, Clark obviously readies himself for another round of terminological subterfuge, is, in turn, to be termed general capital.

Constancy and inflexibility in their reference to abstract capital, Clark gives a hint at what he is aiming with his word game, are to be considered as being most adequately expressed when reference is made to money.

Changeability and flexibility in reference to concrete capital, Clark provides a reverse clue, are to be regarded as being most appropriately brought out when the reference involves production instruments.

As a result of his juggling of terms, Clark comes to present mediums of exchange as essentially unchangeable in character, while means of production emerge from his terminological double talk as fundamentally flexible in character.

The terminological twist at which Clark has arrived at this point permits him to discount the convertibility of money into means of production and to disregard, in turn, the reconversion of production instruments into means of exchange, by claiming that he has provided the terminological means for such disqualification.

By virtue of his terminological tour de force Clark is able to advance the claim that an interrelated view on monetary and non-monetary factors is inconceivable.

He has, in turn, maneuvered himself into a position through his terminological trickery from which he can stage a verbal stunt by proclaiming that a common social and economic denominator for monetary and (non-monetary) production gains cannot be established.

The terminological disarrangement which he has engineered makes it, moreover, feasible for the author of the "Distribution of Wealth" to proffer a renunciation of the observation that monetary and non-monetary income are interchangeable.

The terminological disorientation which he has brought about is well fitted to support his claim that monetary and non-monetary income are socially and economically incongruous.

Some subsequent remarks by Clark look at first glance as an expression of doubt on his part, of whether he should fully subscribe to the just stated conceptual disparity. Some qualifying

125

statements, which Clark brings up, appear at first as an indirect admission on his part that a certain interrelation in the generation of income from money and non-money capital cannot be denied.

His half-hearted backtracking becomes so involved, however, that it defies any signification.

His qualifications become so overlaid with more or less as to lose any definite meaning.

In the formulation which then follows, Clark removes even the shadow of a doubt that he endorses a complete conceptual break between money and non-money capital.

When Clark proceeds to accord income from non-money capital the quality of a material increment and simultaneously moves to deny income from money capital the signification as a material attribute he makes it clear, that he is determined to maintain an unbridgeable gap between the conceptions of money and non-money income which he advances.

When he undertakes to characterize income from non-money capital as naturalistic and goes about picturing income from money capital as non-natural, he makes it clear that he is bent on complete suspension of any links between the conceptions of monetary and non-monetary income.

To make sure a peculiar form of income from money capital is not to play havoc with the conceptual disparity of money and non-money capital which he devises, Clark performs still another terminological trick.

To make sure that interest from money capital is not to be linked with income from non-money capital, Clark perfects an exercise in syntax.

To reemphasize the incongruity of the two income categories, the author of the "Distribution of Wealth" advances a syntactical device.

Capital as a noun is to be reserved for exclusive use in the term abstract capital and its terminological correlate money capital.

For the term concrete capital and non-money capital as its terminological correlate, capital as a noun is to be held fully replaceable with capital used as an adjective.

It does not make any difference, Clark accompanies his just

stated instruction for a syntactical somersault with a refrain, whether non-money capital is being otherwise referred to by the term of capital goods.

The execution of the syntactical somersault in Clark's presentation, to indicate its real impact, brings about another aspect of conceptual disparity.

In keeping capital as a noun reserved for the term abstract capital and having capital reduced to an adjective in his reference to concrete capital, Clark establishes a divergency in scope of the two forms of capital.

Abstract capital referred to as money capital and concrete capital referred to as non-money capital, referred to, in turn, as capital goods, are placed out of each other's conceptual range.

Abstract capital referred to as money capital becomes overabstract as compared to concrete capital, referred to as non-money capital, referred to also as capital goods.

Concrete capital referred to as non-money capital, referred to also as capital goods, is rendered, in turn, overconcrete as compared to abstract capital, referred to as money capital as result of the "operation syntax" undertaken by Clark.

As a result of his syntactic changeover, Clark presumes, money capital becomes so abstract a proposition that it has to cease serving as a specifiable factor of income formation.

Money capital, in becoming a superabstraction, Clark advances an empty argument, all but loses its link with any form of concretization.

Money capital, in becoming a comparative superabstraction, Clark insists, can in particular retain no more than a nominal relationship with money income.

In relating social and economic issues, if they were devoid of any social and economic content, Clark succeeds in having money income referred to also as interest, detached from any socially and economically meaningful relation to money capital.

In treating the subject of income formation as but a terminological device and not as a matter of social and economic differentiation Clark succeeds in having money income, referred to also as interest, assume the character of an income which is removed from any identifiable socio-economic source.

By sheer terminological sophistry, income in the form of interest is being transformed by Clark into an income the social and economic origins of which are unknown.

By sheer terminological tour de force, income in the form of interest is being accorded an economically unrelated and a socially independent form.

By virtue of a terminological twist, income in the form of interest is being frozen into what Clark terms as a static condition.

Under the impact of his syntactical device, Clark expects income in the form of interest to transform itself into a kind of self-perpetuating bonus the socio-economic origin of which is to remain unknown and the socio-economic beneficiaries of which are to be kept hidden.

The overconcretization of money capital, Clark, in turn, suggests, makes it unfeasible to maintain any socially and economically meaningful relation with non-money income.

Since non-money capital comes to be referred to by the term capital goods, there is no need to grant non-money income any social and economic character of its own, Clark argues.

Non-money income can simply be identified as a capital goods increment, Clark turns his terminological screw the other way.

As far as money capital is concerned, to provide a clue for the overgeneralization and overspecification game, Clark had not entirely disqualified its social economic aspect, he had only overgeneralized its social and economic factors; he felt therefore constrained to define money without any direct reference to money capital.

As far as non-money capital and its respective terminological changeover to capital goods is concerned, the social and economic aspect has been entirely lost sight of; and it is exactly the social and economic sterilization of non-money capital on which Clark had staked his literary fame.

Since he was determined to have production identified as a mere physical process, Clark could well afford to have non-money income defined as production increment.

He could be sure that in view of the social and economic designification to which he is subjecting the production process non-money income defined as production increment would provide neither a lead for the social source nor an indication of the economic allocation of non-money income.

In view of the denial of social and economic attributes to the production process to which he is committed, Clark can feel confident, his definition of non-money income as production increment is most likely to be taken as referring to a self-generating increment.

Income from non-money capital emerges from the terminological hide and seek game of Clark as a production premium which is not due to any social and economic effort.

Non-money income emerges from Clark's playful indulgence in overconcretization and overgeneralization as a production premium which is inherent in what Clark cares to call the dynamism of production.

Since his social and economic disqualification of the source of non-monetary income makes it feasible for him to keep that source causally attached to the socially and economically designified form of non-monetary income, Clark feels no hesitation to argue that no further proof should be required that non-monetary income is the incomparably better guaranteed income.

Since, in turn, he had omitted to furnish a social and economic disqualification of monetary capital and had thus felt compelled to deny any causal link between a socially and economically disqualified monetary income and what is commonly regarded as its source, Clark has no scruples to insist that monetary income is the comparatively much unsafer income.

Terminological substitution is thus without any further qualification granted causative efficacy.

Deliberate terminological detachment and attachment is without further explanation being placed on the level of changes which relate to social and economic causation.

Social and economic causation, moreover, is being brought into the context of terminological relations which are not supposed to refer to any kind of social and economic content.

Since, however, Clark has set himself on a course which is not supposed to require any socially and economically meaningful interpretation, he sees himself entitled to continue playing a word game without even offering any excuses.

The safety and steadiness of income from non-money capital to which he testifies on the strength of his inference that terminological and causative relations do not differ from each other in any form and manner, Clark is eager to have terminologically reasserted.

He is anxious to have non-monetary income referred to by a term which has traditionally been associated with steadfastness.

Since stability and continuity have been generally associated with the term rent, Clark finds it opportune to suggest to shift the use of the term rent and have it refer to income from non-money capital which he otherwise terms as income from capital goods.

In sounding the word rent the perfector of a new kind of a theory of distribution of wealth has no intention to subscribe to the social and economic meaning which the term had acquired.

Rent as an indicator of social privilege, rent as a toll demanded and paid for to the owner of land does not in any way enter Clark's scheme.

Since he is set to defy the social signification of any form of income, Clark should not be expected to divulge the social identity of the rent receiver.

Pursuant to his drive for social designification, Clark places the term rent within a purely technological context.

Rent is turned into an indicator of productive efficiency by Clark.

The narrow scope to which rent is being assigned presents but a preliminary stage in Clark's recasting of the rent category.

Subsequently, Clark leaps into an overextended claim as far as the rent category is concerned.

In a rather ominous move, Clark undertakes to assign the crippled concept of rent the role of an overall income category.

The ominous aspect of Clark's designification of rent is brought out by his insistence that rent postulated as a mere technological factor is to be given cognitive preponderance over any and all income forms.

A socially designified rent category, Clark feels undoubtedly sure, can well be used for identification of that increment which accrues in a socially designified production.

A socially designified rent category, Clark is no doubt confident, can be well applied in a move to underscore the denial of any social differentiation within the range of the production process.

The twist which Clark offers in the stated connection pertains to an act of deliberate imputation.

He imputes rent defined as production increments to the production effort as a whole.

He redefines in turn the production effort as a whole as nothing but an expenditure of inanimate energy.

He then proceeds to confer the name of labor on what he just defined as a non-human force.

He thus makes the brusque terminological move to have the non-social aspects of production and its effects expressed by words which had been hitherto used to express human production elements.

As a consequence, Clark feels free to refer to non-human efficiency as if it were human efficiency.

Furthermore, he feels at liberty to refer to a non-human reward, as if it were a human compensation.

He feels unconstrained in using the word wage to identify a material increment.

The only possible objection to his casting of rent in the role of an overall income category, Clark maintains, can be raised only by those who are not willing to reinterpret the "Principles" of Ricardo.

Opposition, Clark professes, he expects only from those who are not willing to go along with a reassessment of Ricardo's rent category.

Exception can be taken only by those, Clark implies with the just stated profession, who are unable to realize that Ricardo's rent category is in need of social disqualification.

The outcry of outrageous misrepresentation can only be hurled against him by those, Clark inadvertently admits, who are adamant in refusing to acknowledge that Ricardo's broad social views on rent are wholly compatible with his, Clark's, subjection of the rent category to managerial manipulations.

What Ricardo had regarded as rent differential, Clark spells out his version of Ricardo's "Principles," has no relation to social conditioning.

What Ricardo had come to define as diminishing returns from the successive use of production implements, has no social bearing to Clark.

The way Ricardo had conceived and conceptualized the need for a productive use of the soil, has no social implication to the author of the "Distribution of Wealth."

The conception of rent differential, Clark insists, is wholly unrepresentative of a social division of income.

The conception of rent differential and its conceptual correlate of diminishing returns, Clark protests, have no relation whatsoever to a socially privileged income form.

The conception of rent differential and its conceptual correlate of diminishing returns, Clark proclaims, are in no way indicative of any particular social and economic condition.

Rent differential and diminishing return as its correlate are ever present according to Clark's declaration.

Rent differential and diminishing returns as its correlate express nothing more than variations in standards of non-human efficiency to Clark.

Rent differential and diminishing returns as its counterpart are slated to become terms indicative of non-human productivity in the nomenclature of Clark.

Ricardo was guilty of a misconception, Clark would have it, when he conceived of rent differential and diminishing returns as being causally related to each other.

It is unpardonable Clark rages, to have rent differential and diminishing returns conceived in terms of social causes and social effects.

Rent differential and diminishing returns are not supposed to refer to any social factors, Clark is adamant.

A comprehension of rent differential and diminishing returns which makes allowance for a socially preceding and a socially succeeding factor in the correlation of the two terms to each other is thus rendered inoperative by Clark.

Rent differential and diminishing returns are not even to be considered as following each other within a non-social range.

Causation just does not become effective in any analysis of the correlation of the rent differential and diminishing returns, Clark would have it.

It does not even make a difference whether the denotations of rent differential and diminishing returns are kept nominally apart or not, Clark insists.

Considering the meaning to which they become reduced by having them serve as indicators of non-human efficiency and non-human productivity, it should not even matter Clark argues, if the two denotations were used as interchangeable.

The social meaninglessness to which he has reduced all terms he uses, makes it logically feasible for him—Clark but underscores his disorienting social and economic position—to have his socially and economically meaningless term of rent differential used as interchangeable not only with his socially and economically designified term of diminishing returns but with any other socially and economically disqualified denotation.

Why not, Clark asks a rhetorical question, have the term rent differential replaced by the term wage differential, since, as he realizes, he has assigned both words which compose each of the two stated terms to the role of expressing the non-social.

Why not, Clark continues to orate, replace, in turn, the term of diminishing returns by the term material increment, since he is aware that he has disqualified each of the two respective terms to serve as indicators of socially and economically relevant factors.

The denotation wage differential as well as the denotation of material production increment come to serve in Clark's terminological followup as references to technological aspects of production.

The terms wage differential and material production increment come to be used by the author of "Distribution of Wealth" for the purpose of denoting varying aspects of physical productivity.

In the non-social context in which Clark places the stated terms, wage differential assumes the character of a self-generating wage differential while material production increment comes to rate as a self-propelling material production increment.

133

Clark on his part does not mind to subscribe to the monstrous implication of self-generation and the self-propelling of income.

He finds it even opportune to emphasize that he is bent on such use of the terms wage differential and material production increments as to create the definite impression that those terms are indicative of a selfsustaining production device.

Wage differential and material increment, Clark protests, are not tied to productivity as such, but to a productivity of a special kind.

In attaching himself to the band wagon of those who had placed the mirage of ever increasing scarcity in the forefront of their argumentation, Clark makes the terms wage differential and material increments expressive of what he calls a marginal productivity of labor.

The term marginal productivity of labor is being designated by Clark to play a major, yet not readily accountable role.

By involving the magic words of marginal productivity of labor, Clark expects each individual laborer to gain the ability to set his own production sights.

Through the mere intonation of the sounds marginal productivity of labor, wage differentials come somehow to fix themselves in Clark's imagination.

In the evolving picture of sweetness and light to which the invocation of marginal productivity of labor is supposed to lead marginal increments are to be found as setting their level in full accord with the degree of the respective individual productive exertion in Clark's fancy.

Clark's conception of marginal productivity of labor, to appraise its logic, is based on the presumption that wages are but correlatives of production increments which each worker attains by virtue of assigning himself his own work schedule.

Clark further presumes in advancing his conception of marginal productivity of labor, that the wage level cannot be possibly raised above the level of productivity attained by the least diligent worker, since each worker is supposed to be responsible for his fellows in regard to their productivity and efficiency over which he is to consider himself duty bound to watch.

The technical lingo Clark uses fits outwardly into the conceptual framework of scientific management.

The larger meaning of Clark's terminology is not however without pre-scientific implications.

The practice of holding all members of a working crew responsible for the work tempo of any single crew member which is called for by Clark's terminological device, is reminiscent of a period when the individual laborer was not yet free to negotiate a personal labor contract.

The device of having one laborer prod another to work to the limit of his physical endurance and beyond, as suggested by Clark, is quite in keeping with the kind of labor discipline which had been in force under feudal bondage.

As he places his own terminology under review, Clark prides himself on having displayed a zeal for the purification of concepts.

He does not find it at all embarrassing to have his terminological duplicity as well as his overindulgence in unqualified substitution of one term for another serve as patent examples of terminological precision.

Nor does the author of the "Distribution of Wealth" find it compromising for himself to have his device of rendering a concept meaningless by depriving it of its social and economic core presented as a demonstration of a purification practice.

What Clark wants to pass as purification can well be described as the practice of making an empty shell out of a generalized observation by making it lose any relevant social and economic content.

Clark feels no scruples to insist that the purer i.e. the emptier a concept is made, the less there is room for a misdirected view.

He has no hesitation to claim that the more precise i.e. the narrower a focal category is drawn, the less is there room for misrepresentation.

Whether he would care to have it cited at this juncture that it is not at all misleading to suggest, as he does, that it does not matter, as far as an understanding of the relevant social and economic issues is concerned, to have the terms wages and rent used as interchangeable, when the subject of wage compensation is under discussion, Clark does not care to specify in the stated context.

Instead the author of the "Distribution of Wealth" goes on to clamor that neither production instruments nor forces of nature are supposed to play any role in the calculation of productive gains as far as they are effected by human efforts.

Instead he goes on banishing material technology and matter itself from any consideration of economic goods.

He would like to make it sure, Clark professes, that material technology and matter itself are to be forever confined within the range of non-economic goods.

Clark's respective terminological strictures provide sufficient indication to prove that he regards the effectuation of goods by way of a productive effort as well as the use of any production tools, raw materials and the soil as being of no social and economic relevance within the range of his conceptualization.

He, moreover, gives a hint with his social and economic disqualification of production tools, raw materials and the soil, that he is bent on refusing to discuss the subject of social and economic appropriation of the means of production in any positive manner.

Clark's terseness in this and many other instances serves him as a convenient means for leaving his formulations under a cloud.

In spite of his proud claim that he is aiming at conceptual precision, Clark continues to present his readers with examples of compounded inexactness and lack of precision.

He demonstrates his claim to conceptual purity, to state but one outstanding example, by proposing to use wages and interest as interchangeable terms.

Were Clark to suggest that the categories of interest and rent are socially and economically alike in the sense that they both refer to socially privileged economic gains as Smith and Ricardo had postulated them, there would be little room for any misunderstanding.

Were he to infer that the taking of interest and the collecting of rent within a broad social and economic perspective represents but two aspects of a single leisure class function as the founders of classical economic thought had postulated it, he would have had no ground for a misconception.

But Clark, on his part, prefers the assertion that the rent category which he has taken out of any social and economic range and has made to serve as an efficiency and productivity indicator, is conceptually akin to the category of interest the social and economic significance of which he shows no inclination to attack.

Clark's claim to exactness in conceptualization comes to sound ridiculous when he advances the proposition that the category of rent which he had reduced to a non-social term, be viewed as congruent and is therefore to be used as interchangeable with the category of interest, the social and economic significance of which is kept in force.

When he, in turn, proposes to have the category of interest, the social attributes of which are left unobstructed by him, regarded as being conceptually derived from a socially obliterated term rent, Clark's clamor that he is consistently precise in the evolving of concepts becomes utterly preposterous.

Clark might not be conscious, it could be brought up as an extenuating circumstance, that he, in referring to incongruous concepts, might not be wholly aware of where his terminological merry-go-round is leading him. He might not be cognizant that he is framing a dual approach to conceptualization, though he is outwardly conforming to a uniform conceptual pattern.

When, however, he publicly avows the syllogistic suggestion which infers that the interchangeability of the terms interest and rent coupled with the interchangeability of the terms rent and wages warrants the conclusion that all three terms are interchangeable, he should not be surprised that the suspicion comes to grow that he has no intention of respecting any cognitive line which provides for a distinction between meaningful and meaningless propositions, that he has i.e. been all along engaged in a deliberate effort to propagate nonsense.

Clark probably suspects that his formulations are self-contradictory. He does not seem to be entirely unaware that his argumentation lacks coherence.

He attempts to erect a protective screen against the accusation that he is evolving nonsensical propositions, by asserting that his conclusions are based on a striking premise.

He tries to protect himself against the charge that he is passing on an array of senseless sounds by insisting that all his deliberations stem from a highly significant assumption.

His whole exposition, Clark wants it to be noted, stands and falls with the supposedly hypothetical proposition that major social and economic generalizations can be arrived at by ignoring social and economic transformations.

His whole approach, Clark wants it to be known, is founded on the presumed postulation that basic social and economic categories can be adequately formulated without reference to the factor of social and economic change.

His whole literary effort, Clark wants it to be accepted as the apex of his attainment as a social and economic theorist, is rooted in the premise that social and economic processes can be fully delineated by presuming that they are at all times static.

The author of the "Distribution of Wealth" does not mind to stake the fate of his entire contribution on the acceptance as incontrovertible assumption of the proposition that social and economic living can be most adequately expressed by having it presented as frozen.

The immobility of social and economic life, as a major postulate for an analysis of a mobile social and economic structure, is not being devised by Clark in the sense of a working hypothesis.

The immutability of social and economic living is not being introduced by Clark as a proposition which is governed by the methodological device of ceteris paribus.

He does not apply his postulate in a manner which provides for a temporary social and economic isolation of a partial aspect of the subject under investigation.

He is conducting his investigation by isolating the entire social and economic framework which he is about to analyze without ever expecting to repair the theoretical damage which such wholesale isolation brings about.

He is evolving or better said dissolving his income formulations —the central theme of his treatise—on the presumption that the social and economic stream within which income is being formed remains frozen for all time.

Clark's half-hearted admission made in a casual remark, that a static preconditioning is to be considered unrealizable is not followed by any significant revamping of his fundamental approach.

When he is ready to readmit a dynamic notion into his static analysis at the very end of his treatise, he does not make any provisions for a weakening of his static assumptions.

He keeps the static framework of his income categories in full force, allowing but for inconsequential dynamic vibrations.

Clark makes sure that his social designification devices are kept intact when he is ready to give the sign by which the flow of social and economic life is to be reopened for investigation.

He has no intention of discarding the non-social capsules with which he inaugurates his treatise after his presumptuous static analysis comes to run its course.

Nothing could be further from Clark than the undertaking of a real and effective move for the abandonment of the social blinds with which he surrounds his terminology.

Clark is fully prepared to maintain the anti-social blockade or more correctly the blockade of social identification throughout.

Within that basic preconception the dynamic notion assumes as unrealistic a character as had the static presumption.

As it stands, Clark is engaged in a literary venture in which he is professedly dedicated to the task of measuring the social pulse of the production process by a device from which the scales by which productive growth could be measured have been eliminated in advance of any measurement.

As it turns out, Clark devotes his literary labor to the dissection of productivity increments through a design, called the static presumption, which is to make it inconceivable to comprehend any production gains.

To bolster his self-contradictory position, Clark takes some pot shots at the basic prerequisites of conceptualization.

In an apparent contest with Menger's and Wieser's attack on time and causation, Clark voices his extreme displeasure with the commanding methodological position which the categories of time and causation continue to maintain.

The category of time, Clark insists, is a highly dubious instrumentality.

The category of time, Clark asserts, is apt to become very ambiguous when it comes to be applied in the course of social and economic conceptualization.

The category of time, Clark has reached the point he is eager to make, becomes particularly inconsequential when it is being used to bring out the objective aspect of a social and economic concept.

The category of time, Clark reaches the climax of his indictment, becomes particularly inane when its application is required in order to qualify an economic concept which had not been in advance emptied of all social content.

He considers the use of the time category to advance a social signification, as having little, if any relevance.

He cannot see what, if any significance, can be attached to having the time category used with reference to any interpersonal matters.

Time is to be regarded as having significance when it refers to individualistic considerations.

Time is to be viewed as having a significant import only when it can be made to bear on an individualistic choice.

Time is supposed to become meaningful only when a subjectivistic preference is involved.

Time to Clark merits consideration only under the condition that it is made to refer to a completely isolated individual who is placed in a position of making a most personal decision.

Time in Clark's formulation is worthy of attention only when it is related to a person who becomes involved in making up his mind about the form of his individual satisfactions.

Time, Clark assures, is only applicable with reference to the resolution of a personal conflict.

Time, Clark asseverates, can only be considered a conditioning factor in a case in which an individual becomes engaged in the ascertainment of his feeling about the disposition of what he considers is coming to him as his earning.

Time, Clark persists, can only be admitted as a qualifying attribute when it pertains to a person who is about to render a highly personal decision with regard to the utilization of what he considers to be his income.

Time in Clark's ultimate formulation is to be permitted to enter as a factor only in such a highly personal decision which the individual is about to make with reference to using his income or parts of it by either slating it for direct utilization or by assigning it or its part to form an addition to what that person is inclined to regard as his income source.

Time, Clark ends up in a major piece of sophistry, is to be rated as an element of essentiality in a socio-economic analysis, when it is pictured as setting itself to work on the mind of a person who is undertaking the task of assuring himself of, whether or not, his feelings could find an adequate expression by the provision he is making to withhold either a part or the whole of his indeterminable income flow to augment, what is to be termed as existing capital.

Clark takes pains to emphasize the subjectivistic sophistry of his formulation, he is careful to rule out objective factors in any consideration of time.

Only the deliberation of the individual with himself is to be considered subject to timing.

Only within the range of the intimate personal character of the decision which pertains to the utilization of either part or the whole of an indeterminable income by way of withholding it, time is to be permitted to be a factor.

As far as the correlation of the highly individual decision to withhold the whole or a part of the indeterminable income with the augmentation of capital is concerned, Clark makes provisions for an added disorientation.

In the generation of concrete capital or, to use Clark's substitute term, in the generation of capital goods, timeliness is to be regarded as being of no essence.

Merely with regard to the life span of what is to be designated as specific capital good by virtue of a highly personal decision, time is to be granted some relevance.

Only the durability the individual considers he is willing to allot a concrete good, is to be considered as coming within the range of time specification.

Any attempt to specify the time required for production and reproduction without specific reference to subjective considerations, Clark finds it necessary to warn, is to be considered foredoomed, since production and reproduction, as far as they do not refer to individual mental gyrations, are supposed to receive an advance rating of being ephemeral by nature.

The effectuation of concrete capital, to revert to the terminology which Clark uses in referring to production and reproduction, is supposed to remain by direction of the author of the "Distribution of Wealth" beyond the range of any socially signifiable time limit.

Clark does not leave himself time to rest, he is obviously unable to regain his peace of mind until he makes sure the socio-economic signification of time is to be subjected to an added ban.

Time, Clark rages, is to be held as being unspecifiable in regard to what he terms as capital per se.

The denotation of capital as such or to use Clark's substitute term, money capital, is to be regarded as being so abstract or i.e. as so wide in scope, that its encompassing by any time span is supposed to fall within the range of the inconceivable.

In this case the very designation of capital is being placed by Clark beyond the range of timing.

Money capital in the very range of its conceptualization, Clark wants to make it sure, is to be so elusive a category as far as its social and economic attributes are concerned, that the very thought of bringing it into any meaningful proximity of time specification is to appear unfathomable.

Money capital is being placed by him so much out of the range of any social economic context, Clark inadvertently admits, as to deprive it of any specifiable social and economic meaning.

In suggesting a correlation of one unspecifiable proposition, as which he parades money capital, to another unspecifiable proposition, as which he treats time in this instance, Clark comes dangerously close again to the propagation of the nonsensical.

As far as the specification of time with regard to concrete capital is concerned, Clark allows for no more than an intimation of the time aspect.

What can be gained in the stated connection with reference to

142

the ascertainment of time by taking recourse to synchronization as Clark belatedly suggests, is difficult to see.

Within the context of Clark's deconceptualization drive as it is directed against the specification of the time category, synchronization can amount only to a device for the correlation of something or other which is not precise with a something or other which is not precise—a contradictio in adjecto.

Within the range of Clark's disqualification of the social and economic aspects of time, synchronization can only refer to the correlation of subjective intimations to each other.

The near obliteration of time, Clark does not give himself a rest, is quickly followed by a specific effort to disengage the category of causation.

Causation is being tied to a rather odd phenomenon by Clark.

Causation, Clark indicates, can only be considered effected when it refers to a peculiar kind of shrinking and a peculiar sort of bulging.

Causation, Clark becomes a little more specific, can be considered as being of some consequence when it refers to either contraction or expansion in the use of, what Clark terms, a given capital.

Clark is willing to have causation remain effective when such effectiveness pertains to the withdrawing of parts of a given capital particle from one point of that given capital and the attachment of those particles or parts to another point of the same given capital.

Causation, in other words, is to have effect only with reference to shifts within a given capital range.

The aspect of causation is i.e. to be excluded from any reference to either any real addition to a given capital or a real diminution of a given capital.

He thus inferentially bans causation, it should be duly noted, from the sphere of capital accumulation as well as the sphere of capital losses.

An added prohibition of causation is being decreed by Clark when he touches upon the subject of material production increments.

He is particularly insistent in that connection on having any causal linkage excluded between an added production increment and an added unit of human effort.

Production increments are specifically to be prevented, Clark wants to make it sure, from establishing any causal relation with differentials of real wages.

In a further move to block a causative explanation of human labor, Clark provides for an obfuscation of the qualitative and quantitative distinctions of respective causative links.

He would like any increase in labor effort to be regarded as unmeasurable.

A measurable effect is to be held as solely attributable to what is to be termed as a given amount of capital.

As far as labor is concerned, it is not supposed to be credited with having any causal relation with quantitatively assessable production gains.

Clark's willfulness in his treatment of the qualitative and quantitative aspects in reference to causation fully matches the capriciousness of his comprehension of the subjective and objective factors in causation.

He is proceeding in the same unprincipled pragmatistic manner in his disengagement from causation which he demonstrates in his disengagement from timing.

The disengagement from causation is executed by Clark, to give its real implication, in order to eliminate the conceptual prerequisites for a focal view on social stratification, while the disengagement from timing as its counterpart is pressed by the author of the "Distribution of Wealth" as a means for the obfuscation of the social factors of production.

From the very onset of his "Distribution of Wealth," Clark gives it to understand that he is determined to set aside any rules of reasoning which might stand in the way of having labor excluded from any accounting for economic gains.

From the very start of his presentation, Clark makes it clear that he is not prepared to tolerate any methodological interference with his set aim of having division of income presented in a form in which no provision is made for the acknowledgement of human effort and, in particular, in a form which provides for the exclusion

144

of any conceivable link between the exertion of human labor and the factor of distribution of wealth.

From the very beginning of his treatise, Clark resorts to indiscriminatory tactics in removing methodological and terminological restraints which conflict with his predetermined aim.

To keep the delineation of income within the narrow range into which he is predetermined to force that category, Clark resorts to a number of questionable designification devices.

He starts off by introducing a rather innocuous term of industrial differentiation.

Industrial differentiation, Clark proffers his formulation, is supposed to relate production stages with regard to the effectuation of a product.

Industrial differentiation, Clark amplifies his stand, is supposed to relate the differentiation between industries in which the entire product is being produced and industries in which the effectuation of but one or another phase in the production of the finished product is attained.

The technological delineation of industrial differentiation which he is devising, Clark wants to have accepted as the social identification mark.

His terming of industrial differentiation, Clark asserts, makes a specific reference to social stratification unnecessary.

His term of industrial differentiation, Clark claims, is all inclusive, it provides for the covering of any specific form of social differentiation which can be thought of.

The term industrial differentiation, when it refers to the effectuation of the entire range of a production within an industry, is to be considered, Clark has no hesitation to insist, as a perfect vehicle for the identification of a major social and economic division.

Clark to be sure, does not state that the static major social and economic division refers to a division of propertied and non-propertied aspects.

He prefers to make no reference to the factor of social and economic appropriation in the stated context. He proceeds to clamor that the term industrial differentiation when it refers, in turn, to the effectuation in an industry of either raw material or a half-finished product or the last stage of a finished product be regarded

145

as the most adequate device for presenting a subsidiary social and economic division of social and economic groups.

Whether in citing social and economic groups Clark has sources of income in mind, he does not care to state without equivocation. He resorts to a terminological diversion, in order to hide the link between a division of social and economic groups and a division of sources of income.

The term industrial differentiation in its reference to social and economic groups, Clark cares to use as a terminological means for fencing in of income allocation.

The term industrial differentiation in its reference to social and economic groups, Clark cares to have applied as a terminological obstruction in the path of a conceivable social signification of income categories.

The term industrial differentiation in its reference to social and economic groups is in particular called upon by Clark to serve as a terminological cage for capital and labor income.

The term industrial differentiation in its reference to social and economic groups is specifically designed to provide a terminological cover for treating capital and labor incomes qualitatively indistinguishable from the product to which Clark imputes them.

The term industrial differentiation in its reference to social and economic groups is, moreover, supposed to furnish the terminological wrapping for the relegation of capital and labor income to the level of material increments.

The term industrial differentiation in its reference to social and economic groups is, furthermore, supposed to provide a terminological frame for having capital and labor income referred to as socially and economically indistinguishable forms in an effort to equate material expenditures and material results by way of statistical devices.

The term industrial differentiation is thus slated to become a terminological shield which is to permit the presentation of capital and labor income in the form of socially and economically undifferentiated production indexes.

The fencing off of capital and labor income Clark follows up with a fencing off of other income categories.

He furnishes terminological obstructions for the tracing of any form of income from its respective source to its receiver.

He starts referring to interest, rent, profit and wages as if they were but different signs for identical social and economic factors.

He thus lays the terminological ground for a socially and economically undifferentiated view on the income receiver.

Since the terms interest, rent, profit and wages are to be considered socially and economically indistinguishable, the use of those terms becomes useless for any social and economic identification.

Since he prohibits the attachment of any specifiable social and economic meaning to any of the four stated income categories, Clark can see nothing terminologically offensive in having any income receiver presented in a quadruple role of an interest taker, rent collector, profit maker and wage receiver. He thus ends up in a compounded meaninglessness.

CHAPTERS 6 and 7

ARRIVING AT NOTHINGNESS

As against the terminological free for all, as against the conceptual looseness of John Bates Clark, the literary offering of William Stanley Jevons strikes one at first as the product of a highly disciplined mind.

The author of "The Theory of Political Economy" does not care to indulge in a terminological hide and seek game.

He does not resort to the overplaying and underplaying device to disparage qualitative distinctions.

Qualitative distinctions, he straightforwardly declares, are being ruled out in advance in his fundamental treatise.

Differences in kind, he unabashedly proclaims, are being relegated to the realm of the unapproachable.

Qualitative distinctions, Jevons decrees without winking, are to be regarded as impenetrable.

Differences in kind, Jevons asserts, are so elusive as to defy any attempt of concretization.

Qualitative distinctions, Jevons unequivocably admits, are bound to become untraceable in any social and economic analysis in which individualistic deliberations become preponderant.

Differences in kind do of necessity vanish, Jevons does not mind confessing, when a social and economic investigation assumes the character of an inquiry into the vagaries of personal feelings.

Under subjectivistic analytical precepts, Jevons realizes, the question of what accounts for differences in kind has to remain forever unanswered.

148

Under the rules of an individualistic analysis, Jevons is aware, qualitative distinctions cannot be traced further than their most immediate effects.

Hence, he holds, it should not be improper to conclude that within a subjectivistic analytical framework differences in kind are observable only to the extent to which they effect a variation in quantity.

He thus invokes qualitative incomprehensibility and causal indistinctiveness to stand guard on the approaches to his "Theory of Political Economy."

In hoisting the presumption of impenetrability of qualitative distinction at the entrance to his exposition, Jevons makes it sure, that any social and economic division he comes to expound does not rate more than a differentiation among graded signs.

The signposts of hedonism with which Jevons introduces his treatise, the symbols of joy and pain which are to pave the way for the "Theory of Political Economy," are not supposed to offer any insight into what makes human senses react.

The physiological aspect of sense perception, the accounting for human sensitivity is something which Jevons attempts to keep out of his "Theory of Political Economy."

In appraising pain and pleasure, Jevons is trying to make it clear, he intends to limit the range of his interest to finding out about the actuality of the squaring of contrary feelings.

In the appraising of pain and pleasure, Jevons wants it clearly understood, he is particularly bent on devoting himself to an ascertainment of the actual emotional balance at which an individual manages to arrive.

The way the individual resolves his emotional conflict, the specific ascertainment of the sum of painful and pleasurable experience which may account for the gaining or regaining of a personal emotional balance, Jevons wants to be left out of consideration.

Any conceivable information which might provide a clue to what prompts an individual's emotional release, Jevons is determined to spurn.

Only in regard to one instant is the author of "The Theory of Political Economy" prepared to lift the veil over the question of how contrary feelings are being composed.

149

Only the split second which precedes the effectuation of a personal emotional release in which a person resolves his inner emotional conflicts is to be made subject to an investigation.

In regard to the moment immediately preceding the resolution of the personal inner conflict, Jevons is willing to give some consideration to the more or less pain as contrasted with the more or less pleasure which the individual experiences.

He invokes in this instance the hedonistic supposition that any person is driven by the unrelenting desire to add to one's pleasure and to detract from one's pain.

He proffers a personal emotional rationale which is supposed to operate by way of weighing down one's unpleasurable anticipations in favor of one's pleasurable expectations.

Too much pain, Jevons amplifies his major proposition, can prove as unbearable, as too much pleasure.

Any added pleasure, Jevons wants to have it inferred, diminishes the individual's desire for more pleasure.

Hence, he argues, any addition to effected pleasures comes to have the tendency of progressively saturating the individual's lust for effecting more pleasure.

When the saturation point in the individual's effectuation of pleasure has been reached, Jevons finds it safe to predict, the anticipation of additional pleasurable experience is not likely to lead the individual to seeking more pleasure.

When the saturation point in the individual's effectuation of pleasure is reached, Jevons is prepared to foretell, the anticipation of additional pleasurable experience is not likely to stir the individual into any action.

Jevons i.e. foresees that the anticipation of more pleasure is most likely to deter the individual from making any move to attain that result in case he has reached the saturation point in the effectuation of pleasure.

In placing his hedonistic argumentation within the frame of decreasing personal utility, Jevons considers he has succeeded in bringing pleasure and displeasure under a common denominator.

He has reduced the distinction of pain and enjoyment, Jevons is satisfied, to a mere quantitative difference.

Depending on quantitative changes, pleasurable experiences are termed unpleasurable expectations in Jevons' formulation.

Unpleasurable anticipations, in turn, come to be termed pleasurable expectations, depending on a quantitative variation, in Jevons' presentation.

Having deprived the words pleasure and displeasure of any qualitative distinctiveness, Jevons proceeds to eliminate the use of one of the two words.

The word displeasure which refers to a painful experience can be safely eliminated from the vocabulary, Jevons orates, since the words pleasurable as well as unpleasurable can both be expressed by having referred to them as more or less pleasure.

The substitution of the term more or less pleasure for the term displeasure and the painful experience it relates make it, in turn, feasible for Jevons to reword the reference to conflicting emotions.

Emotional irresolution and its resulting inactivity, Jevons argues, does not have to be referred to in terms of the contrary emotions of pain and pleasure.

With the term displeasure and the painful experience which it relates made dispensable, emotional irresolution and inactivity as its counterpart can well be referred to as but an unwillingness to indulge in added pleasure, Jevons would like to have it inferred.

How the more or less is to be ascertained, Jevons does not care to say. He but makes a casual reference to the law of averages and the law of great numbers.

How the law of averages is to be applied to the ascertaining of a quantity of pleasure, Jevons does not mention.

Leaving the subject of quantification hinging on his verbal invocation of the law of averages and the law of great numbers, Jevons proceeds to use his reference to more or less pleasure for the evolvement of what he names as the principle of economic principles.

All economic activity comes to be related by Jevons to a desire for personal gratification through added pleasure.

The gratification to which he refers, Jevons is quick to remark, does not refer to any inherent attribute of a good.

Gratification and pleasure derived from it, Jevons insists, is not to be attributed to an essential property of any object.

Self-gratification, Jevons asserts, cannot be interpreted as having any relation to materiality.

Self-gratification comes to express but a highly personal utility in Jevons' formulation.

Personal utility, in the context in which the words are being used by Jevons, is not supposed to refer to any lasting attribute of a good.

Personal utility is but to reflect a passing characteristic of a good.

Personal utility, in the form in which Jevons wants the term applied, is supposed to refer to something or other which the individual might be inclined either to grant or to deny to a good.

Utility in the economic sense—and he means personalized utility —is not supposed to be concerned in any way with the process of production, Jevons wants to make it sure.

Utility in the economic sense, and he again means personalized utility, is not supposed to have any relation to the process of distribution either.

Utility in the economic sense—meaning personalized utility— Jevons offers the subjectivistic refrain, is to be considered expressive of an individual's preoccupation with consumption.

Utility in the economic sense, meaning personalized utility, Jevons amplifies, is to be considered as being determined by what a person fancies himself of being in need.

Utility in the economic sense, meaning personalized utility, comes to relate in Jevons' description, a highly personal preference for the consumption of an indeterminate amount of an indeterminate variety of goods.

Utility in a more specific economic sense, i.e., personalized utility in its more concrete expression, refers in Jevons' presentation to the wavering of the individual between the satisfactions of his cruder and his more refined wants.

Utility in a more qualified economic sense thus comes to be referred to as an agonizing struggle of the individual within himself for the realization of a more elevated personal taste.

His placing of utility within an economic range which disallows a distinctive social evaluation, Jevons proffers as a principal contribution to the purification of the theory of political economy.

Utility deprived of any social content is to be viewed as a key factor in bringing out the uniformity of economic thought.

Utility disqualified as meaningful social designation is to be regarded as a basic presupposition of any fundamental economic law.

In an obvious attempt to demonstrate the purity of economic thought at which he has arrived, Jevons proceeds to reformulate what he considers as the law of economic laws.

In an ostensible effort to justify the claim that the approaches to economic theory have been cleansed by him, Jevons proceeds to relate what he calls utility to the laws of human wants.

In relating utility to the laws of human wants, Jevons finds it necessary to warn, a distinction is to be made between total utility as referred to a whole object and partial utility as referred to a particle of the object.

In relating utility to the laws of human wants, Jevons considers it appropriate to add, due attention is to be given to the impermissibility of establishing a direct causal connection between the material embodiment of an object or any particle of it and the respective utility of that object and particle.

In the redesignation of the laws of human wants with particular reference to personalized utility, it is to be duly recognized, Jevons emphasizes, that it is to be considered unfeasible to relate in any direct form or manner the material embodiment of any product or any particle of it to the respective want that product or particle might be called to meet.

In the redesignation of the laws of human wants, Jevons reaffirms his stand, utility can only be allowed to enter in a form and manner in which the total or the partial utility of the object comes to express itself in self-gratification.

Only a utility which results in self-gratification, Jevons reemphasizes, is to be considered as lying within the range of comprehensibility.

The laws of human wants Jevons moves, are called upon to furnish testimony for the correlation of different phases of self-gratification.

The laws of human wants are specifically to demonstrate the correlation between subjective utility and subjective wants.

A correlation of personal utility with personal wants, Jevons takes pains to caution, is not to be expected to lead to any definite results.

The correlation of the subjective comprehension of utility and a subjective perception of wants within the framework within the range of which Jevons undertakes to demonstrate the laws of economic wants, as he inadvertently admits, does not provide for either a clear discernment of utility nor for a clear assessment of wants.

It should be conceivable to specify the whole of a want, Jevons appears to have a second thought.

It should be possible to arrive at a fairly definite result in the ascertaining of the quantity which is required to satisfy the personal need for nourishment within a limited space of time.

It should, however, be admitted, Jevons remarks in a mood of resignation, that a concretization of a partial want is hardly feasible in any definite form.

An attempt to ascertain the quantity which is required to satisfy a partial want of a person and in particular a partial want for which no specific limitations of space and time are set, Jevons invites the inference, can hardly lead to any conclusive results.

In an ostensible effort to shift the argument, Jevons suggests the use of the term relative satisfaction.

The more specific term of relative satisfaction and its correlate term relative utility, are to take the place of the rather indeterminate designation of partial satisfaction and partial want.

Relative satisfaction and its terminological correlate of relative utility are to be considered relative to a marginal satisfaction.

Marginal satisfaction is, in turn, to be imputed to an infinite particle arrived at by a ceaseless process of decimation of any given object or objects.

Relative satisfaction and relative utility are defined as having a relation to something indeterminable.

Instead of advancing a more exact quantification the substitution of partial want by the term partial utility leads but to a confounding of indefiniteness.

154

At this point Jevons once more calls for the taking refuge in great numbers in his ostensible quest for quantification.

What advance towards quantitative exactness could conceivably be made by a sheer limitless multiplication of confounded indefiniteness, Jevons does not care to mention.

How the degree of satisfaction from infinitely small particles experienced by multitudes is to be ascertained in the face of the indeterminateness of the extent to which an infinitesimal particle affects the satisfaction of a single person, Jevons does not care to discuss.

Jevons proffers to leave the question unanswered of how multiplication of admittedly elusive personal judgments on marginal utility can lead to any degree of concretization.

He leaves the formulation of want and utility in a status of indecision and lack of precision.

The very indeterminateness and unspecifiability of marginal utility serves him as a prerequisite in his approach to value.

Jevons refuses to respect Smith's postulation of the necessity to uphold a conceptual distinction between exchange and use value.

He considers it opportune to disregard Mill's exhortation of economic theorists to be exact in the defining of the category of value.

The category of value, Jevons observes, has come to be defined in too many different ways to retain any significance.

He wants no part in any inquiry which could conceivably uncover the social and economic issues which lurk behind the diverging definitions of value.

He brushes aside the view that the controversy over the definitions of value presents a dispute over the question of what social meaning is to be attached to value.

Jevons wants all definitions of value to be deprived of any social content.

He wants the onus of phrasemongering thrown on any and all value formulations.

A disputation over the proper social place and the proper social weight of the category of value among other economic concepts is being shrugged off as pure verbalism by Jevons.

Jevons does not consider it opportune to admit that his insistence on having the value category declared socially meaningless presents a deliberate attempt to thwart any socially and economically meaningful discussion of a vital subject.

He is satisfied with drawing the nominalistic inference that a social disqualification of the value category makes the uttering of the very word value a useless exercise.

Should it be conceded that the whole discussion over what constitutes value revolves around the question of whether to substitute one socially meaningless tag for another, should it be admitted that the entire dispute over the formulation of value does not involve more than a terminological quibble,—Jevons advances a sophism, —the discarding of the denotation of value could not be considered as an impairment of social and economic understanding.

The significance of social and economic theory, Jevons is led to explain, will not be in any way diminished by the disposition of a dubious word which it should not be disputed, had needlessly troubled the mind of countless social and economic theoreticians.

The subject matter of economic theory, Jevons does not doubt, is not to be at all affected by a ban on the word value which, it should not be contradicted, has caused irritation to all concerned.

To justify his radical step to make his drastic proposal plausible, Jevons invokes the authority of John Stewart Mill.

John Stewart Mill is being cited by Jevons as the economic theorist who has paved the way for the disposition of the category of value.

Mill, Jevons emphasizes, has made great strides towards the designification of the value concept.

By relegating the category of exchange value to a position of relative significance, by expounding the view that exchange value signifies but the manifestation of the value of one good in terms of another good, Jevons points out in defense of his own position, Mill has deprived the category of value of any overriding meaning.

The turning of the social focus on the concept of value, the placing of the value category in a key analytical position, the manner in which Adam Smith and David Ricardo have dealt with value, Jevons is quick to condemn as an allegedly unwarranted preoccupation with an abstraction.

Jevons does not care to recognize any distinction between an

156

abstraction filled with a socially significant content and an abstraction emptied of any social content.

Jevons gives voice to a strictly formalistic comprehension of value when he lauds Mill for the decisive blow which the latter delivered to the absolutistic treatment of the value category.

Jevons refuses to notice the deep social meaning which the category of value had acquired in the exposition of Smith and Ricardo as the latter's most consistent disciple. He derisively refers to a socially meaningful approach to value as the expounding of a meaningless essence.

Jevons bases his commendation of some steps towards the disqualification of the value concept by the latter day representatives of economic classicism of whom Mill is one, on the presumption that the value category had received a mere terminological treatment from Smith on until Mill.

He decries the view which regards value as an essence, he fails to make a distinction in this connection between a formalistic view on essence and essence in the sense of a social essence.

His subsequent derision of Smith's reference to the value concept as an intrinsic category does not make any cognitive distinction between the use of the word intrinsic in an esoteric sense and the use of the word intrinsic in the sense of a pivotal social meaning.

The key social factors which have entered into the conceptualization of value by Smith and Ricardo, Jevons implies, have been thoroughly disqualified by Mill.

Though he is in full accord with Mill's effort to remove the value concept from the key position at which it had been placed by Smith and Ricardo, Jevons, nonetheless, considers that Mill did not go far enough in the deprecation of the social relevance of value.

Mill, in Jevons' view, traveled but half the road towards the designification of the value concept.

Jevons wants to make short shift of all the controversies on fundamental social and economic issues which had centered around the concept of value.

He wants no part in the heated debates on basic social and economic problems which have revolved around the value category.

He is bent on having the controlling concept of value reduced to utter insignificance.

157

He suggests that the once focal category be made wholly meaningless.

He considers it an entirely proper methodological procedure to have all the troubling social and economic complexities to which the concept of value had called attention banned from the analytical picture, by having the denotation of value replaced by another word.

Unsettled social and economic conditions can be kept at a safe distance from theoretical discussions, Jevons presumes, by his granting of the expression of individual self-gratification a key position in systematic economic comprehension.

The relegation of value to a position of a relative concept as it had been suggested by Mill, leaves value a much too specific concept, Jevons complains.

The appraising of the value of one good in terms of another good goes much too far in the admissibility of concretization, Jevons is vociferous in his objection.

A comprehension of value which is not based on the presumption that value has no relation to any material embodiment, Jevons terms as unacceptable.

A comprehension of value which does not deny that there is no cognitive connection between a value and an object is branded as intolerable by the author of "The Theory of Political Economy."

The category of value is to present no more than an empty shell, Jevons wants to make it sure.

Economic value is to be referred to by socially meaningless signs, to please Jevons.

Economic value is to be presented by socially irrelevant symbols, to satisfy the author of "The Theory of Political Economy."

The concretization of the value concept, Jevons insists, is not to go beyond the scope of a socially inexplicable formulation.

The specification of the value category, Jevons appears to be very strict about it, is not to be advanced beyond the sphere of a correlation of socially unidentifiable figures.

After having taken what he regards as requisite terminological steps to deprive the category of value of any meaning, Jevons considers he is justified to ask whether there can be any sense in a continuous use of the meaningless word.

After he has moved for the reduction of the word value to an empty sound he considers it safe to infer that a dispensation with the word value will not impair any social and economic understanding.

Jevons appears to be expressing the conviction that all social and economic problems which had been highlighted by the discussion of value will forever be consigned to the limbo were the controversial word to be dropped from the vocabulary.

In pronouncing a ban on the word value, Jevons obviously presumes, he but rids social and economic theory of a needlessly irritating sound.

Irritation, which the utterance of the word value causes, will not in any way be lessened in Jevons' presumption by having the word value pronounced in combination with another word.

In the combined words exchange value and use value, the word value sounds as irritating, Jevons argues, as if it were pronounced by itself.

He thus feels constrained to have the expressions exchange value and use value included in his order against the very mention of value.

In the wake of the expurgation of the word value, Jevons makes the suggestion, that anything which had hitherto been explained through a reference to the term value can be similarly clarified through a reference to the term ratio.

Jevons obviously considers that he is erecting an effective terminological bar against the reappearance of the socially explosive word value, by placing the socially innocuous sign of ratio in place of it.

In issuing his call to forget about value and to remember only ratio, Jevons somehow shies away from providing much of an explanation.

To the question of ratio of what, Jevons does not care to furnish any satisfactory answer.

He is willing to substantiate the term ratio under the proviso that the word value is not to be used in connection with the term ratio.

Instead he wants the term ratio used in connection with the word exchange.

He implies that the wording exchange ratio suggests something definite.

He wants to convey the impression that the expression exchange ratio conveys something specific.

To those who remain unimpressed, Jevons has little to say.

Those who doubt that the social and economic issues which have found their expression in a reference to exchange value can be as well understood when reference is made to exchange ratio, Jevons is unwilling to enlighten.

The self-styled purifier of economic theory prefers to rely on oratory.

He chooses to head off any respective social and economic inquisitiveness by taking recourse to exaltation.

Ratio, Jevons orates, is a self-explanatory term.

The word ratio, Jevons asserts, constitutes a most tangible expression.

The term ratio, Jevons insists, lends itself to a most facile way of substantiation.

A reference to ratio, and there is to be no doubt about it, on the direction by Jevons, represents a superior form of material quantification.

In pleading for an unqualified acceptance of the term ratio, Jevons wants it to be known that he has not followed anybody's lead.

In trying to focus attention on ratio, Jevons wants it specifically recognized, that he has not treaded in the path of John Stewart Mill.

Mill, Jevons is emphatic about it, does not deserve any credit for the calling of attention to the term ratio.

Since Mill considered it necessary to bring in more than oratory in his quest for a greater specification of a ratio, Jevons does not care to recognize Mill as a proper adviser on the use of equation forms.

Nothing is said by Jevons about the reason which prompted Mill to desist from an unqualified use of the word ratio.

A reference to Mill's argumentation that the compound term

exchange ratio (in the sense in which Mill tries to apply it) presents a cognitive monstrosity, is nowhere to be found in Jevons' treatise.

Not a hint is offered by Jevons in the stated context that Mill was careful in demonstrating that an objectively conceived existing supply of goods and a subjectively inferred demand precludes the placing of the two phenomena under the common denominator of exchange ratio.

Jevons is in particular anxious to refrain from taking any notice of the distinction Mill makes between producible and nonproducible goods.

Neither is the crucial role which costs of production play in Mill's analysis anywhere mentioned by Jevons.

Jevons studiously avoids being drawn into a discussion which might conceivably force him to relate ratio to production.

He is not at all willing to have ratio express a social efficacy in regard to production results.

He is rather inclined to indulge in what he chooses to label as the efficacy of consumption habits.

The thought of having to contend in any positive form with aspects of reproduction of commodities appears utterly distasteful to Jevons.

He wants no part in any discussion which involves material costs of multiplication of goods.

He does not say a single word about the changing efficacy of production costs, an issue which forms the central theme of the contribution of Ricardo.

Nor does he take any notice of the social implications of the efficacy of production costs, an aspect most clearly brought out by John Stewart Mill.

He preoccupies himself with the topic of changes in the satisfactions of consumers.

He overplays the subject of fashioning of the desires of consumers in an obvious effort to draw attention away from the realization that consumption when it is presented without any relation to production can hardly provide any social and economic meaning.

He overstresses consumer's wants in an ostensible attempt to prevent a meaningful correlation with consumption and production.

161

He does, to be sure, qualify the term ratio by having it preceded by the word exchange.

Yet, he refers to exchange as if it were a mode of consumption.

He does not allow for any specific distinction between exchange and consumption.

He but matches the indefiniteness of his characterization of exchange with the indefiniteness which he attributes to consumption.

He evades the task of specifying his formulations of exchange and consumption by disowning the very principle of concretization in the stated context.

Concreteness is ruled out since it is incompatible with extreme subjectivization.

Or, as Jevons put it, in a somehow evasive form, concretization of the highest degree of individual satisfaction is something which eludes the social and economic inquirer.

Concreteness is further disowned since it is not compatible with the cultivation of a personalized emotionalism.

The proposition of an actual rating of consumer's wants is being sidetracked by Jevons with a slurring remark that personal desires cannot be ascertained with any degree of accuracy since they come to be expressed in an overcharged social atmosphere.

He is, of course, not willing to deal in this connection with the question to what objective factors the overcharged social and economic atmosphere might be attributed.

He is satisfied to rest his case against concretization in the stated context with the parry that the attempt to assay a marginal self-gratification cannot lead to any complete results, since it is to be taken for granted that the contest of individual wants is taking place in an overtense economic situation.

He obviously presumes that the erratic emotional fluctuations which manifest themselves in the consumer defy any regularity.

Concreteness of consumer's wants becomes an unmanageable task to Jevons in view of his refusal to bring controllable factors into the analytical picture.

He ends up with imparting the obscurantist advice that knowledge of the haphazard choices of the consuming individual cannot be advanced beyond the realization that such choices are haphazard.

The mode of deconceptualization which Jevons advances is predicated upon the elimination of the principle of contrariety.

The degree of conceptualization which he is willing to allow is not supposed to advance to a stage at which one concept can be contrasted with another.

Conceptual distinctions are not to be carried beyond the nominalistic range, on Jevons' direction.

Differences in social and economic content are to be in particular denied any recognition.

With the stated strictures, Jevons can be sure, the theory he advances will not come to reflect any social and economic contradictions.

Under the stated cognitive provisions, Jevons can safely assume, social and economic conflicts will be prevented from ever entering the scope of his analysis.

The relentless exclusion of objective factors, Jevons can rely upon it, permits him to represent the economy and society as a model of serenity and placidity.

In assuming that he has removed all conceptual and perceptual means by which social and economic disturbances can be registered, Jevons can make it appear as if social and economic life invariably runs like clockwork.

In feeling assured that he has perfected a terminological trapeze the working of which cannot be deterred by any social and economic defections and irregularities, Jevons can consider that he has girded himself against any theoretical eventualities when he proceeds to devise lifeless schemes.

Social and economic changes as represented in either social and economic advances or social and economic retrenchment are at any rate denied signification in Jevons' scheme.

With the social and economic scene presented as an unalterable manifestation of everlasting tranquility, social and economic activity comes to be reduced to an exchange of pleasantries.

Market movements and fluctuations of prices, all the vicissitudes of the acquisitive nexus, are assuming the character of bad dreams in regard to Jevons' harmonious scheme.

Jevons is in particular concerned with having economic instability and social dislocation regarded as something inconceivable.

163

He considers that by refusing to acknowledge any interconnection between the different phases of social and economic life, he can furnish himself with an analytical vehicle for the disestablishment of any interrelation between marketing and nonmarketing factors.

He further assumes that by denying that there exists any connection between individual actions in the social and economic sphere, he furnishes himself with a methodological alibi for an analytical disconnection of any single price item from any other price item.

In subscribing to an extreme form of atomization in the interpretation of social and economic data, Jevons feels certain he can proceed to evolve an ideal marketing pattern in complete disregard of any contravening social and economic factors.

The unrealism of Jevons' scheming is being further boosted by his explicit denial that he is in any way concerned with providing a realistic appraisal of the time element.

He takes pains to stress the timelessness of his theoretical scheme.

He does not have to, he emphasizes, to honor any such conception of time which encompasses the past, since the theoretical framework which he is designing is not supposed to reflect any social and economic situation which either exists or existed or is ever expected to exist.

He defends himself against any charges of analytical inadequacy and, more specifically, against any indictment brought against him on the score of an absence of realism in his comprehension, by insisting that his theoretical scheme is not based on a misrepresentation of either the social and economic conditions as they really are in the present, or, as they had been in the past, or, as they are expected to be in the future.

He, says Jevons, has made no secret of trying to escape social and economic reality in his theoretical design.

In formulating his theoretical propositions, Jevons cites it in his own favor, he had studiously avoided to acknowledge any realistic manifestations of social and economic life.

His theoretical formulations, Jevons has no scruples to confess, are supposed to be unrealistic.

He devises his theories, Jevons does not hesitate to admit, with a view of making them fictitious.

164

He bases his entire theoretical design, Jevons does not mind stressing it, on the fiction that the pulsation of social and economic life has ceased.

His entire theoretical scheme, Jevons is as frank about it as is John Bates Clark, is made to rest on the presumption that social and economic living conditions are static.

Jevons is ready to parry an attack on the principles to which he subscribes by insisting that the very unrealism of his scheme absolves him from paying attention to a criticism which bases itself on a non-fictitious approach to social and economic problems.

He is prepared to refute those who might be tempted to upset the symmetry of his static scheme by insisting that his static preconception frees him from the necessity to honor any test of the social and economic validity of his theoretical design which does not rule out a non-static (dynamic) comprehension.

Jevons, though, wants to be absolved from a direct charge of misrepresentation which states that he did perfect a fictitious scheme in order to hide social and economic reality in a subtle manner.

He does, however, not care to deny that he is indulging in a misrepresentation of the socially and economically existing by using the more crude and direct device of deliberate omission.

He even boasts of failing to encompass any realistic social and economic features.

Whether in turning his back on social and economic reality, he is willingly neglecting the comprehension of vital social and economic problems, Jevons is not prepared to say.

Whether he fully realizes that he is taking an epistemological position which favors the spreading of ignorance on social and economic subjects, Jevons does not disclose.

Whether he is fully conscious that he is committing himself to a methodological stand which is bound to obstruct the advancement of social and economic understanding of vast areas of social and economic knowledge, Jevons does not reveal.

As far as his direct statements are concerned, Jevons does not go on record in protesting against the inference that he is leaving a wide range of social and economic issues unattended.

He shows no signs that he in any way resents the drawing of the conclusion that he is blocking the very recognition of many outstanding social and economic questions.

He appears to be wholly insensitive to a charge that he is engaged in an effort to obscure rather than to enlighten.

An accusation that he had greatly contributed to social and economic obfuscation is not apt to disturb Jevons.

Jevons, on the contrary, seems to be well disposed to accept credit for having hit a high mark in the battle for deconceptualization.

Jevons, on the contrary, gives every sign of being favorably inclined to identify himself with the realization that with him the *disability* of a conceptualization which attempts to encompass whims and the frailty of a terminology which attempts to formulate the indefinite had reached a high point, indeed.

Jevons could hardly be expected to mind, were he to be given to understand, that in his own exposition the ambiguity of the proposition on which the marginal utility theory bases its arguments and the inanity of the perceptions on which a sterile subjectivism had come to rely, had reached climactic proportions.

The self-appointed purifier of theoretical economic thought can well be expected to welcome the suggestion that he has perfected a superior method for the enveloping of sense perception and had masterfully applied that method in enmeshing major points at issue.

The self-styled clarifier of economic theory could hardly be expected to mind, were he to be told that the abject emptiness of his formulations can hardly be surpassed.

He could be expected to relish the perspective of capturing the crown for a superior achievement in the race for arriving at nothingness in his deconceptualization effort. ·

Should an added proof be requested, to substantiate the observation that Jevons' claim to fame is based on his hitherto unattained literary skill of explaining away real and vital social and economic problems, by relating one irrelevant aspect to another irrelevant aspect and by referring one insignificant item to another insignificant item, the rest of Jevons' presentation could hardly fail to be convincing to the stated effect.

Should an added illustration be required, to demonstrate that

Jevons offers nothing but empty phrases, the remainder of his exposition should leave little doubt about it.

Should any added exemplification be requested that Jevons' meaningless conclusions do not add anything to his meaningless premises, should an added test have to be conducted to show that his opinions are preconceived, anything which follows is apt to substantiate the observation, that the author of "The Theory of Political Economy" has attained high mastery in arguing in circles.

The terminological rigmarole or more definitively stated the propagation of truisms which characterizes the performances of Jevons reaches new heights when he continues to elaborate on what he terms exchange ratio.

The terminological squirrel dance turns into a sheer dazzling pirouette when he proceeds to dangle what he presents as an enlarged formulation of exchange ratio before the eyes of a bewildered audience.

The terminological shuttle device of referring one unexplained term to another unexplained term is likely to cause dizziness to anybody who would like to follow Jevons when he proceeds to refer to exchange ratio as inverse ratio.

The hide and seek game, as far as the hiding of the respective social and economic meaning of terms is concerned, reaches a stage at which that pastime appears to be an end in itself, when Jevons comes to refer to the exchange ratio as the inverse expression of the final degree of utility.

The words degree of final utility, Jevons finds it requisite to caution, are not to be interpreted as an expression which is to furnish the term exchange ratio with a social and economic meaning.

In referring to the final degree of utility, Jevons goes on record, he has nothing more in mind than to refer to the term exchange ratio in another socially and economically designified form.

Nothing more is involved in the respective terminological cross-reference, Jevons confesses, than the replacement of the socially and economically meaningless term exchange ratio with another socially and economically meaningless denotation.

The reference to the final degree of utility is to remove nothing from the indefiniteness of the term exchange ratio.

The degree of final utility, Jevons wants to be considered as socially and economically indeterminate a factor as the exchange ratio.

When Jevons proceeds to claim that the exchange ratio is predetermined by the final degree of utility, he does not remove the spectre of social and economic indeterminateness from either of the two factors.

He but further disqualifies the exchange factor from playing any definite or better definable role in the social and economic process.

The final degree of utility which continues to be regarded by Jevons as something socially and economically indeterminate is made to impress itself upon a social and economic effect (referred to by Jevons as a commodity available *after* the exchange has been effected) the social and economic cause of which is not supposed to be inquired into.

The final degree of utility which in Jevons' vocabulary becomes a preconditioning factor, forms but an exemplification of a misuse of words.

The final degree of utility can logically and methodologically not predetermine anything, unless it can be itself determined, Jevons could not have been amiss of realizing.

That Jevons prefers to have the socially and economically indeterminate final degree of utility predetermine something which is to remain socially and economically inexplicable can serve but as an added proof that he delights in a venture of compounding meaninglessness by correlating a reference of nothing about something with a reference of something about nothing.

The know-nothing implication of compounded meaninglessness is not in any way lessened by a subsequent reference to the exchange process.

One can hardly find any social and economic content in Jevons' formulation which describes exchange as an activity which continues until such time at which each of the exchanging parties decides to hold on to what it has.

Nor is any social and economic understanding to be gained by Jevons' elaboration of his exchange formulation in which he refers to exchange as an activity which is being discontinued when the utility of trading further quantities tends to become nil in the eyes of the trading parties.

No meaningful social and economic interpretation is in any form advanced by Jevons' recapitulation of his stand in which he restates that an exchange is taking place when two parties to the exchange act expect an added personal satisfaction from trading a particular good or part of it.

Jevons' reformulation, in which he limits himself to repeating that an exchange is being discontinued when neither of the two trading parties expects any further addition to their personal satisfaction from any continuation of the trading in the particular commodity or parts of it, can only be interpreted as another move to ward off any relevant social and economic explanation.

Jevons' recitation that an exchange is being continued as long as the trading parties consider it useful retains as much of a tautological taint as his declamation that exchange is being discontinued when the trading parties cease to see any use in it.

The question of why, in any social and economic sense, an exchange does, or, does not take place, Jevons wants to make sure, is not even to be asked.

The question of why, if it is to be permitted in regard to exchange, is to be strictly limited to the referring of the way human emotions affect exchange.

The why in regard to exchange is not supposed to refer, in turn, to an exchange which is conceived as a social and economic process but to an exchange conceived as an individual act, within a strictly emotional range of cognition.

Any causal quest into the exchange factor which delves into any other aspect than the one which is circumscribed by the emotional vexations to which an individual is subjected who has to demonstrate how he feels about holding on to what he has, or parting with it, is flatly rejected by Jevons.

Any exploration of the causing of exchange which is based on the admission that an effectuation or noneffectuation of the exchange act, in terms of an emotional reaction, cannot be adequately explained, unless the social and economic antecedents of such reaction are brought into the analytical picture, is being strictly opposed by Jevons.

The causal explanation of the individual exchange act in terms of a personal emotional reaction, Jevons wants to make it sure, is supposed to refer to the behavior of a person who, at the exclusion of anything else, is concerned with deriving a personal satisfaction.

The causal explanation of the individual exchange act, is in other words, to be confined to a cognitive sphere in which one emotional reaction is related to another emotional reaction.

The nonemotive aspect in the causative sequence of the individual exchange act is entered but nominally by Jevons.

As far as the nonemotive aspect in the causal explanation of the individual exchange act is concerned, Jevons is willing to make a certain provision for the assignment of a causative role to goods.

He is quick, however, to warn that such goods which are designated for production or such goods which are slated to serve acquisitive ends are not supposed to constitute a causative factor in any determination of an individual exchange act.

Jevons finds it opportune to explain away the causal effectiveness of goods by insisting that the disregard for a view on goods which is not preoccupied with the consumption aspect of goods is due to some unaccountable peculiarity of human nature.

The "unaccountable peculiarity" of human nature to which Jevons takes recourse refers to a peculiar contempt on the part of the author of "The Theory of Political Economy" not only for the aspect of distribution and production in the kind of economic analysis he suggests, the "unaccountable peculiarity" of human nature on which Jevons offers to rely embraces a peculiar contempt for any objective social and economic considerations and in particular a contempt for nonsubjective factors which have a bearing on consumption.

The "unaccountable peculiarity" of human nature, on which Jevons wants to depend, expresses his utter unwillingness to recognize any other effect of consumption on the individual exchange act than the one in which consumption is made the playball of individual fancies.

When Jevons insists that only goods, the consumption of which, the individual considers, have any relation to his most immediate consumption desires, are to be allowed to take a place in any analysis of exchange, he Jevons, gives expression to the crudest form of sensualism.

In recording his explicit approval of the notion that goods which are not lying within the purview of the most immediate sense reaction of the individual are to be excluded from any causal analysis of the exchange act, Jevons takes his place among the outstanding spokesmen of emotional primitivism in the realm of economic theory.

The role of social and economic conditions in shaping an individual attitude towards consumption is fully ignored by Jevons.

The question of what part have social and economic relations in bringing about an interpersonal exchange of goods, Jevons does not even care to ask.

Any attempt to detect a social and economic sequence in personal acts is ruled out of order by Jevons.

Any inquiry which acknowledges a contradistinction between a present, a past and a future in the social and economic sense, is strictly forbidden by the author of "The Theory of Political Economy."

A specific prohibition is issued by Jevons against the admission of the factor of time sequence in any effort to relate one individual exchange act to another.

A consecutive correlation of time spans as a means of gaining a social and economic understanding of individual exchange acts, is held impermissible by Jevons.

The use of designated time intervals as means to furnish a social and economic perspective for the play of individual emotions, appears to be utterly distasteful to Jevons.

Jevons wants time to be reduced to the level of a fleeting notion.

He wants time to be regarded as nothing but an array of instances.

Instead of providing a means for explaining an individual exchange act, time is to be used for confounding such explanations.

By insisting on a formulation of time as an unaccounted and unaccountable instantaneousness, Jevons wants to make sure that reference to such a perception of time is to leave individual notions about consumption and exchange in a state of compounded social and economic disarrangement.

An individual exchange act, Jevons stresses it over and over again, is to be considered as an activity which has no relation to any span of time.

An individual exchange act is to be viewed as an action which is taken at the spur of the moment.

An individual exchange act is to be regarded as but a manifestation of an instantaneous resolution.

Any queries of what brings the instantaneous resolution about, Jevons wants to put to rest by a reference to an all embracing generality.

Any question of what prompts the individual to indulge or abstain from exchange, Jevons wants to be answered by way of a citation of the word equilibrium.

The providing of the word equilibrium with any social and economic attribute, Jevons holds superfluous.

He does not consider it requisite to have the word equilibrium filled with any social and economic content.

To have the word equilibrium used in a sense of an objectively conceived social and economic balance, is something which Jevons wants to avoid.

Jevons finds it safe to rely on the sound effect of the word equilibrium.

He finds it opportune to presume that the mere mention of the high sounding word is to have the magnetic effect of resolving all doubts about the propriety of having the exchange act presented as a matter of an instantaneous resolution.

He finds it appropriate to imply in his presumptuousness that the mere pronouncing of the word equilibrium is likely to create such an irresistible impression upon the reader that any questioning which had hitherto taken place, in an attempt to determine the social and economic causes which prompt an individual exchange act, will instantly cease.

As soon as Jevons puts the characters which constitute the word equilibrium on paper, to give credit to his singlemindedness, he does not spare any effort to render that transcript socially and economically meaningless.

The word equilibrium, Jevons insists, is to be used exclusively for an indication of personal sensitivity.

The word equilibrium, Jevons demands, is to be applied as a sign of nothing more than an indication on the part of a single person that he has gained a feeling of certitude that for one single instant he had managed to square his personal feelings in spite of their ambivalence.

In committing the word equilibrium to the subjectivistic fold, Jevons makes certain that a reference to that word does not lead to a socially or economically significant explanation of the individual exchange act, the advancement of which he is determined to obstruct.

The word equilibrium in the sense in which Jevons wants it used, becomes but another reference to personal self-gratification.

The word equilibrium, in the formulation which Jevons gives it, assumes the role of but another signpost for the describing of an instantaneous saturation of personal satisfaction.

A personal equilibrium is reached by an individual, to apply Jevons' formulation, at the instant at which that individual comes to feel that any further engaging on his part in an exchange act, will not add to his personal gratification.

By the same token, a person who continues to feel that by engaging in further exchange acts, he can derive added self-gratification, is presented by Jevons as an individual who is afflicted with a sense of a personal disequilibrium.

That this kind of reference to equilibrium is pregnant with any social and economic meaning, hardly anyone will venture to suggest.

In tying equilibrium to personal self-gratification, Jevons is but compounding the utter meaninglessness of his exposition of the exchange factor.

By enmeshing the word equilibrium in a web of phrases which are devoid of any social and economic meaning, Jevons adds but another roadblock in the path which may conceivably lead to a social and economic explanation of what accounts for either the engagement or disengagement of the individual, as far as exchange transactions are concerned.

Jevons' subsequent disavowal of any objective factors in his reference to equilibrium is but reemphasizing the social and economic designification of the exchange factor.

His subsequent disclaiming which denies the concept of equilibrium any objective bearing, is but restressing his quest for social and economic disarrangement.

His reference to an equilibrium in any objective sense as a nonexisting situation, clearly demonstrates that he is determined to tolerate only such use of that word which makes it terminologically feasible for him to evade the social and economic issues which he is not willing to face.

His bare-faced assertion that the use of the word equilibrium in a sense in which that word comes to express an objectively given demand situation, constitutes a consciously contrived fiction, shows that in his drive to eliminate all nonsubjective factors from conceptualization, he has arrived at the point at which he is denying himself the application of a cogent criterion which sets the real apart from the unreal.

Equilibrium in the form in which Jevons presents it, turns out to be a conceptual dud.

As such the disqualified category of equilibrium takes its place alongside the emasculated concept of exchange.

Instead of providing a guide for a comprehension of what accounts for an individual exchange act, the citing of the equilibrium in the form in which it is done by Jevons makes the exchange act appear as more unaccountable than ever before.

A correlation of concepts, in the way it is undertaken by Jevons, is not meant to provide a clue for a more conclusive observation.

He refers one general conception to another general conception in an effort to extend the range of inconclusiveness.

The kind of conceptual correlation which Jevons promotes, is not intended to effect an extension of the frontiers of knowledge.

He piles up one socially and economically meaningless concept upon another in an obvious attempt to arrest thought and stifle social and economic inquiry.

Jevons' brand of obscurantism though, has some peculiar features of its own.

The tactics which Jevons uses to prevent any social and economic enlightenment, has some very special characteristics.

Jevons does not care to attack the validity of social and economic reasoning which stands in the way of his presumptions by way of denying that the social and economic factors which have given rise to the reasoning which he sets out to invalidate, have ever made themselves felt in social and economic life.

He is content with drawing attention away from the social and economic issues which have come to underly the generalizations which he sets out to emasculate.

He relies on the tactics of looking the other way on vital social and economic problems when, in the course of pursuing his sterile form of conceptualization, he arrives at the point at which he has to exclude relevant social and economic factors from his generalization in order to keep it empty.

He leaves the obscure, obscure in the path of his methodological tour de force.

The unclarified remains unclarified in the wake of the devastation of a socially and economically meaningful conceptualization wrought by him.

He succeeds in linking the uncertain to the uncertain.

He is no less successful in relating the indefinite with the indefinite.

The kind of concretization in which Jevons indulges becomes, in turn, a manifestation of his intention to demonstrate the representativeness of the nebulous.

The quantifications which he undertakes turn out to be a device which is applied with a view of lending added weight to the unreal.

Jevons' mathematical configurations are so devised, as to provide added support for the improbable.

His most precise formulations are supposed to constitute nothing but envelopments of the unknown.

The highest of the postulates the proposition which is supposed to form the keystone in the new approach to economic conceptualization, the fundamental concept of final utility, emerges as but a shadow of itself from the literary hands of Jevons.

The favored instrumentality of the subjectivistic school of economic thinking, the device of having the marginal utility of the part determine the value of the whole, comes to be all but useless, when it emerges from the treatment which it receives from Jevons.

In contrasting the whole and the part Jevons engages in a game of playing up the notion of the infinitesimally small against the immeasurably large and vice versa, with the result that he is having everybody puzzled what, if any criterion, he is prepared to allow for having the whole distinguished from the part and vice versa.

In the examples of the infinitesimally small and the immeasurably large which Jevons proffers, the whole becomes as unspecifiable as the part.

In exemplifying the infinitesimally small as a way of melting to nothing, Jevons wants to bring out that it is humanly impossible to determine when a part vanishes.

In representing the immeasurably large as a form of the limitless, Jevons wants to point out that it is humanly unfeasible to ascertain when a whole assumes such proportions as to become incomprehensible.

Jevons is desirous of leaving the impression that it is futile to try to determine what is a part since the measuring of the part in terms of infinitesimal numbers can be carried to a point at which nothing is left that can be made subject to measuring.

He wants, in turn, to impress the reader with the notion that it is senseless to try to ascertain what is a whole since the measuring of the whole, in terms of the immeasurably large, cannot be kept within comprehensible proportions.

Jevons uses the mathematical devices of the infinitesimally small and the immeasurably large as an added promotion device in his drive for the dissolution of the social and economic concepts, which he is aiming to destroy.

In his use of the mathematical devices of the infinitesimally small and the immeasurably large, Jevons but underscores it, that the denial of any social criterion in the cognition of an object makes it logically imperative to deny the whole of that object and any part of it any socially and economically meaningful role.

176

In playing up the infinitesimally small against the immeasurably large, Jevons but underlines the realization that his denial of social signification to an object, leaves the whole of that object as well as any part of it without any means of social and economic identification.

In his taking recourse to the mathematical devices of the infinitesimally small and the immeasurably large, Jevons but re-emphasizes that in case an object is denied any social relevance, as it is done in his treatise, a reference to the object, whether to the whole of the object, or part of it, is rendered senseless.

In the way in which he applies the mathematical devices of the infinitesimally small and immeasurably large, Jevons accomplishes the feat of demonstrating that an object which is emptied of social and economic content is most likely to lose itself in a maze of social and economic shapelessness.

In the form in which he employs the mathematical devices of the infinitesimally small and immeasurably large, Jevons is providing a test that an attempt to impute marginal utility to a whole or a part of such an object which is held to be socially and economically indeterminate cannot have any other effect than the one which results from relating something to nothing.

Jevons appears to be intellectually honest to the extent of not trying to hide the irresolution which he is promoting.

He possesses enough integrity to desist from an attempt to camouflage the social self-abdication to which he subscribes.

The self-designated purifier of political economy does not shirk from acknowledging that he is engaged in an effort to engineer a full scale retreat from the social signification of economic concepts.

He does not even mind boasting of his signal role in having concepts deprived of any social meaning.

He is even prepared to make a show of his defeatist stand in regard to economic conceptualization, by proffering to demonstrate its usefulness.

Jevons expresses eagerness to have the notion that it presents a hopeless undertaking to try to imbue economic abstractions with social content extended to his theory of labor.

Labor, the self-professed purifier of economic theory intones, is not to be regarded as a socially motivated effort.

Labor is not to be viewed as a socially determined force.

Labor is not to signify anything else but a physiological reflex.

Labor is not to have any other meaning than that of a mental and physical reaction.

Labor, Jevons directs, is to be assigned no other role than the balancing of individual pleasure and pain.

The duration of labor, Jevons would have it, is not to be considered as a factor which is basically determined by social conditions.

Time spent on labor, the purifier of economic theory becomes emphatic, is not to be treated as an aspect which is fundamentally affected by techno-economic conditions.

The continuation or discontinuation of a given labor effort, Jevons does not hesitate to insist, depends entirely upon the personal sensitivity of the respective individual.

Whether a given labor effort is pursued further or not, Jevons feels no scruples to assert, depends completely upon the personal reaction of the individual to the interplay of feelings within himself.

Jevons is carefully refraining, it should be noted, from making any statement about the initiation of the labor effort.

He is studiously avoiding saying anything about the social and economic conditions under which an individual labor effort is being started.

Jevons is persistently referring to a labor effort which has come to be in progress.

He does not care to pay any attention to anything which lies outside the confines of personal emotional stresses of the worker who is found working.

Jevons designates as a key to his labor theory the proposition that should a personal pleasurable anticipation outweigh the personal unpleasantness which a current labor effort causes the performing individual, that individual is likely to be emotionally predisposed to go on working.

He likewise proffers, as a key formulation, the reverse proposition, which states that should, in turn, the expectation of future satisfactions not outbalance the disagreeableness which the individual ascribes to his current labor effort, the individual is likely to become emotionally predisposed to stop working.

The propositions which he offers as a key formulation, Jevons is eager to have guarded against what he considers to be a misrepresentation.

The anticipated personal pleasure as a stimulant for a continuous individual work effort is not to be interpreted in a way which relates such work stimulus to objectively verified overall production results which loom in the future.

Nor is a personal displeasure and its arresting effect on the individual work effort to be understood in a form which refers such work deterrent to any overall production results which have been currently attained.

Individual emotions which prompt the individual either to continue or discontinue his work effort, are supposed to remain completely unchanged by any ascertainable social and economic currents, on Jevons' direction.

The emotional disposition of the individual to either continue or discontinue his work effort is to be considered as being formed in a complete social and economic vacuum, on orders by Jevons.

The duration of a given labor effort, Jevons continues to spin his labor theory, is to be exclusively related to a play of individual emotions as they come to express themselves in the intensity of labor.

Labor intensity, Jevons wants it to be noted, has nothing to do with technological advances.

Labor intensity, Jevons finds it necessary to warn, is not to be regarded as a correlate of productivity.

The comprehension of intensity of the individual labor effort as well as its duration is placed by Jevons within the cognitive range of a person's emotional amplitude.

Nothing else is supposed to be knowable in regard to causal factors of individual work duration than the realization that the individual is likely to cease to work when the unpleasantness of intensive work outweighs in the emotional reaction of that individual

179

the comparative pleasureableness he expects to derive from what he regards as the fruits of his labor.

Nothing else is supposed to be knowable about the causal factor of individual work intensity than the realization that the individual is likely to cease working when an increasing fatigue outbalances, in the individual's emotional reaction, the agreeableness the person expects from what he considers to be the result of his work.

The continuation and discontinuation of the labor effort assume in the stated presentation a wholly voluntary character.

The laborer continues or discontinues his work wholly unhampered by anybody and anything in Jevons' formulation.

The worker's decision to pursue the work task in which he is engaged or not to pursue it, is presented as a manifestation of that laborer's free and unhindered will.

Jevons arrives at this turn at a voluntaristic interpretation of the work effort.

The aspect of hiring of labor as well as the factor of assigned work schedules go unmentioned by Jevons.

Nor is the factor of ownership of production instruments by others than those who work those instruments accorded any recognition in Jevons' treatise on Political Economy.

Jevons does not acknowledge the disposal of goods by others than those who are engaged in productive labor.

Labor as a social burden, labor as a form of social imposition, is an unknown subject for the author of the "Theory of Political Economy."

Labor, Jevons insists, is not to be regarded as being in any way different from what is generally referred to as play.

No baffling problems of a social or economic nature will ever come to trouble the economic theorist, Jevons obviously presumes in this instance, were labor to be presented as a kind of time passing.

The social and economic complexities which for generations have occupied the searching minds of outstanding theoreticians will lose all their import, Jevons is apparently presuming, were labor to be treated as a delayed action game.

In the case of labor effort, Jevons is at hand with an amplification, the effect might not be as immediate as in the case of a play exercise; as far, however, as the fundamental conception of the two factors is concerned, Jevons reasserts it is not to be granted that laboring differs in any way from playing.

Labor and play, Jevons states his position, both refer to a striving for the attainment of a personal emotional equilibrium.

Jevons does not care to have a cross reference attached to his formulation which represents labor and play as means of squaring personal emotions.

Jevons does not appear to cherish at all the prospect of being reminded in the stated connection, that he has effected a social disqualification of the labor performance.

Nor does he give any sign that he wants to have it recalled at this turn that he has committed himself to a denial of any social attribute to the bearer of the labor performance, the live laborer.

Jevons could hardly be expected to be anxious to hear that by having the concept of labor turned into an empty symbol, he has made it cognitively unfeasible for himself to advance any socially and economically meaningful formulation of the labor effort.

His assertion that his identification of the socially disqualified conception of labor with a socially unqualified conception of play, constitutes a step towards a highly significant conceptual integration, Jevons could hardly care to be told, sounds like a highly pretentious contention.

His insistence that by confining laboring and playing to the emotional fold, he is placing the analysis of human labor on hitherto unattained heights, Jevons could hardly want to be made aware of it, does not appear to be at all convincing.

His subsequent deliberations do, nonetheless, not bear out his pretentions that he has advanced a cogent formulation.

The demonstrations which are supposed to back up his claims do not support his contention that he has forged a potent analytical device with the form of conceptualization which he suggests for labor.

With a highly professional air, Jevons declares, however, that he is willing to concede that it might not be possible to determine in advance the exact point at which a personal emotional balance will be reached by an individual who becomes engaged in labor.

It might, moreover, not be feasible, Jevons relates with aplomb, to calculate beforehand the exact time and the specific intensity at which a personal emotional release will make the laboring individual cease working.

It should be feasible, however, Jevons tries to console himself, to ascertain the degree of painfulness to which the laboring individual feels subject.

It should not be impossible, Jevons maintains, to determine whether more or less pain is being experienced by the individual in the course of his work.

The longer a person labors, Jevons argues, the more painful the work will become for him.

The more intensively an individual works, Jevons maintains, the greater will be the unpleasantness which that person will feel in effecting the work.

Increasing pain which comes to be felt by the person engaged in labor, Jevons proffers to foretell, is of necessity to lead to a decrease in the appreciation of the respective work product by the laboring individual.

Increasing unpleasantness in the exercise of labor, which the individual comes to experience, Jevons ventures to foretell, is, in turn, to result in a reduction of that person's regard for the respective material embodiment of the work product.

Jevons does not shrink in the stated instance from according to what he regards as the degree of personal labor pain a certainty which only a major economic determinant had hitherto come to command.

He has no scruples, in the stated instance, to the according to what he views as a degree of individual unpleasantness of work the role which had hitherto been assigned to a controlling social influence.

The extent to which the individual is painfully affected by his work effort, Jevons does not hesitate to claim by inference, represents the decisive factor in the regulation of production.

The extent to which work is felt to be personally disagreeable to the individual work performer is paraded by Jevons as the unquestionable determinant of the production level.

Production, by the same token, is carried on only to the extent that it pleases any given individual who pursues productive labor tasks.

The extent of unpleasantness of work which the individual work performer feels, Jevons insists lays the basis for that individual's production curve.

The degree of individual painfulness, Jevons enlarges his claim, forms also the basis on which the production curve of one individual can be related to production curves of other individuals.

He suggests something akin to a standardization of like degrees of painfulness as means of comparing individual production records.

The like degree of individual painfulness of work in the form of standardized personal feelings is simultaneously offered by Jevons as a means of relating personal exchange records to each other.

By keeping accounts for the emotional outgo and intake of different individuals, Jevons considers one can record the flow of interpersonal exchange.

Jevons does not take the trouble of denying that the placing of the calculation of production and exchange data on a personal emotional basis, as he suggests, constitutes an invitation to inexactitude.

He does not dispute that an attempt to express the degree of painfulness in any quantitative form could hardly lead to any definite results.

His formulas, Jevons makes it known, are not to be considered as a device for the facilitation of concretization.

Nothing in his formulations, Jevons does not mind pointing it out, is to be taken as a means for advancing concretization in any form.

Anybody who would be inclined to interpret his quantitative deliberations as a search for a more precise form of either concretization of the whole of a given good or the specification of a part of a good, cannot but have misread him, Jevons announces.

Not a single one of his quantification devices, Jevons takes pains to emphasize, is to be credited with pointing to a kind of agglomeration of products which is based on a cognitive acknowledgement of either a separate existence of a single product in a multiplicity of products or the separate existence of a single part in a multiplicity of parts.

He does not recognize, Jevons wants it reemphasized, that a form of cognition could be advanced which could make it feasible to gain a clear comprehension of what is a whole and what is a part.

Nor does he concede, Jevons wants it restressed, that an objective basis can ever be furnished for the effecting of either a division or multiplication of a product.

Jevons insists on ruling out any concretization and quantification which does not restrict itself to the effort of providing an individual accounting scheme for personal feelings.

He places a ban on the evaluation of goods in regard to their size and their amount which does not confine itself to the task of evolving individual scales of personal pain.

The narrowing of the cognitive range to which Jevons commits himself forms a fitting prelude to the introduction of the scarcity scheme by the author of the "Theory of Political Economy."

The degree of scarcity, in the treatment which is accorded to it by Jevons, comes to play the role of an amplifier of the degree of pain.

Any individual, Jevons spells out his marginal utility stand, is at liberty to determine his own wants by his own free will.

Any single person is, in turn, always free to satisfy his wants in Jevons' version of the marginal utility tenet.

Any single person, Jevons wants it to be taken as a socially and economically undeniable proposition, is imbued with having the inalienable power to meet what he considers are his needs.

Should a social and economic impossibility to satisfy one's needs have to be admitted at some instance, Jevons wants it interpreted as but a form of personal maladjustment.

Scarcity becomes a form of a personal psychic imbalance, in Jevons' version of the marginal utility theme.

Scarcity is presented by the author of "The Theory of Political Economy" as a painful experience which any single person has it in his psychic power to overcome.

Scarcity is in particular treated by Jevons as a factor which expresses a personal emotional tension.

The words *degree of scarcity* are made to refer by Jevons to the degree of pain to which the individual considers himself subjected.

The words degree of scarcity lose any meaning of their own in the formulation advanced by Jevons.

The expression degree of scarcity is presented by Jevons as one which is identical with the expression the degree of pain.

Obviously sensing that his suggestion, to use the words the degree of scarcity and the degree of pain as interchangeable, does somehow violence to the meaning of either of the two words, conceivably realizing that the word scarcity cannot possibly be employed without any reference to objective factors, Jevons suddenly switches from the word scarcity to the word privation.

The word privation, Jevons no doubt realizes, has always carried a subjectivistic flavor.

Privation and pain, Jevons is right in assuming, are somehow more suited for being used as alternate conceptions.

Privation, in Jevons' strictly subjectivistic interpretation, does not constitute a factor which is brought about by outer circumstances.

General conditions do not play a role in the effectuation of privation, Jevons is prepared to assure.

Privation is made to play the role of a manifestation of personal inadequacy in Jevons' presentation.

Privation presents an expression of individual failure in the formulation which is being proffered by Jevons.

Privation, Jevons wants it recorded without any further qualification, comes to be visited upon those persons who do not care to strain themselves.

Misery, Jevons wants it to be accepted without any further question, is being suffered only by those individuals who do not want to labor.

Privation and misery are pictured by Jevons as forms of individual frustration.

Privation and misery testify but to a personal inhibition, in the characterization of Jevons.

Jevons, though, is not prepared to go as far, as to deny the existence of poverty as a factor which is not completely emotional.

He is quick, however, to prompt the assertion that poverty cannot be considered as a factor which has any relation to a given social pattern.

Neither is poverty to be regarded, Jevons wants to make it sure, as a factor which has any connection with a given economic system.

Poverty, Jevons falls back on his all out subjectivism, is wholly a matter of individual volition.

Poverty to Jevons relates a condition to which a person succumbs out of his own free will.

Suddenly, as if he had come to realize that he has been expounding an untenable position, Jevons makes a move towards switching his stand.

Without caring to notice that he is merely suggesting the substitution of one form of misrepresentation for another, Jevons reverts from an unqualified indeterminism to an unqualified determinism.

In contradicting his previous assertions, Jevons proceeds to insist that privation and misery are invariably rooted in the bio-psychic constitution of the individual.

At this juncture, Jevons presents privation and misery as predetermined by a person's physical and mental makeup.

Poverty at this stage of Jevons' presentation comes very close to being identified as a manifestation of a subnormal being.

Poverty, in this reversed characterization, comes close to representing a psychophysical attribute of an inferior human being.

Widespread poverty, in a case in which it is impossible to deny its existence, comes to assume in Jevons' reversed formulation the character of a mass expression of an unhealthy psycho-physical predisposition of the individuals concerned.

Large scale misery, should its existence have to be admitted, comes to be imputed in Jevons' deterministic version, to a spreading of inborn personal indolence and apathy.

Progressive impoverishment, an increase in misery, Jevons is at pains to stress, are not to be considered as being attributable to any general stagnation in trade.

A general imbalance between production and consumption, a general disequilibrium between demand and supply, presents a condition which defies observation, according to Jevons' directive.

An intrinsic economic imbalance, a disequilibrium which is rooted in a fundamental social division, Jevons wants to be postulated as incomprehensible.

An imbalance between production and consumption, Jevons wants to be viewed as but an incidental factor.

A disequilibrium between demand and supply, Jevons wants to be regarded as but a wholly insignificant partial obstruction.

Nothing, Jevons becomes particularly emphatic on that point, is ever to be credited to a kind of loss in the social balance which cannot be regained by means of individually conceived manipulations.

A disestablished economic equilibrium, Jevons wants it accepted as an undeniable analytical proposition, can be reestablished without fail by way of an individualistic emotional readjustment.

There should not be any doubt about it, Jevons pontificates, that a social and economic equilibrium can be brought about by a proper personal management of individual emotions.

A socio-economic balance, Jevons considers himself particularly competent to reassure, can be fully attained by way of the voluntary submission to labor pain.

The painful exertion to which an individual is willing to subject himself, invariably results in a material yield for that individual, Jevons proffers an exemplification of his labor theory.

Changes in the degree of a painful experience express themselves most fully in the increment of the respective yields, Jevons wants it to be taken as an illustration of his theoretical stand on labor.

The extent of painful exertion to which the individual is prepared to submit comes to assume, in Jevons' formulation, the role of an indicator of the rate of personal rehabilitation of a person who had come to experience poverty and misery because he had caused himself to become emotionally upset.

Jevons is eager to have the suffering of labor pain accepted as a sure device by which nature is made to yield its forces.

187

He wants the suffering of individual labor pain to be looked upon as a factor which predetermines the extension of the benefits which nature is made to yield.

The material results of one's labor, Jevons proclaims it as a major tenet, cannot be diverted.

The material yield of the individual sufferer, accrues to him in Jevons' presentation, with a certainty of the law of gravitation.

The material yield is as certain to fall into the lap of the individual laborer, as the apple which falls to the ground, Jevons wants it accepted without any challenge.

The subject of social and economic appropriation is not a fit theme for discussion to Jevons.

Since he is carefully evading to have anything discussed which pertains to what takes place before and after a person exerts himself in work, he considers he can be fully excused from ever raising the question of the appropriation by those who do not labor.

Even a conjecture about the alienation of the product is nowhere to be found in Jevons' treatise.

The possibility that a person whose painful experience results in a material yield, could be deprived of the enjoyment of the full fruits of his labor, is not admitted by Jevons.

The conception which regards labor reward as a reflection of social relations, Jevons confines to the realm of the unknown.

The viewing of labor reward as an expression of social and economic power, constitutes something which the author of the "Theory of Political Economy" ignores.

Wages, as a category which concerns itself with hired labor, is being consigned to the limbo by Jevons.

Wages, as a concept which is rooted in the recognition of the social division of income, has obviously not registered with the self-advertised purifier of economic thought.

Wages, moreover, as the kind of income which takes a monetary form, does not merit any mention by Jevons.

The subject of social identification of labor reward is being selected for inaction by Jevons.

The aspect of social signification of labor compensation Jevons prefers to leave unattended.

He finds it opportune to deny income derived from labor any social signification.

Jevons' attempts, to make the category of wages appear socially meaningless, are followed by his effort to reduce the societal consequence of other income categories.

His onslaught against the social aspects of labor reward is followed by an assault on the social imputations in regard to income derived from sources other than labor.

A material yield, Jevons introduces a new twist, is not only to be attributed to personal exertion. Individual strain is not to be considered as the only factor to which a material yield is to be held imputable.

Material yields, Jevons goes on record, are to be viewed as being due to more than labor pain.

Land and capital, Jevons is willing to recognize, also contribute to the effectuation of material yields.

Such admission on his part, Jevons is, however, quick to warn, is not to be interpreted as a concession to a societal point of view.

Whether the factor to which the material yield is to be held attributable is of a personal or of a nonpersonal nature, such factor is to be considered as lacking any social characteristics, Jevons insists.

Jevons is at pains to deny any social quality to either labor or land or capital, in regard to their respective role in the effectuation of the material yield.

Only a quantitative distinctiveness is being granted by Jevons to the factors of labor, capital and land, as far as their respective contribution to the effectuation of the material yield is concerned.

The quantitative differentiation of labor, capital and land as they come to affect the material yield, though granted in principle, is never put to a test by Jevons.

An effort to effect a quantitative differentiation of material yields of labor, capital and land, Jevons is apparently conscious, might not be feasible without furnishing in its aftermath some leads for a social distinction of the differentiated yields.

Even an exclusively quantitative identification of the material yields of labor, land and capital, Jevons appears to be fearful, might provide some lead for a support of a reaffirmation of an existence of a social division of labor and nonlabor income.

To forestall such contingency, to insure himself against any reopening of the question of the social qualifications of forms of income, Jevons makes an added move to obscure the socially explosive aspect of labor, land and capital; the question of how income is formed is not to be granted any relevance.

Income whether it is formed by labor, capital or land, is not to be made known in a form which acknowledges the specific characteristics of each of the three income forms.

Income, whether it is formed by labor, land or capital, is to be referred to by the undifferentiated term of material yield.

Jevons wants the term material yield to supersede the terms labor yield, capital yield and land yield.

He wants it restressed that economic gains, regardless of whether they are due to labor, capital or land, are physical and not social in nature.

The deliberate undifferentiation of income categories is advanced a step further by Jevons outright refusal to continue to use the term wages.

The category wages, no matter how emasculated, appears to have unwanted social connotations to the author of the "Theory of Political Economy."

His sensitivity to social connotations is much less pronounced, when he comes to deal with the category of rent.

Though he is firm in his rejection of a specific social interpretation of the rent category, he is, nevertheless, willing to keep rent in his vocabulary.

Rent in the sense of a yield attributable to the fertility of the soil, is made to play an important role in Jevons' theory.

Rent in a socially disqualified form, is being groomed by Jevons for application as a multiple indicator.

Rent reduced to social meaninglessness, is being slated by the author of "The Theory of Political Economy," to mark the material yield of land as well as labor.

The yield of the soil as well as the yield of personal labor, Jevons

190

wants to have considered as identical yields of a single generative process.

Gains of the soil as well as the gains of human labor, are both to be regarded as mere fruitions of organic nature.

To use Jevons' terminology, labor performed by the soil and labor performed by the human, form a wholly undifferentiated and by inference, undifferentiable expression of a one and only natural law.

The conception of social law, it should be duly noted, remains alien to Jevons.

The possibility of a diversion of the forces of nature by social forces is being ruled out by the author of "The Theory of Political Economy."

In Jevons' apodictic stand, the natural law in its reference to humans, is not permitted to have any social implications.

Jevons makes it a point to cite Ricardo in favor of his own naturalistic conceptions.

Ricardo, in Jevons' allegation, has ignored social factors in conceiving his "Principles of Political Economy."

Ricardo, Jevons makes the paradoxical charge, had paid no attention to property relations in his formulations.

Jevons refuses to see that the law of decreasing yields, as defined in Ricardo's "Principles," presents a generalization which bases itself on the observation of social and economic malappropriation in agriculture. Jevons, on his part, wants the law of diminishing returns stamped as a natural law, which has been formulated without any regard to social relations.

Ricardo, Jevons maintains, would have no objection to a reformulation which denies any social relevance to his, Ricardo's, major generalization.

Ricardo, Jevons insists, could not be expected to protest a formulation which disregards the social division which sets the land owner apart from the propertyless laborer.

Ricardo, Jevons implies, would have heartily agreed to a presentation in which diminishing returns are linked without any further qualification to labor which is so to speak, performed by the soil as well as to labor which is performed by the human.

Ricardo, Jevons wants to have it inferred, would have fully accepted his, Jevons' view, that his, Ricardo's law of diminishing returns, was intended to demonstrate that the factor of increasingly decreasing yields has no social significance whatsoever.

Ricardo would have preferred to see his law of diminishing returns rephrased in a manner, Jevons presumes, which would permit the production effort which in Jevons' wording is inherent in the soil and the production effort which, to speak Jevons' language, is inherent in the human to qualify as identical factors the successive employment of which is made to account for increasingly decreasing yields.

In an ostensible effort to instill some degree of concreteness into the version of Ricardo's law, which he Jevons, is propounding, the author of "The Theory of Political Economy" makes a reference to units of labor and units of soil.

He studiously refrains saying anything, however, on the subject of how a unit of labor and a unit of soil is to be detected.

He carefully avoids making any clear statement in regard to the question of how units of human and nonhuman effort, to which he makes reference, should be constituted.

He prefers to remain vague, when called upon to implement the suggested concretization device which is supposed to lead to a more specific comprehension of human and nonhuman effort within an asocial range.

He restricts himself to lamenting the unavailability of conceptual means which could establish a clear distinction between the efforts of an individual laborer and the collective effort of a labor team.

He indulges in deploring that a conceptual distinction between a single and multiple human act lies beyond the range of human comprehension.

An inquirer who would attempt to establish a conceptual delineation between individual and collective labor efforts, Jevons takes it upon himself to foretell, is to find himself increasingly lost in a maze of shapelessness.

In the absence of an exact counting procedure, Jevons creates a mood of despair.

Anyone who would be willing to undertake the task of numbering human efforts, Jevons insists, will discover that he is increasingly pursuing the will-o'-the-wisp of numberlessness.

An attempt to ascertain a unit of effort, Jevons is at pains to stress, is of necessity to end in compounded indistinctiveness.

In his bent for indefiniteness, Jevons reaches a stage at which he has no alternative but to embrace nihilistic conceptions.

He provides a stark demonstration of his conceptual nihilism, when he proceeds to insist that any attempt to determine with any degree of precision the effort of a multiplicity of workers has to become invariably deadlocked due to the inability of the human mind to conceive how an effort of a measurable number of laborers can be set apart from an effort of an immeasurable number of workers.

He makes his conceptual nihilism no less evident, when he goes on to proclaim that any try which is made to determine with any degree of exactness and effort of a single worker has to become stalled due to the inherent incapability of the human mind of knowing how any unit of an effort of an individual laborer can be singled out from amongst the infinitesimally small parts of which the labor effort of any single person consists.

Jevons' plea for an unqualified acceptance of his presumption that the ascertainment of either a whole or a part of a labor effort lies beyond the power of human cognition furnishes ample testimony, if any further proof were needed, that he has firmly committed himself to an escape into conceptual nothingness.

Labor effort, i.e. applied labor, is treated by Jevons, as if it constituted an undetectable emanation.

Labor effort is treated by the author of "The Theory of Political Economy," as if it presents an indistinctive eruption.

Labor effort is pictured by the self-appointed purifier of economic theory as an endless stream, neither the initiation, nor the cessation of which can ever be determined.

Jevons is not willing to permit labor effort to count for anything more than a demonstration of a ceaseless energy.

The personal aspect of labor, the subjective limitation of the human effort is brushed aside in this instance.

The emotive aspect of labor to which Jevons gave such a big display when he referred to labor in the abstract, is ignored by him, when he deals with the factor of realization of labor.

Labor as expression of joy and pain is nowhere referred to in Jevons' analysis of the actualization of labor.

The major attribute of Jevons' general postulation of labor is thoroughly missing in his treatment of the concrete manifestation of labor.

He disavows the essence of his general formulation of labor when he is called upon to test its application.

The incongruity between labor in the abstract and labor in the concrete can hardly be regarded as an oversight on the part of Jevons.

The creation of a conceptual gap between the theory and practice of labor in Jevons' exposition, can scarcely be ascribed to a sudden lapse of mental power which had overtaken Jevons.

The arrival at the social and economic discrepancy between what labor *is* and what labor *does* constitutes a part of a highly contrived stratagem.

Jevon's disregard for the individuality of the carrier of human labor power, when he comes to deal with the subject of effectiveness of human labor, is part and parcel of a well devised scheme.

His discounting of the bearing of human personality when, in the course of his deliberations, he advances to the stage at which he is called upon to ascertain the efficacy of human exertion, constitutes a strategically placed move on the part of Jevons.

His discounting of the human aspect of labor effort forms a high point in Jevons' persistent drive towards the dehumanization of conceptualization in Political Economy.

Jevons' dehumanized formulation of labor effort provides him with a logical stepping stone in his taking the position that human and nonhuman effort are indistinguishable.

In advancing a dehumanized conception of human performance, Jevons, moreover, furnishes himself with a methodological stand which enables him to gloss over the conceptual division between a personal and an apersonal contribution of labor.

A dehumanized view on human exertion makes it, in turn, feasible for Jevons to enter a formalistic denial that the effectuation of tamed forces of nature as they affect human labor can be held apart from the effectuation of untamed forces of nature in their bearing on human labor.

Jevons' dehumanized view of human performance is, moreover, fully in keeping with his subsequent formulation which terms labor effort as an indeterminable flow of energy.

Jevons' dehumanized view on the realization of human labor is completely in line, as far as formalistic reasoning goes, with his refusal to provide for a distinction between a manifestation of living and nonliving nature.

A dehumanized view on the results of a sustained human work, Jevons can claim with particular satisfaction, is wholly consistent with a formulation which disallows any differentiation between the force of nature as it expresses itself in the productiveness of the human and the force of nature as it manifests itself in the productiveness of the soil.

In making his conception of dehumanized human energy as well as the conception of nonhuman energy express nothing but an indivisible flow of energy, Jevons can well pride himself on having well advanced towards a synthetic presentation of his asocial formulations.

In having the productiveness of the human and the productiveness of the soil presented as identical manifestations of a natural force, Jevons can well boast of having made great strides indeed, in the sphere of social evasiveness.

The case of social designification, which Jevons is trying to defend receives an added impetus by his slurring remarks on causation.

He has no scruples of glossing over the conceptual distinction between subjective and objective causation.

He does not hesitate to deny the determinability of causation and imputation, as far as their respective range and import is concerned.

Jevons takes it upon himself to rule out any attempt to record a cognitive distinction between a cause in terms of a verifiable objectification and a subjective imputation which refers to personal desires.

He suggests that any interrogation into causative aspects and in particular any social and economic interrogation of causative factors be labeled as unqualified conjecture.

He prefers to see any question which pertains to causation and imputation, including questions which involve the ascertainment of social and economic causation and imputation, get lost in a maze of indecision.

The application of causation and imputation as effective analytical tools is placed within the range of the inconceivable by Jevons.

He takes pride in being instrumental in creating insurmountable methodological difficulties in the path of an attempted correlation of specific causes and concrete effects.

Since he has directed that causation and imputation are not to refer to anything particular, Jevons reasons, he has made those two analytical tools become utterly useless for any attempt to answer the question which could conceivably be put to him, with regard to his formulation of the actualization of labor, what specifically is effected by what particular manifestation of energy.

Since he has ordered that causation and imputation are not to have any connection whatsoever with the factor of social and economic relations, Jevons finds it safe to argue that he has made those two analytical tools wholly inapplicable as means for effecting a social and economic correlation of yields and efforts.

Since he is not inclined to permit any social and economic aspect to enter into the consideration of either causation or imputation, Jevons can credit himself, he is preventing the two analytical tools from ever being used in an attempt to have the effect of an effort linked to any social factor.

In dealing with causation and imputation, Jevons takes particular pains to forestall the contingency that the effectuation of a yield is conceivably to be attributed to social forces.

Jevons' treatment of causation and imputation is so designed as to have the question of how and to what extent a yield is effected, placed within a naturalistic scope.

His disqualification of causation and imputation is so devised as to make it logically feasible for him to have any yield presented as an immediate manifestation of the force of nature, regardless of whether the yield in question involves the realization of human or nonhuman energy.

In his social and economic designification of causation, it should be noted, Jevons is guided by the consideration of having yields of human productiveness as well as yields of the productiveness of the soil confined to the range of physical yields.

A dehumanized view on the human effort, Jevons has reason to feel confident, is greatly conducive to the prevention of any conclusive inquiry on the subject of whether it has or has not any social and economic relevance that he denies the distinguishability of what he terms natural yield from the soil and to what he refers as natural yield from human exertion.

After the social disqualification to which he has subjected the categories of rent and wages, Jevons can feel reasonably sure that it will be comparatively easy for him to keep a cloud over the meaning of his direct and indirect references to those emasculated categories, in having them fitted into his dehumanized view on the human effort.

All differences between yields from human productiveness and yields from the productiveness of the soil, Jevons wants to have presented as nothing else but physical variations.

He insists that all distinguishes yields of human productiveness from yields of nonhuman productiveness is to be analyzed, as if it constituted nothing more than physiological and biological divergencies.

The attributes which make yields effected by animate nature differ from yields effected so to speak by inanimate nature, Jevons wants it stressed, are not to be accorded any great significance.

The distinguishing characteristic which sets yields from human nature apart from yields of nonhuman nature, Jevons is at pains to emphasize, are not to be regarded as having much of a meaning.

The dehumanization of the view on human effort, Jevons is well able to invoke the inner logic of his reasoning, forms an effective bar against any attempt of social signification of labor.

The dehumanization of the view on human effort, Jevons can again bring formal logic to his side, serves as a patent impediment to have labor imbued with any social and economic meaning.

A dehumanized view on the human effort cannot be maintained, Jevons has reason to claim, unless the reasoning, which is founded on it, continues to be extraeconomic and asocial in character.

A dehumanized view on human exertion cannot be sustained, Jevons can well cite the inner logic of his argumentation in his favor, unless all formulations which are derived from such a dehumanized view are deprived of any social and economic content.

A dehumanized view on human exertion, Jevons should not hesitate to admit it, presupposes that the human can ascertain as little about himself as about the sphere of the nonhuman.

A dehumanized view on human exertion, presupposes furthermore, Jevons should be frank about it, that no ascertainable distinction can ever be made between what constitutes and what does not constitute a conscious realization on the part of the human.

A dehumanized view on human labor, moreover, presupposes, Jevons should see no reason to deny it, that it is not feasible to draw a distinction between what characterizes and what does not characterize human sensibility.

A dehumanized view on the human effort, to give its practical implications to Jevons, forms a suitable terminological and methodological device for blocking any attempt to ascertain what forms and what does not form a social and economic issue.

A dehumanized view on the human effort is well fitted to serve as terminological and methodological deterrent in any attempt which sets out to determine what generalization has as its criterion a manifestation of social and economic life and what generalization does not have such a criterion.

A dehumanized view on the human effort forms in particular a well geared terminological and methodological vehicle for making it appear uncertain whether a human effort calls for a human reward or not.

A dehumanized view on the human effort constitutes an excellent terminological and methodological instrumentality for making it appear doubtful whether the category of wages has any meaning or not.

A dehumanized view on the human effort can be used as a perfect terminological and methodological screen for an assertion that it is impossible to distinguish between human and nonhuman returns.

A dehumanized view on human effort can well be applied as a terminological and methodological alibi for an insistence that it is unfeasible to determine whether the conception of social and economic values is or is not of any import.

A dehumanized view on human effort, there can be little doubt, is, in Jevons' design, supposed to obstruct any effort to make certain whether the subject of social costs deserves any analytical consideration or not.

A dehumanized view on human effort, there can be hardly any doubt about it, is supposed to preclude in Jevons' scheme, any discussion of the subject whether the substitution of the word natural yield for the word wages has any social and economic significance or not.

A dehumanized view on the human effort is, in Jevons' design, supposed to reduce any dispute on the question of what lies behind the substitution of the general designation of income by the designation of natural yield to social and economic meaninglessness.

Jevons though, is hesitant to refer to rent as a form of labor compensation. He is reluctant to have the category of rent used for the identification of wage payments.

He has no hesitation, however, to refer to interest as a proper form of labor reward.

He has no scruples to suggest that the category of interest be used to denote labor compensation.

He is unequivocally in favor of disguising payments of wages as interest payments.

Interest is pictured by Jevons as a kind of delayed action yield.

The realization of interest is presented by the author of "The Theory of Political Economy" as a form of effectuation of a self-unwinding mechanism.

The accruing of interest is made to appear as a cumulative yield of work.

Interest, in Jevons' general formulation, presents payments made in the future out of income which is formed in the present.

Interest, in Jevons' more specific formulation, represents payments to be made in a future time to come out of currently earned wages.

The operation of interest payments comes to play the role of a wage withholding scheme, in Jevons' formulation.

The word interest comes to stand for deferred wages, in Jevons' subsequent presentation.

His terminological equation of interest and wages rounds out Jevons' formalistic reasoning.

The presentation of an anticipated payment of deferred wages in the form of expected interest payments, it should be acknowledged, is wholly consistent with the asocial character of Jevons' formulations.

Jevons' use of the word interest instead of the denotation wages, is quite in keeping with his disregard for the social core of the economic process.

To Jevons it does not appear improper to term wages interest since he labors under the presumption that social factors do not play any role in the formation of any kind of income.

He can find nothing terminologically objectionable to having interest denote wages since he has pledged himself to the denial that the very concept of income has any social relevance.

In having the category of interest take the place of the category of wages, to look for sense in Jevons' stratagem, he makes a move to bring his proposition of natural yield into a focal position.

In his discounting of the conceptual difference between interest and wages, he lends added weight to his conception of a socially undifferentiated allocation of income.

In glossing over the conceptual division between interest and wages, Jevons reemphasizes his notion that the effectuation of the natural yield is a natural and not a social process.

In blurring the distinction between interest and wages, Jevons restresses his presumption that natural yields can be had for the asking.

In passing over the social attributes of either interest and wages, Jevons underscores his supposition that the disposition of the natural yield depends upon nothing else but the timing of individual consumption.

Time is signified by Jevons in the stated connection only in relation to the disposition of the natural yield.

The sphere of the effectuation of the natural yield does not in connection with the stated formulation rate as a factor which merits a direct acknowledgement that time is involved.

Only in regard to consumption is time to be permitted to play a distinct role.

In production, Jevons rules, the time element is not supposed to become apparent.

As far as the process of production is concerned, the time involved is to be regarded as but an extension of the time span allotted for consumption, or to use Jevons' own terminology, the time involved in the effectuation of the natural yield is to be regarded as but an extension of the time span allotted for the disposition of the respective yield.

The designation of time spans as production periods, Jevons considers out of order.

Production periods as such, Jevons does not care to acknowledge.

The delineation of time in its relation to production is supposed to remain submerged in the designation of time with regard to consumption, in Jevons' dictum.

In disqualifying production as a specific time factor, Jevons is offering a demonstration that to him consumption presents the only factor which assures the continuity of social and economic life.

In denying that time in production merits a specific signification, Jevons deprecates the significance of reproduction.

In assigning to consumption the role of an overriding time factor, Jevons expresses in a very distinct form the supposition that production requirements are no more than incidental.

Yields designated for consumption are thus accorded a superior reality by Jevons.

Yields used for production are, in turn, made to subsist in a cognitive twilight sphere.

Yields assigned for productive purposes are deprived of any specific meaning by Jevons.

He even denies yields assigned for productive purposes a term of its own.

With his denial of social and economic identification to yields assigned to productive purposes, Jevons, it should be noted, creates a very special case of social designification.

In having yields for productive purposes deprived of any economic mark of their own, it should be realized, Jevons makes it logically feasible for himself to advance the proposition that it is terminologically unfeasible to use any such unspecifiable yield in connection with a social and economic argumentation of a wider range.

After having yields for productive purposes deprived of a term of its own, he can consider himself terminologically free to drop that denotation, when he puts the discussion of accumulative designs on his agenda.

In refusing to grant producer's goods a name of its own, Jevons precludes the possibility of having producer's goods identified as capital.

If the producer's goods are not identifiable as such they cannot be identified in a special manner, Jevons can well argue.

If producer's goods do not have any name at all, they cannot be renamed. He thus is able to reserve the word capital for a referring to something which is not identified as a yield of producer's goods.

He is thus in a position to use the denotation of capital with reference to his identification of the labor yield.

He can consider himself terminologically at liberty to insist that the word capital is to be used only with reference to the identification of effected work.

He can claim that he sees no terminological obstacle in the way of his demanding that the word capital is to make reference to a promise which is held out with reference to currently effectuated work.

He can feel terminologically unconstrained to insist that the word capital be used in the sense of an anticipation of future satisfaction out of presently executed work.

After having the issue of producer's goods sidetracked by way of a terminological tour de force, Jevons has reason to claim, as he does, that he has created the proper methodological prerequisites for having the word capital applied for the expression of a social and economic radiation which emanates from a pile of consumer's goods.

The fancifulness of Jevons' presentation is not in any way lessened by his venture into quantification at this point.

Though he voices a demand for precision, he does little, if anything, to implement such demand, as it has become customary with him.

Though he requests strict measurement, he does little. if anything, to make such measurement feasible, as it has become his custom.

Though he asks more specifically for the most exact determination of the yield from what he refers to as capital, he does not proffer an adequate instrumentality for a respective ascertainment.

Though he asserts that the yield of the whole to which he refers as capital can be fully determined on the basis of the yield of its least efficient part, he fails to provide a clue for a clear distinction of what he wants to be considered as capital as a whole and what he cares to have treated as a part of capital.

Jevons gives but evasive answers to the question of what is to be included in the whole of capital and what and how much of the whole of capital is to be rated as part of the whole.

He remains as ambiguous, as ever, on the question of whether all capital, regardless of time and place, is to be regarded as the whole of capital.

He prefers to leave everybody baffled in regard to a possible answer to the question of whether the whole of capital termed by him as such is supposed to refer to all present, all past, as well as all future capital and whether a part of the whole of capital is supposed to constitute a part of such all embracing whole.

He chooses to have everybody remain puzzled who would undertake to interrogate at what particular time and under what specific social and economic conditions that part of the whole of capital, so termed, which merits designation as the least efficient particle is supposed to be ripe for detachment.

He is satisfied to leave it to everybody's guess, how the extent of the marginal particle of the whole of capital, so termed, is ever to be determined.

Jevons' insistence that his mental gyrations which have found expression in his formulation of capital, can be measured in the most precise manner by the mathematical device for the determination of the immeasurably large and the infinitesimally small can hardly be taken seriously.

No mathematical procedure, no matter how subtly it is devised, will make his immeasurable mental acrobatics measurable, Jevons should have realized, or did he.

The mathematical procedure for the assaying of the immeasurably large and the infinitesimally small, is not applicable in such an indiscriminate manner, as to measure anything and nothing, Jevons should have known, or did he.

The undertone of self-gratification, which forms the ultima ratio of Jevons' formulations, presents so vague a notion as to defy any and all attempts to lend it precision.

The sublimation of self-gratification which emerges from Jevons' treatise as the net effect of social and economic activity, is much too indistinct a factor for any effort to concretize it.

Jevons, though, can rest content, with having scored a high mark in compounding meaninglessness.

He can pride himself on outdoing Menger and Wieser in the dexterity of making the indistinct refer to the indistinct.

He can well boast of having come close to perfection in devising techniques for the designification of social and economic concepts.

He can well claim that in the art of dangling empty social and economic concepts before the eyes of a bewildered audience, he has yet to be matched.

He can well contend that the obstructions to a social and economic understanding which he has piled up, have yet to be surpassed.

The dissolution of objectified economic thought, to give Jevons his due, was all but complete after he had effected his literary effort.

Social and economic generalizations have come to mean next to nothing, after Jevons had his say.

The comprehension of social and economic life, had come to be reduced to a hunting for the non-essential.

In a way the literary nihilism practiced by Jevons is comparable with the conceptual free for all to which John Stewart Mill, had given rise.

Protestations of empiricism, promises of concretization which abound in the works of Jevons as well as Mill, have not prevented either of the two literary figures from engaging in a spreading of a lack of precision in social and economic expressions in the consummation of their literary tasks.

A precise delineation of social and economic factors can hardly be advanced, Jevons as well as Mill should have realized, through the use of an unselective cognitive approach in regard to the gathering and interpreting of data.

The major characteristics of social and economic living, can hardly be brought out by a method, which is supposed to record everything and nothing, as Mill as well as Jevons should have known.

The key factors in society and economy can hardly come to be highlighted by indiscriminate observations, as Mill, as well as Jevons, could have learned.

The empiricistic device to the perfection of which Mill had dedicated his literary labor, could hardly result in anything else but the distorted analytical picture which Jevons has given it.

The piling up of facts, becoming an end in itself, cannot fail to create a sense of social and economic misdirection.

The spurning of any objective criterion for the validation of data cannot but have the effect of disorienting social and economic inquiry.

Subjectified social and economic interrogation has to avoid any objective conceptual safeguards against social and economic misrepresentation.

Subjectified social and economic theorizing has to steer clear of any objectified conceptual standards by which a social and economic miscasting can be detected.

UNDERLYING FICTIONS

The three presumptions which underly the schemes which characterize the climax of economic fictitiousness—

a) Boehm-Bawerk's presumption that one who is incapable of being effectively frugal does not deserve any fare

or, by implication, that the one who is actually engaged in productive work should not be entitled to eat

b) John Bates Clark's presumption that the one who is consistently diligent is receiving the fare he deserves

c) William Stanley Jevons' presumption that the one who is consistently straining himself really gets what he wants to get

are but variations of one unvaried theme.

All three presumptions are but varied expressions of a single minded endeavor, they express but different forms of negation.

1) The departure into the Paradoxical

2) The approaching of Meaninglessness

3) The arriving at Nothingness,

as the three presumptions can be identified, present but different ways of explaining away accumulation.

The intonation of frugality by Boehm-Bawerk,

as well as the invocation of diligence by John Bates Clark,

as well as the incantation of self-gratification by William Stanley Jevons,

echo but apparent social and economic differences, all those tunes are set to the tenor of presenting acquisitive distinctions in a nonacquisitive dress.

The real distinction between the schemes evolved by Boehm-Bawerk, Clark and Jevons, can only be found by looking behind the screen of such nonacquisitive symbols which have been deprived of their social economic content by the respective three writers.

Real differences in the presentations of Boehm-Bawerk, Clark and Jevons can hardly be determined on the basis of the pre-acquisitive images which the three authors use in a form which is lifted out of the socio-historical context.

The social and economic realities have to be dug out from amongst a pile of empty words and meaningless phrases.

Some very up to date acquisitive practices come to emerge by way of a thorough scrutiny of the nonacquisitive fences.

A scrutiny of the factors which each of the three proponents of marginal consumption is most anxious to hide makes it possible to gain a lead to learning what were the real differences in the social and economic scheme to which the three stated authors refer.

Concentration on the particular aspect which each of the three deconceptualizers is eager to underplay, can well provide a lead to the real distinctions between the social and economic conditions which prompted the literary labor of each of the three exponents of economic fictions.

Even from the way in which each of the three designers of economic fictions places obstacles in the path of social and economic identification, something can be learned about the real dissimilarity of the social and economic features to which each of the three exponents of economic fictitiousness refer.

The Neo-Idealism and Neo-Positivism of Boehm-Bawerk, the paradoxes which he invokes, can well be taken as indication that he considered a particularly fanciful screen necessary to guard against the disclosure of the real factors to which he refers.

Boehm-Bawerk's compounded fictions can well be taken as an expression of a desire to provide for a double insurance against the threat of any possible lifting of the veil from the social and economic features which he was desirous of hiding.

The elimination of all but the name of the category of means of production, which constitutes a social and economic disqualification of the machine, furnishes Boehm-Bawerk with a roundabout way of trodding a path on which he can extinguish any qualitative distinction between income derived from production and income linked with nonproductive tasks.

If wealth embodied in production facilities is made to appear socially and economically indistinguishable from wealth related to aspects of consumption, the factor of aggrandizement for the sake of aggrandizement becomes hidden, Boehm-Bawerk was well aware.

The denial of cumulative accumulation signification as a factor of social and economic life, makes it, in turn, logically feasible to have the category of capital deprived of any social and economic content, Boehm-Bawerk was keen to realize.

Taken out of the social and economic context within which it has a meaning, capital becomes but an innocuous word in Boehm-Bawerk's formulation.

Capital as a socially and economically designified term becomes all but useless in Boehm-Bawerk's presentation as a key factor for the identification of any function of social and economic life.

Capital conceived in a socially and economically emasculated form, can hardly provide an analytical clue for any social and economic practice.

A conception of capital which is deprived of its function of identifying major processes, can hardly recapture much, if any, of its lost social and economic meaning by having it used with reference to an intermediate acquisitive practice.

A conception of capital which is not supposed to acknowledge a conceptual dividing line between production and consumption,—Boehm-Bawerk's assumption to the contrary,—could hardly serve as a yardstick for the appraisal of the social and economic bearing of the acquisitive practice of investment.

A socially and economically disqualified designation of capital can hardly reacquire its character as a conceptual guiding post on the strength of a syntactic device, contrary to what Boehm-Bawerk has to say on that subject.

A mere prefixing of the adjectives invested and uninvested to the word capital after the shadow of social economic indifference has been cast upon that category,—the practice in which Boehm-Bawerk indulges,—can hardly be interpreted otherwise than another verbalistic move designed to skirt the issue of a realistic social and economic identification.

Boehm-Bawerk's attempt to envelop the factor of investment with the most intricate verbal fence provides, nevertheless, some indication with what in particular Boehm-Bawerk was anxious to deal.

Boehm-Bawerk is apparently most concerned with providing a reassurance to those who are engaged in the placement of capital.

Those who indulge in investment of capital are given a broad hint by Boehm-Bawerk that they can take solace in the realization that he, Boehm-Bawerk, has destroyed the category of capital as an effective analytical weapon.

In the absence of capital as a potent cognitive instrument, those who derive income from managing investment can assume that they are at liberty to disregard controlling social and economic influences in the handling of funds entrusted to them.

The social and economic undifferentiation and social and economic designification of the category of capital, to which Boehm-Bawerk takes recourse, constitutes a patent device for making the concept of capital cognitively insensitive to fundamental factors of social and economic life.

The social and economic insensitiveness of the concept of capital can, in turn, be interpreted in the way Boehm-Bawerk makes use of it, as a rationalization of a social and economic immunization of those who undertake to place capital into the stream of social and economic life.

The social and economic designification of the category of capital on the part of Boehm-Bawerk, finds its counterpart in his social and economic designification of investment.

The social and economic twilight in which the category of capital is left to linger precludes the throwing of much if any social and economic light on the factor of investment.

In rendering the social and economic impact of investment unascertainable in any meaningful form, Boehm-Bawerk provides the go-between in the flow of capital—to be specific the investment broker—with the logical basis for claiming that he cannot see any necessity for furnishing a socially and economically relevant accounting for his deals.

The studied nonchalance, the ostensible incoherence, to take up John Bates Clark, form but a variation in a scheme designed to be-cloud fundamental social and economic issues.

The pragmatistic treatment, the unbalanced views which in Clark's case are not far from approaching meaninglessness, present but a change in the form of laying a fog over basic social contours.

The picturing of the producer as the maker as well as the user of the tools he makes, on the part of Clark, presents no departure from the basic theme.

Clark's portraying of the worker as the consumer of goods which the worker himself produces, constitutes but another form of enveloping the factor of capital accumulation.

Clark's insistence that production has no social implications, his reduction of the production process to the analytical level of an efficiency device, presents but another form for the covering up of acquisitive designs.

For purposes of his own, the professor of the distribution of wealth considers it opportune not to imitate Boehm-Bawerk and deny the relevance of the mechanical means of production.

Clark finds it suits his own design to acknowledge that the machine has a certain impact.

He is quick though, to add a request that no social and economic conclusions should be drawn from such an acknowledgement.

As far as social and economic designification is concerned, Clark is no less devoted to it, than Boehm-Bawerk.

He injects a new quirk into the technique of social and economic disqualification of concepts by refusing to move head on on his target.

He prefers not to indulge in a direct onslaught in his effort to designify means of production.

The professor of the distribution of wealth cunningly directs his blow at the social and economic effects of the production implements.

He disqualifies the economic efficacy of the means of production, he uses his ingenuity to explain away the social and economic impact of mechanical implements.

He thus uses an indirect method to render the machine socially and economically meaningless.

He squares the dated image of the producer who makes and keeps his own tools with the notion of the machine functioning as a kind of automaton, to bar any kind of meaningful social perspective.

In reducing the complexity of production technology to the level of the self-revolving mechanism and by presenting, in turn, the producing subject in the role of a silent bystander, Clark pairs the speechless inanimate nature with the inarticulate in the human.

In a kind of backdrop picture, Clark discusses the subject of work attitude.

The vicissitudes of the market, the professor of the distribution of wealth would like to make believe, will be held at bay by individual fortitude and personal perseverance.

Questions relating to the alienation of the product of human work are not supposed to become acute, as long as the worker remains diligent.

The diligent worker is to consider himself assured of receiving the compensation due to him.

The problem of the division of the effected product is not supposed to arise, sources of income other than work are not to be granted any recognition.

Clark is obviously trying with the stated argumentation to impress the factory worker with the notion that the latter can avoid the social and economic problems of an acquisitive industrial society by readapting the work attitudes of the artisan who owned his own tools.

Since he has blocked the social differentiation of the participants of the production process and refused to recognize conflicting social and economic claims, Clark obviously assumes that his unhistorical approach will remain unchallenged.

Since he has denied the presence of owners and nonowners, Clark can well presume that his espousing of the artisan work attitude will appear enticing.

Since he does not permit other than productivity gains to express themselves in any apparent manner, Clark can further create the impression that the worker's reward constitutes nothing more than a recognition of that worker's efficiency rating.

The worker in this instance is again cast in the social image of a self employed artisan.

Clark makes the producing laborer emerge from his treatise in a role in which that laborer cannot be quite sure whether he is a wage earner or a profit taker.

Taking cognizance that all sources of income have been socially disqualified in the "Distribution of Wealth," there is no conceptual obstacle left to prevent the Clarkian toiler from claiming that he is the exponent of a unique social and economic symbiosis.

The social designification of capital implements is, in particular, conducive to giving rise to an illusion on the part of the laborer that he is not just a propertyless worker, but an owner of capital as well.

Clark does not look at all askance to alluding that any hard working toiler is fully justified to believe he is creating wealth for himself by his very exertion.

The author of the "Distribution of Wealth" is not at all averse to make the toiler believe that by virtue of his, the toiler's diligence, he transforms himself into a capital owner.

To prevent any disenchantment of the worker who is stimulated to exert himself to the limit of his physical capacities and beyond, Clark sees to it that those who hold titles to wealth by virtue of pecuniary acquisition are not to become subject to any social and economic scrutiny.

To disorient the worker and sustain his illusions about his social position and economic opportunities, Clark excuses those who enjoy a privileged position in productive undertakings from ever appearing for a social and economic questioning.

Those who derive an income without the physical exertion required from the manual laborer are given a convenient leave of absence when Clark proceeds to discuss what he terms as the basic dynamic factors of the distribution of wealth.

Since he has been instrumental in all but dissolving all categories of income, since labor as well as nonlabor income have been deprived by him of any specific social meaning, the absence of those who hold shares to the riches in the productive generation of which they do not have to take any direct part, will not make any difference in an analytical way, Clark can be sure, as far as his exposition is concerned.

The ostensible evasion, the deliberate obfuscation of social and economic contours in which Boehm-Bawerk and Clark indulged, reaches a point of high theoretical perfection with Jevons.

A studied formalism represented by a parading of skeletonized concepts appears to be coming into its own in "The Theory of Political Economy."

The questioning of the admissibility for unexplainable notions to take the place of an explainable hypothesis, a cognitive problem which Clark and Boehm-Bawerk did not entirely rule out, is not considered as meriting any attention by Jevons.

Doubts about the propriety of supplanting of a proven regularity with unprovable hunches are not permitted by the author of "The Theory of Political Economy."

By ruling out a whole range of cognitive problems, the self professed purifier of economic theory is able to establish a semblance of orderliness in the array of conceptual shells.

His is a scheme which places emptied social and economic categories into some sort of relation to each other.

Jevons has work termed as a form of a game to preclude any kind of social and economic identification.

He denies any social and economic signification to either laboring or playing, to render it cognitively impossible to differentiate those living by their toil from those whiling away in leisure.

Jevons' methodological and terminological strictures make a socially and economically qualified analysis inconceivable.

In lieu of a social and economic explanation of work, Jevons feels methodologically unconstrained to parade the unqualified observation that everybody exerts himself exactly to the point to which he desires to strain himself.

As far as the social and economic exploration of leisure is concerned, Jevons considers he has methodologically freed himself from advancing beyond the point of observing that everybody discontinues his exertion by the time he feels like foregoing any further strain.

His elimination of a social delineation of the propertied as well as the propertyless and his omission of the factors of ownership and non-ownership of wealth come to place the subject of social appropriation and its cause, as well as the subject of economic accumulation and its effect beyond the range of Jevons' inquiry.

His formulation of the production effort as but a consumption device, his presentation of the process of production as but an extended consumption sphere, provides the basis for Jevons' allegation that a socially selective approach to the production output is cognitively improper and that an economic signification of products which are being used for the generation of other products constitutes a highly objectionable device.

By his denial of social and economic relevance to means of production, he has sufficiently disqualified the core of social and economic systematization, to suggest a confinement of the choice between toil and leisure to the exclusive purview of individual wishes.

The self-appointed purifier of political economy can well credit himself with having removed any terminological and methodological obstructions to his assertion, that the succession of work and idleness expresses nothing else but a succession of individual emotions.

Since he rules out in advance any social and economic evaluation of labor and leisure, he can claim to be consistent when he proffers a formulation according to which labor and leisure stand for nothing more than minus and plus signs through the medium of which the individual assures himself of the degree of the emotional adjustment of which he is capable.

Since he has postulated self gratification as the key factor in social and economic analysis, Jevons can see no reason why he cannot assert that an improper balance between work and idleness constitutes but a factor of personal maladjustment.

Those who lack work as well as those who lack leisure, Jevons feels unconstrained to insist on the basis of his key presumption, cannot place the responsibility for their condition on anything and anybody but their own lack of emotional self control.

Just as those who carry an excessive load of labor or those who are privileged to indulge in excessive leisure, Jevons feels no hesitation to assert on the basis of his major presumption, cannot find any other reason for the respective excessiveness in anything else but the high tension of their emotional amplitude.

Only those who attain a self-gratification which is characteristic of an attitude taken by a self assured bond holder, Jevons' presentation suggests, can escape the excesses of joy and pain.

Only those who gain the self-assurance of which a bond holder is capable, Jevons' treatment indicates, can place themselves above the factors which are involved in the apportionment of labor and leisure.

The literary pace of Jevons' presentation, to compare it with that of Clark, bears an air of reserve.

As compared with the shrillness of Clark's declamation, Jevons' presentation appears almost placid.

As contrasted with the aggressiveness which permeates Clark's formulations, Jevons' argumentation has the flair of resignation.

The unruliness of Clark's presentation is fully in accord with his willful means to promote production.

His cramped style is indicative of his high pressure drive to spur production gains.

His literary turbulence is, moreover, well fitted to express the feverish activity of unruly stockholders.

Jevons' disenchantment, in turn, can be considered as being highly appropriate for expressing gratification over secured production gains.

The rather detached presentation of "The Theory of Political Economy" reflects a mood of calmness which befits a spokesman for the unruffled bond holder.

Part 3

The Anti-Climax of Extreme Subjectivism

CHAPTER 8

INTUITIONISM

With income categories reduced to insignificance, with sources of income deprived of any particular meaning, the systematic edifice of the classical school was coming apart at its seams.

With propertied and nonpropertied income tagged as interchangeable, with appropriated and unappropriated resources marked as socially and economically identical, little was left intact of the theoretical foundations on which Adam Smith and David Ricardo had built their thought.

With social barriers refused acknowledgement, with economic division declared untraceable, the social and economic structure to which the classicists had borne testimony, could hardly be recognized anymore.

With the conception of time and space made subject to individual capriciousness, with the comprehension of sequence and quantification placed under the dictate of a personal whim, social and economic theory had acquired the character of a personal escape mechanism.

Social and economic conceptualization had come to serve as an instrumentality for the mirroring of personal feelings.

With major social and economic categories reduced to conceptual shambles, with the systematic framework of social and economic comprehension all but wrecked, social and economic theories were giving way to a playful introspection.

The loosening of the categories, the drive for the dismantling of concepts which had been initiated by Menger and Wieser had come into high gear with Boehm-Bawerk and Clark.

The undermining of the key concepts, the demolition of the fundamental outposts of systematic thought, had come to reach a climax with Jevons.

Wishful thinking as underlying factor of all social and economic reasoning was blossoming out. The superseding of realistic conceptions by fictions was coming into full bloom.

Theoretical presentations became noticeable for their omissions; literary presentations came to mean largely what they did not say.

The major task of deconceptualization had come to be completed. The drive for the reduction of social and economic reasoning to a meaningless phrasemongering had come to run its course. Any sequel to the empty talk with which Boehm-Bawerk, Clark, and Jevons had amused themselves, could only have the impact of an anti-climax.

Those who readapted the destructive deconceptualization practices in which Boehm-Bawerk, Clark, and Jevons had excelled, are but pursuing a beaten track. No matter how important the latter day admirers of Boehm-Bawerk, Clark and Jevons would like to sound, they present but faint echoes of the noise made by the three conceptual master wreckers.

Schumpeter, to refer to one of the more contemporary deconceptualizers, fully acknowledges his debt to those who had engaged in the task of the dissolution of social and economic concepts before him. Schumpeter, to introduce a leading literary figure among those for whom Boehm-Bawerk paved the way, starts out with an explicit tribute to those who had been instrumental in the removal of the links which had assured a coherence in social and economic reasoning. Schumpeter goes on record in acknowledging his debt to all those who have littered the approaches to social and economic theory with an array of crippled categories.

His forerunners, Schumpeter gratefully acknowledges, have evolved the basic procedures of social and economic designification which he as a latter day disciple is fully willing to accept. His predecessors in the drive for the subjectivistic subversion of classical economic thought, Schumpeter dutifully attests, have furnished the general prescriptions which he, as a latecomer, has no intention of contesting.

His own contribution, Schumpeter appears to be modest in his claim, is to serve but as an elucidator of the social and economic designification which went before him. His own literary offering, Schumpeter modestly claims, is to offer but an addendum.

His own literary labor, Schumpeter states his ambition, is but to add a note of dynamism to the predominantly static presentation, in which he considers the professed subjectivistic detractors of classical economic thought had engaged before him.

Economic development, Schumpeter opens his major opus, constitutes but a manifestation of a personal attitude. Economic development, Schumpeter comes to lean on Menger and Wieser, presents but a course which follows an individual predilection.

An economic development, Schumpeter directs, which takes place, either, within the social and economic confines of tribalism, or, within the social and economic range of artisandom, or, within the social and economic framework of modern industrialism, should be rated as being indistinguishable from each other, as far as the essential features of each such development is concerned.

Economic development within each of the three cited social and economic systems, Schumpeter's directive implies, is not essentially affected by the fundamental social and economic as well as technological factors which constitute the distinguishing marks of any of the three nexuses.

The assumption should be ruled out, Schumpeter would have it, that a given social structure can exercise a marked influence on economic development. A fundamental bearing of an economic system on the pattern of economic development is to be, furthermore, discounted nor is it to be considered feasible for a given status of technology to affect the patterning of economic development in any significant manner.

Any economic development, Schumpeter wants it stressed, is tied to the availability of specially endowed persons. As basic factor in all economic development, Schumpeter postulates the emergence of a qualified economic leadership.

He assigns the key role in any and all economic development

to persons who are endowed with a certain capacity for spontaneous generation.

Those persons on whom economic development rests, Schumpeter cautions, are not to be credited with inventiveness as such. Those persons on whom economic development depends, are but to be credited with the ability to actualize inventions and to realize new discoveries.

A capacity to put across new combinations, an ability to act quickly and resolutely, a capability of breaking routine, are listed by Schumpeter as the specific personal characteristics by virtue of which economic development is brought about.

In a way, Schumpeter tries to elucidate, it is the capacity to brave opposition, in a sense, it is the ability to flaunt customary opinion and traditional ways of thinking which makes a person fit to bring about economic development.

Lest he be suspected that he is extolling such personal qualities which might enable a person, so endowed, to advance an economic development which involves overall changes, Schumpeter comes out with a number of qualifications.

The personal ability for breaking customs and traditions, Schumpeter issues a warning, is not to be viewed as an individual capacity for bringing about breaks which go all the way. The personal aptitude for breaking customs and traditions is not to be regarded as a personal predilection for radical moves in the social and economic sense. The personal inclination for breaking customs and traditions is, furthermore, not to be looked upon as an individual's bent for bringing about revolutionary technological changes.

The personal capacity for breaking customs and traditions to which he refers, Schumpeter likes to sound reassuring, does not take into consideration anything going beyond the range of the individual's predisposition to make rearrangements of this or that. The capability of the individual to break customs and traditions, in the context in which he applies it, Schumpeter wants it to be known, concerns itself with nothing else but a personal predilection for new variations in manipulations. The individual capability of breaking customs and traditions, Schumpeter wants it understood, is at the most to be taken as a personal capacity for the demonstration of new forms of combining managerial skills.

220

Lest it be inferred that he is referring to anything fundamentally new within the limited scope of manipulations, Schumpeter enters a few qualifications.

The kind of newness the individual manipulator is supposed to advance, Schumpeter is trying to explain, refers but to a newness in form. Newness in the manipulated sense, Schumpeter amplifies, does not relate a newness with reference to any meaningful content. Newness in the manipulative sense, Schumpeter points out, relates but an incidental newness. Manipulative newness, Schumpeter finds it opportune to stress, relates but a newness which stops short of any essential newness.

Manipulative newness, Schumpeter proffers a subjectivistic obfuscation, constitutes but a newness in the manner of an individual self-realization. Manipulative newness, Schumpeter obscures the issue still further, presents but a newness in the form of personal self-fulfillment.

Lest it be implied that newness in the manipulative sense does not entirely exclude objective social and economic factors, Schumpeter makes a few more qualifying statements.

Manipulative newness, stipulated as newness in the manner of individual self-realization, as well as manipulative newness, in the form of personal self-fulfillment, is not to be interpreted as a newness which leaves room for wider social and economic aspirations.

Manipulative newness stipulated as newness in the manner of self-realization, as well as manipulative newness in the form of self-fulfillment, Schumpeter directs, is not to be considered as indicating anything else than a way in which an individual finds himself compelled to act for the sake of acting.

Manipulative newness, stipulated as newness in the manner of self-realization and newness in the form of self-fulfillment, Schumpeter wants to make it sure, are not to signify anything more than a way in which a person feels constrained to make his actions revolve for the sake of revolving.

Manipulative newness, Schumpeter hesitantly admits, does have some relation to economic factors. Manipulative newness, Schumpeter half-heartedly concedes, has to allow for some link with the acquisition and exchange of goods.

The economic aspect is, however, Schumpeter unhesitantly declares, supposed to remain an extraneous factor in regard to any manipulative newness.

Production and distribution of goods are directed by Schumpeter to be no more than incidental factors in any manipulative newness.

Social and economic factors are not supposed to have any direct bearing on a kind of newness which is stipulated but as a newness in the manner of self-realization and the form of self-fulfillment, Schumpeter wants to make it sure.

Manipulative newness is to be held as being basically determined by an inexplicable inner force by which an individual finds himself driven.

Manipulative newness is to be regarded as fundamentally effected by some inner compulsion by which a person finds himself seized.

Manipulative newness is to be considered, on Schumpeter's request, as being brought about by an individual who aspires to acquire and exchange material goods for the sake of giving expression to his innate dynamism.

Dealing in material goods on the part of an individual who seeks expression for his dynamism, Schumpeter wants it stressed, is supposed to exclude the proposition that such dealing is being undertaken out of economic considerations.

Dealing in material goods by a person who is imbued with dynamism, Schumpeter restresses it, rules out the postulation that such dealing is motivated by the desire to satisfy material wants.

The dealing in material goods on the part of a dynamically endowed person, and here Schumpeter dares to deviate from his subjectivistic teachers, is not to be attributed to the pleasure which that individual would like to derive from consumption. A dynamically endowed person is not to be rated as a person who is attracted by any kind of restful satisfaction.

A person endowed with dynamism, Schumpeter amplifies, is not to be regarded as a kind of person who can ever attain an emotional balance. A dynamic person is not to be viewed as a sort of individual who can achieve any individual happiness. A person endowed with dynamism, Schumpeter underscores it, cannot be considered as a person of a hedonistic type.

A dynamic person, Schumpeter ends up with a pleonasm, is a person who never rests. A dynamic person, Schumpeter rephrases his pleonastic refrain, is but a person who is never satisfied with himself.

A dynamic person, Schumpeter offers another pleonastic version, is a kind of person who is never gratified with what he can possibly attain.

A dynamic person, Schumpeter offers a compounded pleonasm, is a kind of person who can only derive joy by way of expressing his dynamism.

In trying to keep any social and economic content from entering any of his pleonastic pronouncements, Schumpeter becomes so engrossed in the sound of his activistic jargon, as to become unaware of what he is really saying.

He is obviously not aware that he is giving his word game away when he caps his phrase-mongering with the assertion that a dynamically endowed person is a person who is capable of losing himself somewhat.

A person who by his very nature is predisposed to losing himself, Schumpeter should have realized, is not a person who can either attain or sustain a sense of social and economic direction.

Completely unaware of his inadvertent verbal faux pas, Schumpeter exposes his pleonastic wording still further to the implication that he advocates the cultivation of a sense of social and economic misdirection.

When he characterizes a dynamic person as a person who is capable of divesting himself of his surplus of personal energy by way of self-abandonment, Schumpeter is not exactly espousing an individual who knows where he is going.

Whether Schumpeter considers that he can relieve the kind of dynamic person, whom he characterizes, from carrying the onus of being a socially and economically misguided and misguiding person, by insisting on having social and economic factors denied any specific signification, as far as the character of the dynamic person is concerned, he, Schumpeter, does not care to mention.

He appears to be caught in the net of his sophistications, when he proceeds to refer to the acquisition and exchange of goods as but a means by which a dynamically endowed individual can realize his dynamism.

He does not seem to be fully aware that his referring to the acquisition and exchange of goods as but a means by which a dynamically endowed person can realize his dynamism, might come to be regarded by his readers as an attempt to erect a screen of words behind which any conceivable social and economic misuse of goods can be hidden.

He does not seem to be fully conscious that by pleading for acceptance of a formulation in which production and consumption are pictured as but instrumentalities which enable a dynamic person to consummate his supply of energy, he is proffering a wording which is open to any conceivable misconception about the social and economic aspects of production and consumption, their causes and their results.

He does not, on the other hand, appear to be fully convinced that the verbalistic trappings which he furnishes for the dynamic individual, will turn out to be entirely fool-proof.

He gives the appearance of wanting to protect his exposition against the raising of embarrassing questions by seeking added protective devices.

As if to ward off a possible accusation that the social and economic meaninglessness of his pleonastic characterization of the dynamic individual has been conceived by him in a deliberate effort to promote a general social and economic misrepresentation, Schumpeter plunges into an irrational conception.

As if he were troubled by the prospect of being told that his parading of the individual to whom he ascribes dynamism, forms a highly misleading proposition, Schumpeter undertakes to shift his cognitive frame.

As if he were aware that the treatment he had accorded the proposition of the individual to whom he ascribes dynamism, can hardly stand the test of a socially and economically meaningful argument, Schumpeter is ready to deny he has kept within the framework of reasoned argumentation.

224

The compulsion under which the dynamic individual labors, Schumpeter bursts out, cannot be perceived in any rational form. The inner drive to which the person imbued with dynamism finds himself subjected, Schumpeter exclaims, cannot be explained in a logically reasoned manner.

The individual whose dynamic endowment predestines him to become an economic leader, Schumpeter outshouts himself, is not to be considered as being rationally motivated.

The individual who by the very nature of the dynamism with which he is supposed to be imbued, is bound to rise to economic leadership, Schumpeter becomes ecstatic, is not to be regarded as being capable of steering clear of irrational ends.

The individual who is imbued with dynamism and is, by the same token, endowed with the predisposition to become an economic leader, Schumpeter is trying to spell out his exclamation, cannot even be regarded as being able to account to himself whether he has scored a social and economic success or not.

Schumpeter obviously expects the individual who is imbued with dynamism to become so entranced in the realization of his compulsion to engage in irrational ventures, as to be unable to grasp anything rationally.

A person who is predisposed to irrational ventures is, according to Schumpeter, not a person who has the psychological make-up for making it certain whether he has received an adequate social and economic reward or not.

The question of whether he is receiving an adequate social and economic compensation or not, is not supposed to even arise in a person who feels sure his predilection for irrational undertakings predestines him for economic leadership, according to Schumpeter's interdict.

A person with a dynamic endowment derives a perfect satisfaction from any chance he gets to indulge in irrational ventures, Schumpeter asserts.

A person imbued with dynamism, whose very nature impels him to become an addict to irrational adventures, is expected by Schumpeter to conduct himself in a manner of a happy-go-lucky individual.

A person imbued with dynamism is being pictured by Schumpeter as a person bubbling with energy, who is happy he can manifest his exuberance.

Success in any material sense, Schumpeter is justified to claim, cannot have any definite influence on a dynamically predisposed person, as long as that person remains insensitive to a rational perception.

Any particular success, Schumpeter has reason to assert, cannot make a dynamically driven person pause, as long as that person continues to be seized by his addiction to irrational undertakings.

Since Schumpeter's dynamically endowed person is by the very irrational nature of his dynamism divested of the ability to register any specific attainment, the author of "Theory of Economic Development," has reason to infer that such a person could not conceivably ascertain in any rational form whether he is entitled to take a rest or not.

The person endowed with dynamism who realizes his dynamic nature by way of an irrational addiction, Schumpeter has reason to maintain, can at best gain an irrational feeling about an attainment.

As long as a person labors under the impact of an irrational compulsion, Schumpeter is reasonably correct in expecting that person to be incapable of correlating a particular expenditure with any particular result.

A person who acts under an irrational dynamic compulsion, Schumpeter is justified to infer, can never arrive at a rational sense of satisfaction.

An irrationally acting person is by the very nature of his acting saddled with the inability of ascertaining whether he has really succeeded or not.

A person, whose dynamic predisposition catapults him into an irrational activity, finds himself under a spell, Schumpeter relates, he has no choice but to keep acting, he has no alternative but to go on and on with his actions without any prospect of a let-up.

The inability to assure himself of whether he has scored a real success or not, Schumpeter divests himself of another piece of sophistry, compels the dynamically predisposed person to commit himself to a perpetual race of catching something which he can never catch.

In its counterpart the inability to ascertain in any rational form of whether he has attained a success or not, condemns the dynamically endowed individual to the inability to ascertain his failures in any rational form.

A person who is unable to determine in any rational terms, whether he has really succeeded or not, is, by the same token, Schumpeter spins another sophism, a person who is unable to ascertain in any rational terms whether he has really failed.

A person who is unable to offer a reasoned account of his successes, Schumpeter elaborates on his sophism, is, by the same token, a person who is unable to proffer a reasoned explanation of his failures.

Neither failure nor success, Schumpeter sums up his sophisms, can ever be registered in any definite form by a person whose inner dynamic quality drives him into irrational ventures.

Since knowledge of his failures and successes, in any definite form, is not supposed to lie within the capabilities of the person endowed with dynamism, the way of knowing, whether he has ever earned a rest, is not open to him.

The irrationally acting person who is unable to furnish himself with an accounting of the results of his actions, finds himself compelled to continue acting for the sake of acting.

The person who is committed to a ceaseless irrational activity, might be able to get a faint glimpse that success had been denied him, Schumpeter has a second thought.

Such glimpse might come to the irrationally acting person, Schumpeter qualifies his back-tracking, as indication that an *initial* success had been denied to him.

Such indication, should it come to the irrationally acting person, Schumpeter is quick to fall back on his general rule for obfuscation, could not possibly have an arresting impact on a person who labors under an irrational compulsion.

An irrationally acting person on whom it might dawn that he had not been successful at the first attempt, Schumpeter reinvokes his more recent obscurantist device, continues to be unable to account to himself for his failure due to the inherent irrationality of his action.

Schumpeter makes sure that his initial proposition which leaves the irrationally acting person no alternative but to undertake one irrational venture after another, remains in full force.

Not to be forgotten in this connection, is to be Schumpeter's identification of the irrationally driven person as the person whose dynamic predisposition qualifies him for the capturing of economic leadership.

There might be a thread of truth in the thought which relates the sheer limitless activity of the person endowed with dynamism, to a lust for power, Schumpeter seems to be ready to admit.

Some relevance might be granted to the contention, Schumpeter finds it opportune to state, that the self-abandonment by virtue of which the dynamically endowed person realizes his dynamism constitutes but a realization of a domination by those individuals who are dynamically predisposed over those who are statically inclined.

Such domination, were it to be proven, Schumpeter is quick with a qualifying clause, is not, however, to be interpreted as referring to any particular social and economic structure.

The domination of one dynamic individual over many static persons, should that fact be confirmed by an inquiry, Schumpeter insists, it could not conceivably be interpreted as having any relation to the impact of a given social and economic system.

Schumpeter is unreservedly committed in this case to microscopic observations of a microcosmic range at the exclusion of a macrocosmic outlook.

He adamantly refuses to validate the general along with the particular in this case.

Domination of a dynamic person over a multitude of static individuals, should the existence of such a domination be accepted as a fact, Schumpeter finds it necessary to issue a direct warning, is in no way to be interpreted as having any socially and economically meaningful relation to either time or causation.

After having issued the warning, Schumpeter busies himself

228

with the turning of the phenomenon of domination over to time-lessness.

He wants it to be regarded as inconceivable that it can ever be determined when a domination starts and when it ends.

He wants it, moreover, to be viewed as unfeasible that it can ever be ascertained what generates a domination and what makes it cease.

The fact of domination, should it be established as such, Schumpeter rules, is to be interpreted as being no more than an accidental factor.

After having done anything conceivable to deprive the factor of domination of any socially and economically discernible content, Schumpeter continues to refer to the empty shell he had made out of the socially and economically meaningful category of domination, as if he had done nothing to detract from its meaning.

In spite of his doing his utmost to have the commonly accepted meaning of domination, in the sense of a relentless social and economic rule, distorted, he continues to use the word domination, as if he had done nothing which was aimed to destroy its objectified meaning.

Though he continues to use the objectively conceived word domination, he is actually referring to the subjective conception of domineering.

The ostensible reference to domination on the part of Schumpeter, while he is actually talking about domineering, is not without a significance of its own.

In refusing to draw a denotative division between the factor of domination and the aspect of domineering, Schumpeter provides himself with a terminological license to pretend he is referring to a broad range of social and economic direction, while he is, in fact, relating the very narrow and limited implications of personal manipulations.

Schumpeter's terminological duplicity which denies domineering a term of its own, comes in handy, when he proceeds to deprecate the subject of social and economic change.

The terminological misrepresentation of the subject of domineering by way of the unwarranted use of the term domination, makes it feasible for Schumpeter to advance a nominalistic challenge to the effectiveness of social and economic change.

Domineering paraded under the name of domination serves Schumpeter well, when he is about to take the essential conceptual core out of the factor of social and economic change.

He has only to render the words social and economic change as empty of relevant social and economic content as the word domination, to be able to advance the formal argument that domination in its socially and economically emptied form is as indeterminable a factor, as the factor of change of domination in its socially and economically emptied form.

Schumpeter is not found remiss in saddling of the denotation of social and economic change with as many qualifications as possible, in order to make the word change as socially and economically meaningless, as he had rendered the word domination.

Schumpeter runs true to form when he applies the concept of social and economic change in the same manipulative sense in which he employs the concept of domination.

In the course of his efforts to reduce the concept of social and economic change to a manipulative range, Schumpeter is completely losing sight of the aspect of a fundamental social and economic change.

Caught in the web of the manipulative terminological strictures of his own making, he considers himself at liberty to claim that change has no relation whatsoever to what is generally called social and economic progress.

The kind of social and economic change which Schumpeter presents is manipulative in character, it refers to a kind of moving which comes from nowhere and moves to nowhere.

The social and economic change, which Schumpeter characterizes as manipulative, refers to a movement which has no specific social and economic source and no particular social and economic direction.

A manipulative social and economic change, as the one premeditated by Schumpeter, is, in turn, wholly insensitive to any meaningful social and economic relation with either time or space.

A manipulative change, Schumpeter appears to have an afterthought, would have to be regarded as a rather ephemeral change, were there to be no means available to implement it.

A manipulative domination would have little to show in any concrete form, Schumpeter continues his second thought, were there to be no instrumentality in existence to effectuate that domination.

What would a dynamically possessed person be able to get out of his manipulative devices, Schumpeter appears to be troubled by the thought, were there to be no objects at his disposal, by means of which he could realize his manipulations.

The person endowed with dynamism, who is driven towards an irrational venture, could hardly be expected to pursue his activity indefinitely, Schumpeter is forced to concede, were he to be denied all access to ponderables.

The person whose dynamism drives him to action would consider he is wasting his time, Schumpeter continues to appear agitated, were he to be refused the opportunity to reach out for economic power.

The person who is committed to a boundless activity, Schumpeter begins to sound as if he were not himself, could hardly consider it is worth his while to exert his energy were such exertion not to lead to the establishment of any potent social claims.

The person who is applying his dynamic qualities, Schumpeter begins to talk as if he were another person, could hardly be expected to apply his natural gifts were such application not to promise him any potent claims on goods and services.

Those who would surmise, that Schumpeter is ready to perform an about face are in for a disappointment.

He is making it unmistakably clear that the revalidation of objective social and economic factors is the last thing he is willing to permit.

The subjective dynamic predilection, Schumpeter falls back on his initial argument, can be realized only to the extent to which the dynamic person is able to lift himself out of the static social and economic sphere.

The lifting out of the static social and economic sphere, Schumpeter proffers an amplification, refers to an application of personal dynamism in which the dynamic individual shows his resolution to resist any regularization, save the one he is willing to set for himself.

The lifting out of the static social and economic sphere, Schumpeter implies with the just stated amplification, relates an exercise of personal dynamic qualities in determined opposition to the very principle of regularity in social and economic life.

Dynamism in this instance becomes a sort of social and economic nihilism.

The dynamic person emerges, in turn, from the stated characterization as a kind of unprincipled go-getter.

As if he were anxious to reenforce the impression that he looks with favor on the promulgation of a social and economic nihilism, Schumpeter insists that the person who possesses dynamic qualities becomes untrue to his dynamism when he expresses unwillingness to discount the periodicity of annual returns.

To show that he is quite pleased with the prospect of being identified as a promoter of an unprincipled go-getter, Schumpeter volunteers the assertion that the dynamic person could not possibly realize his dynamic disposition were he not determined to dismiss the social and economic relevance of the continuity of production.

What else than an attainment of a general social and economic disorganization, could Schumpeter have in mind, when he submits a proclamation that the dynamic person would betray his dynamic nature were he to refuse to make it crystal clear that he is to have no track with a conception which keeps an unremitting social and economic link between a current replenishment of goods and services and the respective replenishment of such goods and services which had taken place in the past.

What else than a go-getting with a devil-take-the-hindsight attitude, could Schumpeter have in mind, when he declares, that a dynamic person would render his dynamic endowment useless, were he to be reluctant to dispel the sense of security which is rooted in a certainty which refers to what had occurred in the past.

Schumpeter's subsequent insistence that the dynamic person is called upon to demonstrate his dynamism by girding himself against the uncertainty which lies in any future, does not in any way justify the indiscriminate disqualification of the social and economic past on the part of the author of the "Theory of Economic Development."

Schumpeter's subsequent assertion that the dynamic person can most effectively apply his dynamism by braving himself against the risks which the uncertainty of the future entails, does hardly warrant a discounting of any objectified past experience.

Personal dynamism can find a true expression, Schumpeter is ready with an equivocation, in having the person endowed with dynamism act contrary to what is to be considered static.

A dynamic person, if he were to remain true to his dynamic nature, Schumpeter insists, could not do otherwise than to mark the static self-supply procedure as his number one target of attack.

The dynamic individual, Schumpeter immediately enters a qualification, is not, however, to view the very principle of self-supply as being his static target.

The dynamic person, Schumpeter qualifies his qualification, is to set himself merely against the realization of a perpetually balanced self-supply.

According to the multiple qualification of Schumpeter, the dynamic individual is not supposed to war against the self-supply scheme as such. The person endowed with dynamism is to be concerned merely with a manipulative variation of self-supply.

The person endowed with dynamism, Schumpeter issues a warning, is in particular to guard himself against attacking the pattern of self-supply on the ground that such pattern does not square with a commitment to selfaggrandizement.

The thought that the upsetting of an even keel of self-supply cannot be avoided due to the uncertainty prevailing in the acquisitive social and economic nexus is, on Schumpeter's instruction, to be considered as being far removed from the mind of the person endowed with dynamism.

An admission on the part of the person, whose dynamic endowment predisposes him to economic leadership, that his bent on keeping the self-supply scheme out of balance has any objective causal connection with a realization on his, the dynamic person's, part, that a continuously balanced self-supply cannot be maintained in a system which is grounded in the accumulation of individual wealth, is specifically forbidden by Schumpeter, for the paradoxical reason that it would constitute a most misleading fiction.

Schumpeter's dictum that a reference to the acquisitive social and economic nexus is fixtitious, can only be explained with regard to his ruling that the person endowed with dynamism is not supposed to consider anything as being real which is not manipulative in character.

Only the kind of person whose dynamic quality, on Schumpeter's advice, is supposed to come to fore in the form of social and economic blinds which render him incapable of seeing and acting upon fundamental social and economic factors, could possibly consider anything related to a social and economic vista which extends beyond a manipulative range, as being wholly unreal.

The manipulative range of Schumpeter's argumentation is underscored by his insistence that the dynamic endowment of the individual go-getter is supposed to refer to nothing more than a personal predisposition to shift goods.

The prime function of the dynamic go-getter, Schumpeter directs, is to consist in the undoing of what to that go-getter appears as a static demand and supply situation.

By virtue of his inherent dynamic quality the individual who feels predisposed to become a go-getting economic leader, is to consider himself supremely fit, on instruction by Schumpeter, to upset any given demand and supply situation by detaching the future from the past in his highly personal evaluation.

A nondynamic person, a person who by the very nature of his disposition cannot become a go-getting economic leader, is to view himself by contrast, on Schumpeter's direction, as being constitutionally unable to undo a static social and economic condition.

Whether a nondynamic person is expected by Schumpeter to hold himself disqualified from the task of upsetting a given demand and supply situation in a manipulative sense, since he as a "static" person is supposed to have a disposition to look with distaste upon an evaluation of a given supply and demand situation without the gaining of an interrelated view of social and economic factors and whether such distaste is to be interpreted as a distaste on the part of the "static" person for the socially and economically unreasonable, the author of the "Theory of Economic Development" does not care to say.

Nor is Schumpeter prepared to make an outright statement on whether he expects a nondynamic person to be disinclined to discard any link between the present demand and supply and the respective demand and supply situations in the past and future, since he, as a nondynamic person, is supposed to have a natural disinclination to carry out erratic propositions.

The difference between static and dynamic, Schumpeter wants it underscored, does not refer to anything else but to a difference in an individual's disposition.

A social and economic balance is not supposed to be due to any extrapersonal conditions nor is a social and economic imbalance to be due to any nonsubjective factors, Schumpeter would like to make it sure.

Whether a given demand squares with a given supply or not, is to be held fully explainable in terms of the temperaments of the individuals who become concerned with it.

The inclusion of objectified elements in any social and economic analysis which attempts to dissect the problem of social and economic dislocation, Schumpeter wants it particularly emphasized, is to be rated as a major fallacy.

No objective social and economic deterrents are supposed to be granted existence which could conceivably be regarded as major factors of obstruction in either the phase of production or the phase of consumption.

No objective social and economic obstacle is to be given recognition, Schumpeter is ready to see to it, to which a lasting general disruption of the social and economic process could be possibly traced.

A basic disturbance in the flow of social and economic life, Schumpeter wants to be regarded as inconceivable.

A general social and economic breakdown is to be regarded as being out of question. The social and economic process is to be looked upon as a self-perpetuating circular flow.

To sustain the picture of an unhampered circular flow, Schumpeter perfects a special device.

To bolster his proposition of an inherent social and economic equilibrium, Schumpeter comes up with an ingenious scheme.

Each participant in a production performance, irrespective of his social and economic position, is to be handed a scrip which is to be related to his production record.

The scrip is to be issued in a form in which a certain amount of the person's effected production is to command a certain amount of personal consumption as its equivalent.

The scrip holding scheme is to serve as an indicator of an equitable mode of social and economic relations. The scrip holding device is, in particular, to testify to the absence of any social and economic stratification.

As far as the operation of the scrip holding scheme is concerned, it is to be based on the proposition that each scrip holder is to be free to exchange the consumption equivalent to which his scrip entitles him with another consumption equivalent of another scrip holder.

Scrips are to be made exchangeable with each other, Schumpeter passes on the instruction, in the expectation that the consumer's share of each scrip holder can be had on call from some community warehouse.

The community warehouse is supposed to constitute the place in which all produced goods come to be stored away to wait for those who are ready to redeem their scrips.

The exchange operation of the scrip scheme is no doubt to convey the notion that production is not in any way socially and economically removed from consumption.

The exchange operation of the scrip scheme, as can be readily seen, is being based by Schumpeter on the presumption that production as well as consumption are conducted in the form of a communal undertaking in which no place has been provided for any acquisitive aspirations.

The scrip holder's claim to his share in consumption might conceivably be convertible into money, Schumpeter appears to be willing to concede.

Should such conversion take place, Schumpeter is quick to caution, it is not supposed to affect in any basic form the working of the essentially nonaquisitive scrip holding scheme.

He is devising the scrip holding scheme, he then comes out with a startling announcement, in order to make it serve as an instrumentality for deception.

His scrip operation is but to serve as a vehicle, Schumpeter unabashedly declares, by which those with a static temperament can be made to hold on to an illusion to which their static disposition predisposes them.

Those static minded simpletons who can be made to believe that by exchanging their scrip for money they are but exchanging one certificate which entitles them to a certain share in consumption for another certificate which assures them of an equivalent amount of consumption, Schumpeter does not feel any scruples to make it known, can be made to submit themselves with ease to the conniving of those who consider themselves dynamically endowed.

By having those with a static frame of mind believe that they are exchanging one specific share in consumption for another when they trade their scrip for money, Schumpeter brazenly declares, those with a dynamic bent of mind can turn the working of the scrip scheme to their full advantage.

Those with a dynamic bent of mind are specifically instructed by Schumpeter, to make every effort to prevent the statically minded from realizing that, by exchanging the scrip for money, they are partaking in the disruption of the static social and economic flow, the sustaining of which is of vital concern to their static predisposition.

It is incumbent upon those with a dynamic bent of mind, Schumpeter amplifies his instruction in deception, to keep any information from the statically minded which might indicate to those with a static predilection that by consenting to exchange their scrips for money they express willingness to become holders of promissory notes.

It is in particular to the interest of the dynamically disposed, Schumpeter expands his instruction in deception, not to let the statically minded discover that the money they are willing to take in exchange for their scrip can well be used for the diversion of goods and services from the phase of replenishment to which they had hitherto been designated.

It is specifically to the advantage of a person with a dynamic predisposition, Schumpeter perfects his technique for deception, not to have it dawn upon the static minded simpletons that the money which is being offered to them in exchange for their scrips with the understanding that it presents an equivalent of a certain purchasing power might well turn out to stand for nothing but a fictitious claim.

The person with a dynamic bent, Schumpeter reveals some anxiety about the effectiveness of his instruction in deception, is to use his wits to quieten the suspicion the static minded might express that they are being asked to exchange their claim to a definite quantity of realized goods for a claim the materialization of which is to be greatly in doubt.

The person with a dynamic endowment, Schumpeter seems to be really troubled by the thought that his elaborate deception technique might not work after all, is to employ his ingenuity in taking the mind of those with a static predilection off the speculation that the money they are prevailed upon to accept in exchange of what they consider as certificates of established claims, might well turn out to be an offer of a series of promissory notes with a highly questionable redemption prospect.

The exchange of scrips for money units, — Schumpeter is trying to regain confidence in his deception technique by attempting to boost it, — is to be welcomed by the dynamically endowed since it provides a good opportunity for playing on the naivete of those with a static frame of mind.

The exchange of scrips, for money, Schumpeter is again in a confident mood about his propagation of deception, can well be seized upon by the dynamically minded as an opportune occasion for misleading the statically minded simpletons about a factor the social and economic nature of which is not to be made known.

Schumpeter expects those with a dynamic bent of mind to impress upon the statically minded that monetary resources do not present means for accumulation of wealth.

Money, the dynamically endowed are expected by Schumpeter to make the statically minded believe, is but an instrumentality which operates within a consumer's range.

Money constitutes but a means through employment of which a consumer's satisfaction can be delayed, Schumpeter expects the dynamically predisposed to make the statically inclined presume.

The dynamically endowed are to dissuade the statically minded from ever undertaking a close social and economic scrutiny of money, on Schumpeter's instruction.

The dynamically endowed are expected to leave with the statically minded the impression that money has all the earmarks of a natural bounty.

The dynamic person is supposed to preclude any inquisitiveness into the social and economic origin of money on the part of the static minded, Schumpeter directs, by issuing a declaration that money is at all times readily available through a kind of Santa Claus who is to be known by the name of a benevolent banker.

The banker, the dynamically endowed is to be prepared to testify, is the kind of person who does not shrink from clinching the most adventurous deals by proclaiming himself the guarantor of such engagements.

The banker, the dynamically endowed is to consider himself free to maintain, is the sort of man who does not mind subscribing to sheer unlimited risks.

The banker, the dynamically endowed is to feel unconstrained to proclaim, is the one person whose benevolence makes it feasible to acquire natural resources and services (Leistungen) for their respective dynamic utilization.

The banker, the dynamically endowed is not to be ashamed to intone a song of praise, is the one unmatched financial wizard who underwrites non-existing production and serves as guarantor of a non-existing product.

The banker, the dynamically endowed is not to hold himself back from bursting into a panegyric, is the financial miracle man who furnishes purchasing power without requiring any equivalent.

The dynamically endowed is being made to express his unbounded admiration by the author of the "Theory of Economic Development" for the way in which the banker is effecting a purchasing medium without assuring himself, in turn, of the availability of either goods or money or any other collateral.

The banker emerges from the treatment by Schumpeter as a person who is by his very temperament eager to back a promise.

The banker, in the form into which Schumpeter compresses his image, appears as a kind of individual who by his very psychophysical make-up is anxious to uphold a questionable commitment.

The banker is in Schumpeter's presentation imbued with a compulsion to step forward in order to invite public trust in a venture to which a dynamically predisposed person might feel inclined.

It is a kind of meeting of temperaments which in the explanation of Schumpeter accounts for the eagerness with which the banker is expected to seize upon the opportunity to back any venture of a person with a dynamic predisposition.

The banker, Schumpeter stresses, does not want anything but to make it sure that the dynamically endowed individual receives a chance.

The banker, Schumpeter emphasizes, places purchasing power within the reach of the dynamically predisposed for the reason that it pleases him to see the dynamically endowed person realize his dynamism.

The banker, Schumpeter amplifies his characterization, is not supposed to be identified with all the decisions and all the actions which the dynamic individual might be inclined to undertake.

The selection of components for the establishment of an enterprise is not to be considered as lying within the competence of the banker.

Nor is the operation of an established enterprise to be viewed as the province of the banker.

The decision about the kind of technological devices which are to be used, as well as the choice of the ways in which economic calculations are to be applied are to be regarded as lying outside the banker's range.

The person with a dynamic bent is to be left free to demonstrate, Schumpeter directs, whether he was or was not worthy of having brought the banker to his side.

It should be up to the dynamically endowed individual to show by his deeds whether he is to rate as a success or a failure.

The dynamic individual is to be rated as a success, should he be able to show that he possesses the ability of transforming the purchasing medium which has no relation to any existing goods and available services into a purchasing medium which refers to transactions in realized goods and effected services.

The person with a dynamic bent is to be marked as a worthy go-getter, Schumpeter gives the impression of being specific, should he be able to return the purchasing medium which had been advanced to him to the person from whom he had received it.

Should the person with a dynamic bent be unable to release the ostensible guarantor of his, the dynamic person's, initial purchasing power from the obligation, the guarantor has assumed towards him as a dynamic person in time, the dynamic individual is not to mind being described as a failure.

Should it become apparent that the dynamic person has used the fictitious media of exchange which had been made available to him without being able to transform them into real goods and services, the dynamic individual is not to object to being regarded as a person the confidence in whom has been misplaced.

Should it, in particular, become evident that the dynamic person has come to leave it to the banker to supplant the fictitious purchasing power which he had advanced with an equivalent of real purchasing power, the dynamic individual is to be forced to plead guilty to utter breach of trust.

The banker, on his part, Schumpeter concedes, could not fully escape from being called to account.

The banker could not flatly deny that he is responsible for the bet he was willing to make.

By underwriting the dynamic individual's fortune, by taking his stand behind the dynamic person, the banker is definitely giving the impression that he is ready to make good for any resulting failure.

Ultimately, Schumpeter does not hide it, somebody has to learn the lesson that social and economic life cannot function on the strength of mere promises.

Ultimately, Schumpeter does not conceal it, someone has to be burdened with making amends for using purchasing media, the economic equivalent of which remains unrealized.

The social and economic responsibility for the institution of fictitious purchasing power, Schumpeter makes no attempt to deny it, rests with the banker.

That the ultimate social and economic payoff involves also those who have come to place their trust in the banker is, however, not being indicated by Schumpeter.

That the ultimate social and economic burden has in the net result to be borne by those statically minded simpletons who are persuaded to accept promissory notes in exchange for their realized production shares, Schumpeter does not care to mention in this instance.

In omitting any reference to the stake of the statically minded in the manipulation of fictitious purchasing power into which they are drawn, Schumpeter studiously avoids a squaring of all social and economic accounts involved in the matter.

By discounting the social and economic role of individuals or groups of individuals who are being cajoled into providing funds for the banker, Schumpeter effects no more than an apparent closing of the social and economic gap between fictitious and real purchasing power.

In reality, Schumpeter is but inviting the banker whom he presents as the generator of fictitious purchasing power to unburden himself by passing on an added installment of fictitious purchasing power after the initial flow of fictitious purchasing power had lost its effectiveness.

That it is not the banker but the mass of the static minded simpletons who in the final reckoning are to be deprived of real assets which Schumpeter expects them to exchange for unrealizable claims, the author of the "Theory of Economic Development" does not care to divulge.

Any such banking which would allow for an all around social and economic accounting, Schumpeter wants to be branded as extraneous.

He intimates by that stricture that he is opposed to having the full social and economic implications of his banking scheme revealed.

Any form of credit which is in particular predicated upon rational economic calculations, Schumpeter, — in further pursuance of his tactics to preclude the disclosure of the real social and economic consequences of his lending device—wants to be labeled as non-essential.

Any form of banking and credit which is in particular based on other considerations than the temperamental predisposition of the dynamic individual and his banker towards irrational ventures, Schumpeter wants to be termed as superfluous,—in an obvious effort to block by terminological strictures even the raising of the question as to who is called upon to carry the real social and economic burden of his scheme for the operation of fictitious purchasing power.

After having assured himself that he has given all the necessary instructions for having banking and credit made to serve the perpetuation of fictitious claims, Schumpeter proceeds to fashion the formulation of capital in a manner in which that concept could be fitted into the realm of the fictitious.

After having divested himself of an unrealistic conception of capital functions, Schumpeter brings a studied unreality to bear on the constitutional elements of capital.

Capital, Schumpeter is quick to underscore, cannot be regarded as something real.

Capital, Schumpeter emphasizes, cannot be viewed as something which consists of material goods.

Capital, Schumpeter insists, cannot be appraised as something which finds expression in either land or labor or mechanical implements.

243

Capital, moreover, Schumpeter wants it stressed, cannot be referred to as something consisting of money.

Capital, Schumpeter directs, is not to be permitted to express anything but the shifting of goods and services.

Capital, Schumpeter wants it proclaimed, is not to be allowed to refer to anything but an indication of a means by which purchasing power can be exerted and, let us not forget to add, fictitious purchasing power at that.

Capital, Schumpeter implements his declaratory statement, cannot be said as constituting a strictly monetary term.

Money, as far as it is required for sustenance, Schumpeter amplifies, cannot be viewed as forming a part of what he wants to be regarded as capital.

Cash, for whatever it is being designated, Schumpeter further elaborates, cannot be held as forming any part of what the term capital is supposed to stand for.

Capital, Schumpeter at last divests himself of a semblance of a positive commitment, is to be formulated as something which consists in the main of promissory notes.

The bulk of capital, Schumpeter would have it, is to be represented as consisting of promissory notes of a strictly monetary character.

However, Schumpeter finds it opportune to caution, promissory notes of a character which provides for future money payments cannot be said as accounting for all capital.

The term capital, Schumpeter prefers a more ambivalent formulation, is supposed to refer to some promises to pay in money as well as to some actual money.

Capital, Schumpeter reinvokes his most favored terminological trapping, is supposed to refer to any circulatory media which are designed to initiate dynamic production.

Some circulatory media, Schumpeter draws at last near to what he is driving at, are not, however, to be classed as part of capital.

Circulatory media which are reserved for those who operate in a static manner, Schumpeter brings up the specific angle of his terminological merry-go-round in this instance, are not supposed to belong to capital.

Circulatory media which are put aside for the mere exchange of goods and services, Schumpeter wants to make it sure, are not supposed to form any part of capital in any functional use of the term.

The sphere of production which is run by those who are statically minded as well as the sphere of exchange which is being conducted by those with a static disposition, Schumpeter gives notice, are not supposed to fall within the range of utilization of capital.

Nor is the sphere of exchange of goods and services which is operated by those with a dynamic predisposition be considered as lying within the analytical scope of employment of capital.

Capital taken in the functional sense, Schumpeter finally discloses what he is after, is to be formulated as an instrumentality which is supposed to act as a lever for something non-existent.

Capital in the functional sense is to be termed as a medium which is supposed to serve as a diverter of goods and services from the sphere of the realized and the real into the realm of the unrealized and the unreal.

In the final resolve, the function of capital thus comes to be regarded by Schumpeter as a device by the use of which the flow of fictitious purchasing power can be set into motion.

Capital, Schumpeter considers it opportune to add a postscriptum, does not constitute a category of a national economic dimension.

Capital, Schumpeter lectures, is not to be regarded as a concept of societal magnitude.

Capital, Schumpeter raises his forefinger, is to be viewed as a concept of an exclusively private economic relevance.

The category of capital, Schumpeter wants to make it sure, is to be kept within a merely subjective range,—to make that category a pliant medium, let us add, for his Schumpeter's flight into unreality.

Objective social and economic considerations, Schumpeter wants to play safe, are to be ruled out as factors involved in the conceptualization of capital,—in order to enable him, let us add again, to be unrestrained in referring to capital as a lever for the non-existent.

With the category of capital conceived as a subjective medium for the manipulation of fictitious purchasing power, the determination of capital gains and capital losses in any non-subjective form is rendered inoperative by Schumpeter.

With the objective social and economic core of capital denied identification, the identification of social and economic increments and decrements of capital in any objective manner is cognitively blocked.

To comply with the subjectivistic strictures which he has placed in the way of the conceptualization of capital, Schumpeter is readily conceding that the manipulation of fictitious purchasing power for which his category of capital is supposed to serve as a medium, does not necessarily guarantee any real gains,—and to complete Schumpeter's train of thought for him in this instance, in the absence of real capital gains any attempt of cognitive specification of such gains can be disposed of.

The specific gains which a dynamic individual makes, Schumpeter is eager to sustain the tie between subjectiveness and fictitiousness, cannot be held as being attributable to the means which enable him to acquire productive forces.

The particular gain which the dynamic person scores, Schumpeter reemphasizes the link between subjectivistic and fictitious conceptions, is not to be viewed as being subject to any causative linkage with the productive mechanism of which the dynamically predisposed individual is making use.

The gains of the go-getting person, Schumpeter reemphasizes the tie between subjectivism and fictitiousness, are not supposed to be looked upon as gains which arise from the material which the go-getter comes to use in production.

The gains of the go-getting individual are under no circumstances to be appraised as being generated by production implements.

Neither are the gains of the go-getter to be presented as gains which are derived from the labor which the go-getting individual employs.

The gains of the go-getter, Schumpeter is but demonstrating anew the use which he is making of the subjectivistic approach, are to be held as being attributable to nothing else but the peculiar way in which the go-getter avails himself of the uses of the fictitious purchasing power which is placed at his disposal.

The gains of the go-getter, Schumpeter adds a note of meaninglessness to which his subjectivistic approach gives rise, are to be ascribed to nothing more but the odd kind of use of productive equipment and labor of which the go-getter is alone capable.

The gains of the go-getter, Schumpeter compounds the obscurantist position to which his subjectivistic preconception leads him, are to be considered as being linkable to those unidentifiable subjective notions which are, as he, Schumpeter, puts it, a peculiar characteristic of those who are dynamically predisposed.

The gains of the go-getter are referred by Schumpeter to that unexplainable intuition by which a person endowed with dynamic go-getting qualities finds himself seized.

It is an odd manner in which a personal notion in the form of an individual intuition takes possession of the go-getter, Schumpeter recites.

He wants zest for the extraordinary, flare for the untried, preference of the unexperienced, zeal to upset existing combinations, listed as the outer forms in which the intuitive manifests itself.

The go-getter who is led by his intuition, Schumpeter proffers as an observation, finds himself compelled to arrange things in a hither-to untried manner.

The go-getter, Schumpeter enters what can be taken as a rationalization, owes his income to the way his intuitive notion makes him reorganize production in a hither-to unexperienced fashion.

The go-getter, Schumpeter continues to rationalize, earns his income through the intuitive compulsiveness with which he effects a realization of a new production or brings about an introduction of new products.

The specific income to which the go-getter is to hold himself entitled, is not by any chance to be attributed to the technological innovation which the go-getter might have originated, Schumpeter finds it necessary to warn.

Nor is the specific income which the go-getter is apt to claim to be linked to the effect of the new way of disposing of the product of the technological innovation to which the go-getter might have given rise.

The special gains to which the go-getter is to be entitled to lay claim, Schumpeter wants to make it sure, are to be ascribed solely to the unique suggestiveness which is supposed to constitute the outstanding characteristic of a go-getter.

Schumpeter imputes the income of the dynamic go-getter to the way in which the go-getter takes it upon himself to undertake willful actions.

The income of the go-getter is turned by Schumpeter into an expression of social and economic irresponsibility via the route of blocking the cognition of the social and economic source of that income.

The go-getter's income is presented in Schumpeter's formulation as difference between an outgo which is calculable and an intake which is incalculable.

Anything calculable is supposed to be included in the go-getter's outgo.

The go-getter's outgo is supposed to contain all production expenditures.

Every item in a balance sheet is to be given a place in the go-getter's outgo.

Credit and debit items are to be added up for inclusion in the go-getter's outgo without any provision for a cognitive distinction between the factors of who owes and who owns anything.

The go-getter's outgo, Schumpeter directs, is supposed to cover all technological production expenditures, regardless of the way the expenditures had been procured, as well as regardless of the rate at which a utilization of material is taking place.

The listing of the go-getter's outgo is, moreover, to include the rent for the land which the go-getter might conceivably own.

The go-getter's outgo is furthermore to have a place for the listing of interest on capital which the go-getter might possess.

The outgo of the go-getter is in addition to contain a column for the listing of an adequate premium for the risk the go-getter might be willing to entail.

The go-getter's outgo is also to carry a column for the entering of the reward for the managerial services which the go-getter is prepared to claim as wages of management.

The go-getter's outgo to attempt a summation, is presented as a hodge-podge of innumerable items which reasons not readily disclosed, Schumpeter is willing to grant accountability.

The intake of the go-getter is, by contradistinction, confined by Schumpeter to the realm which he wants to be regarded as unaccountable. Since a subtraction of an unaccountable intake, regardless whether the unaccountable is willfully designated as such or not, from the accountable outgo, regardless whether the outgo is arbitrarily listed as accountable or not, cannot result in anything accountable; the size of the go-getter's income, Schumpeter can rest assured, is bound to remain anybody's guess.

The dynamic go-getter, Schumpeter is willing to say that much, is getting *his* by arranging something which the static minded simpletons have not thought of.

The dynamic go-getter, Schumpeter is ready to state, is getting *his* by way of organizing something in a manner the indolent static minded have not cared to do.

The dynamic go-getter, Schumpeter does not mind bringing it out, is getting *his* by catching the unsuspecting statically minded off guard.

The dynamic-go-getter, Schumpeter demonstrates the application of his technique for deception, is getting *his* by startling those who had become accustomed to static production and traditional products.

The dynamic go-getter is getting *his,* Schumpeter shows how his technique for deception can be put to work by way of shocking those who have been accustomed to regard static production implements, a static production process and a static way of offering products as the only feasible forms of running an enterprise.

To make it sure that the income of the go-getter is not to be made objectively accountable, Schumpeter goes out of his way to caution that a sudden introduction of a new production device or an announced realization of a new product in the form in which they are presented in his "Theory of Economic Development," do not account for any income of the dynamic go-getter on the strength of the material effect of those innovations.

It is but the personal imbalance, it is but the emotional upset, Schumpeter finds it opportune to stress, to which the statically minded come to be subjected by the dynamic go-getter which provides the go-getter with an assurance of his gain.

No part of the gain to which the dynamic go-getter is to be entitled to lay claim, Schumpeter sounds another warning, is to be ascribed to a shift in the use of production factors.

The shift of land and labor to a use in a dynamic way, Schumpeter is ready with a qualification of a qualification, does not warrant any increase in the respective value of those two factors.

Any increase of value which might accompany the dynamic utilization of hither-to static production factors, Schumpeter forewarns, is to be ascribed solely to that unique intuitive quality which constitutes the personal characteristic of that dynamism which expresses itself in go-getting.

For the identification of any such gains which the go-getter is apt to make in such enterprises which come under his sway Schumpeter assigns the term profit.

He consigns, by contrast, such enterprises which are not held under the go-getter's sway and in particular such undertakings which are conducted by statically minded persons to the range of a-profitable undertakings.

Undertakings on which the statically minded leave their mark, undertakings in which the outgo and intake respond to a rational calculation, Schumpeter finds it necessary to point out, do not by their very nature constitute undertakings which could conceivably show a gain which would merit a profit rating.

Economic undertakings which are conducted by those with a static disposition and which, as Schumpeter implicitly admits, show a clear contradistinction between debit and credit items in their accounting procedure are being consigned to the fold of such undertakings which by their very essence are kept from scoring any net gains.

Schumpeter refuses to regard undertakings in which the static mind rules supreme as enterprises in the proper sense of the term.

He denies the undertakings which are bearing the stamp of a static mind any acquisitive properties.

An undertaking in which a person with a static disposition engages Schumpeter wants to be viewed as an undertaking which is bound to be a-acquisitive in character, in the sense of being conducted for the sake of balancing a given supply and demand of consumer's goods.

Schumpeter does not expect the static minded person who is conducting an economic undertaking to seek any profit.

It thus is not supposed to occur to the static minded individual to claim that his legitimate gains are being encroached upon by the profit making activity of the dynamic person who becomes engaged in an enterprise.

Neither is any other income receiver supposed to get the notion that the dynamic enterpriser might be cutting into his, the other income receiver's rightful earnings.

Neither the wage earner nor the rent receiver could conceivably come to claim, Schumpeter would have it, that they are being short-changed, no matter how exorbitant the profits of the dynamic enterpriser might turn out to be.

Neither the wage earner nor the rent receiver, Schumpeter considers he has made it sure, will ever think of the possibility of being placed in a position in which they would have to contest the claims of a dynamic enterpriser.

Wages and rent, there should not be any question Schumpeter directs, are to be considered fundamentally static regardless of whether they accrue in a static undertaking or in a dynamic enterprise.

Wages and rent are basically predetermined in Schumpeter's conception.

He does to be sure, concede that in a dynamic enterprise run by a go-getter, wages and rent can be regarded as not entirely frozen. He appears to be qualifying his fundamental conception of rent and wages when he argues that in an enterprise in which a go-getter has his say it might not be warranted to regard wages and rent as wholly unflexible.

He reasserts his fundamental position on wages and rent, however, when he demands that the variations in wages and rent are to remain within the confines of the accountable.

Wages and rent, regardless of the extent of their fluctuations, Schumpeter insists, are not supposed to move beyond the manageable range.

Increases and decreases of wages and rent are supposed to be left within the purview of the go-getting enterpriser, on Schumpeter's explicit order.

The granting of increases and decreases in rent and wages is i.e. made subject to emotional considerations by the author of the "Theory of Economic Development."

Actual increases in wages and rent are to be granted in conformity with the degree of emotional release which the go-getter is willing to grant the wage earner and rent collector, on Schumpeter's instruction.

How he squares his notion of the wage earner and rent collector whom he conceives as statically predisposed and thus emotionally balanced persons with his expectation of an emotional tension on the part of the wage earner and rent collector in anticipation of a rise in their earnings, Schumpeter does not care to explain.

Nor does he care to state, how he would conceivably square his insistence on the characterization of the wage earner and rent collector as persons of a-acquisitive placidity with his expectation that the wage earner and rent collector become concerned with an increase in their earnings.

He is satisfied with proffering the reassurance that the emotional imbalance of the wage earner and rent collector is not to be expected to get out of control.

The go-getter will see to it, Schumpeter is sure, that the emotional vibrations to which the wage-earner and rent collector give expression, when wage and rent increases or decreases are involved, will be adjusted without any challenge to his, the go-getter's sway over all those to whom he ascribes a static predisposition.

Increases and decreases in wages and rent, Schumpeter reaffirms his stand, can never be permitted to rate as a qualitative difference.

The rating qualitative change is to be reserved for the sphere of profit making, on Schumpeter's direction.

Qualitative change, in the way Schumpeter uses the words, becomes but another way of endorsing the unaccountable.

Qualitative change, in the context in which Schumpeter uses the expression, becomes but another terminological vehicle for covering up the irrational.

By making profits subject to qualitative change while restricting wages and rent to a quantitative differentiation, Schumpeter but reinforces his dictum which demands of the wage earner and rent collector that they remain answerable to the profit maker and absolves the profit maker, in turn, from ever accounting for anything to those who earn wages and collect rent.

In keeping wages and rent on this side of rationality while transferring profits to the irrational sphere, Schumpeter blocks a wholly rational correlation between rent and wages on one side and profits on the other.

Schumpeter is persistent in denying any socially meaningful correlation between rent, wages and profit, he thus provides the go-getter with an assurance that he can treat the income of the wage earner and rent collector as a socially predetermined cost item with equanimity, while he, the go-getter himself, can consider himself free of any social and economic limitations in his grasping for profits.

The duality of Schumpeter's position, the propagation of double social and economic standards receives further emphasis in Schumpeter's dealing with interest.

Interest within the static range is viewed as abnormal by Schumpeter.

Interest, should it generate in a social and economic sphere which is dominated by the static minded, Schumpeter wants to be regarded as but an accidental occurrence.

Within the social and economic sphere in which static mindedness comes to express itself, all income is regularly to rate as wages and rent, on Schumpeter's insistence.

Within the social and economic range in which the static mind leaves its imprint all income is to be normally imputed to what Schumpeter calls soil and labor performances (Boden und Arbeitsleistungen).

Only in the social and economic sphere in which the dynamic mind comes to rule supreme interest is to be accorded an essential role.

Although Schumpeter uses identical terms he is apparently referring to different propositions when he respectively relates interest to the static and dynamic spheres.

When he uses the word interest with reference to what he presents as the static social and economic range, he is apparently applying the denotation of interest in relation to a concrete production factor.

In using the word interest with reference to the static sphere, Schumpeter is presenting interest as a correlate of a lasting production element.

In Schumpeter's treatment of interest in the static sphere, the subjectivistic angle is but super-imposed. The static mindedness, is in this instance, accorded the force of a qualifying but not of a disqualifying proposition, as far as the objective factors of production are concerned.

When, by contrast, Schumpeter makes reference to interest in the dynamic sphere, the term assumes a predominantly subjectivistic form, or better said, formlessness.

Interest in the dynamic sphere is treated by Schumpeter as a category which has but a remote relation to any nonpersonal factors.

Interest with reference to the dynamic sphere relates not much more than the personal dynamic quality of the go-getter in Schumpeter's presentation.

Interest in reference to the dynamic sphere is being imputed by the author of the "Theory of Economic Development" to nothing else but the intuitive in the go-getter.

The ambivalence of Schumpeter's treatment of the factor of

254

causation and imputation in regard to interest is not in any way lessened when he proceeds to deal with the function of interest.

Interest in the functional sense is assigned by Schumpeter the role of a special stimulant which the dynamic person is supposed to apply as a bait in order to overcome the opposition to dynamism on the part of those who are statically minded.

Interest is assigned by Schumpeter the function of providing a kind of premium which the go-getter is to take upon himself the liberty to offer the statically minded in an effort to break the grip that the latter are holding on production.

Interest is to assume the form of a special reward, on Schumpeter's direction, which the go-getter is to consider himself entitled to promise those among the statically minded who consent to refrain for the time being from a static reproduction of materials and products to which they hold title.

Schumpeter is candid enough to concede that the promise of a reward to which the statically minded are expected to respond does not constitute a guarantee that the promised reward shall be fully forthcoming.

The go-getter who is making the offer of a reward, Schumpeter is ready to admit, cannot be sure that he will be able to furnish the premium the promise of which he holds out to the statically minded.

The promise of a reward to the statically minded, Schumpeter does not conceal it, is but intended to help the go-getter to start.

The go-getter is not expected to fulfill the obligation he is taking on towards the statically inclined, Schumpeter does not mind being outspoken in this instance, since the basis on which the go-getter makes his promises is a faulty one.

The novelty of the dynamic way of doing things to which the go-getter is supposed to ascribe an interest bearing potency cannot but wear itself out, Schumpeter states with resignation.

The innovation in the way of doing things on which the go-getter is supposed to base his expectation of being able to pay interest, Schumpeter comes out into the open, does not refer to any basic change in material factors, nor does that innovation relate an invention or discovery.

The innovation in the way of doing things on which the go-getter is supposed to base his expectation of being able to pay interest does not present anything else but a manipulative stunt, Schumpeter is quite frank about it.

The manipulative stunt might initially have the desired effect of stunning those whom interest payments are promised; the effect of the stunt is, however, not likely to last, Schumpeter makes no effort to deny it.

The large promises which the go-getter is to feel unconstrained to make to those statically minded who have a hold on the material elements of production, thus comes to loom but as another effort on the part of the dynamic aspirant to create with his irresponsible promises an atmosphere in which he can unload upon those unsuspecting statically minded another avalanche of fictitious purchasing power.

Schumpeter to reassess the significance of his "Theory of Economic Development" has succeeded in bringing about a major theoretical debacle.

The incessant drive towards deconceptualization to which Schumpeter fell heir assumed the character of a major theoretical breakdown in his discourse.

With his "Theory of Economic Development" Schumpeter succeeded in striking a fatal blow to systematic economic reasoning.

In consigning his chosen concepts to the irrational fold and holding his less favored rational concepts in captivity to his most favored irrational postulations, Schumpeter can well pride himself of having made a striking contribution to social and economic disorientation.

In turning the categories of profit and interest over to "dynamic" unreason and keeping the "static" concepts of wages and rent in a position of subjection to the propositions, which are not supposed to be reasoned out, Schumpeter has made a decisive step towards incoherence in social and economic thinking.

On the surface to be sure, Schumpeter expounds two forms of conceptualization, on the surface, he concedes that rationality has a place alongside irrationality in the formation of concepts.

But the co-existence which he grants to irrationality and rationality is only granted on the condition that the rational submit to the irrational.

256

The keeping of rationally arrived at concepts alongside of irrationally contrived propositions, with a view of having the rational proposition submit to the dictates of the irrational, provides but an added note of ambivalence.

Schumpeter tolerates rational propositions only under the condition that they be drowned in the flood of unreason.

In postulating the intuition of the go-getter as an all embracing factor, Schumpeter delivers a death blow to social and economic conceptualization.

If no valid distinction is to be maintained between a concept which is conceived within the range of reason and concepts which are turned over to unreason, how is one to know what distinguishes conceptualization from deconceptualization.

Intuition to take a brief look, at the turbulent history of that postulate which looms so large in Schumpeter's exposition, has come to play a key role in the struggle between intellectualism and anti-intellectualism.

Descartes used intuition in his struggle for the supremacy of the rational, he made a supreme effort to clear intuition of supranatural connotation.

Schelling, on his part, applied intuition in a drive to have the irrational tower over the rational, he resupplied the irrational connotation of intuition which had been lost by Descartes.

Since Thuenen intuition as an irrational proposition has become implicit in the drive towards subjectivization of social and economic thought.

It was not until Schumpeter, however, that the intuitive was granted explicitness in the subversion of social economic thinking to irrational whims.

Schumpeter was no doubt led to an explicit use of the term intuition by the realization that intuition in the irrational sense has gained currency through the widely applauded literary effort of Henri Bergson.

Schumpeter was no doubt pleased to seize the opportunity of extending the wave of anti-intellectualism which had come into full force with Bergson by having it envelop the entire range of social and economic theory.

CHAPTER 9

ALOGISMS

At this advanced stage of dissolution of systematic economic thought, the lure to earn a thorny crown by compounding tortuous twists of social and economic reasoning appeared to be greatly enticing. At this phase at which aberrations in social and economic thinking have come to rule supreme, the tortured notion of making an all but hopeless tangle more hopeless seemed to have dazzling prospects. The period was at hand when the weirdest configurations could be made to serve the wildest of surrealistic pretensions. The stage was set for a piecing together of a ramshackle theoretical construction, as Keynes came to realize, by using conceptual debris as the formative elements of such makeshift erection.

John Maynard Keynes takes great pains to restress the logical and methodological unreliability of any conceptualization. All logically derived knowledge, any perceptually conceived insight, is to remain forever confined to the area of the improbable, if Keynes is to have his way. The most accurate presentations, the most refined mathematical counts, are not to lead to any degree of certainty, Keynes wants to make it sure in his "Treatise on Probability."

The most exact calculations are not to approach the range of the possible; the most refined form of quantification is not to touch upon the realm of the probable in Keynes' dictum. Keynes is bent on conveying a sense of futility, he is set on having doubting for the sake of doubting accepted as the keystone of all reasoning. He is determined to envelop all methodological considerations in an air of supreme scepticism.

Since everything and anything is rated as improbable by Keynes, social and economic sequence and uniformity are rendered inoperative. Since unpredictability is made to serve as an overriding maxim in any analysis proffered by Keynes, an inquiry into social and economic life appears to signify no more than an investigation into a play of chance.

In contradistinction with Laplace who was determined to draw a line between the range of the probable and the sphere of the improbable, Keynes sees it as his task to enlarge the area of the improbable to sheer limitless proportions. In contrast with the laborious effort, which the initial deviser of the theory of probability had undertaken to provide a glimpse of certainty, the latter day theorizer of probability uses all his ingenuity for the furnishing of devices by which reasoning is to be kept forever in complete uncertainty.

Laplace's efforts to restrict the bearing of uncertainty were obviously motivated by his desire to have the frontiers of knowledge advanced. Keynes who, in turn, is dedicating his labors to have uncertainty applied without any limitation was apparently concerned with turning much of the range of the knowable into the realm of the unknowable.

Laplace's dealing with probability is so devised as to provide vehicles for forming a firmer grip on the controllable aspect in any sphere of knowledge. Keynes' treatment of probability is, by contrast, so designed as to serve as instrumentality for a weakening, if not for the losing, of the very sight of controlling factors.

Elements of knowledge, analytical particles emerge as mere subjective projections from Keynes' "Treatise on Probability." Thought comes to express an assortment of wistful schemes in Keynes' version of probability. Human beings and their relations to each other come to represent a world of shadows. Scheming appears to have no limit within Keynes' range of probability.

Phantasmagorias are left without restraint by Keynes' methodological exercises. Keynes' excursion into general methodology provides him with the authorization to present unrelated comments as the apex of coherent reasoning. He is well able to use his methodological looseness to have casual remarks paraded as the very essence of a systematic treatise. A personal impression becomes indistinguishable from an apersonal meaning, in Keynes' approach to scientific formulations. An intangible personal attitude comes to carry as much weight in an argumentation as an apersonalized conceptualization, in Keynes' way of reasoning. Subjective utility and objective utilization become indistinguishable. Value in terms of personal emotions and value in the sense of a societal appraisal are not differentiated in the approaches which Keynes furnishes for economic thought.

Keynes is not at least hesitant to chide the classical objectivists for the social and economic distinctiveness of their presentations in the opening passages of his "General Theory of Employment, Interest and Money." He is completely at ease in berating the classical economic thinkers for their insistence on a clearcut social and economic identification. He feels he owes it to himself and his methodological professions to call the standard bearers of classical economic thought to order for having missed their real calling by having erected and maintained conceptual obstacles which prevented them from losing themselves in a subjectivistic web.

Oddly enough, Keynes opens up his treatise on the "General Theory of Employment, Interest and Money," by pointing out that the classicists try to draw a line between the essential and the nonessential in their presentations. For some unspecified reason,—Keynes appears irritated,—the classical economic thinkers make an effort to distinguish between the lasting and the passing. The classicists, Keynes is irked, insist on signifying the real as against the apparent. The classicists, Keynes is greatly disturbed, adhere to a peculiar device of holding an intrinsic nonmonetary value apart from an extrinsic monetary value. In classical theory, Keynes becomes disconsolate, monetary values have come to be subordinated to nonmonetary values.

Keynes refuses to consider that Smith's and Ricardo's design to uncover the social bearing of production had been greatly advanced by their theoretical move which consigned all monetary values to the fold of the apparent. Keynes does not care to acknowledge that a socially relevant analysis could not have been carried out by the major classicists had they not confined non-monetary values to the range of the nonessential. In chiding Smith and Ricardo, Keynes fails to realize that the two writers who had laid the groundwork of classical economic thought, could not have retained a focal view on the complexity of social and economic relations, had they not treated monetary values as a transitional phenomenon.

In his underhanded attack on Smith and Ricardo, Keynes seems to be eager to leave the impression that the designation of non-monetary values as real values is apt to prevent the realization of the social implications of money operations. Keynes appears to be anxious to convey the feeling by his castigation of Smith and Ricardo that a signification of nonmonetary values as essential values by the two major classical economic thinkers was conceivably undertaken with a view of hiding something which is essential to production. Keynes is apparently intent to press for a forced conclusion, he would like to have the rather perplexing inference drawn that the analytical device which singles out nonmonetary values as a lasting factor, has the effect of ruling out a balanced appraisal of productive and nonproductive factors. In the view which Keynes would like to impose, Smith and Ricardo had treated monetary and nonmonetary values in a discriminatory manner because they considered such discriminating treatment as a convenient form for the misconstruing of the utilization of productive resources.

By keeping monetary aspects apart from nonmonetary aspects in the respective bearing of those two aspects on production, the two thinkers who had laid the groundwork of classical thought, Keynes lodges a specific complaint, have become instrumental in preventing a proper explanation as to what factors are involved in the nonutilization of resources. Smith and Ricardo stand accused by the stated allegation of having turned their analytical backs on idleness. Smith whose inquiry into the "Wealth of Nations" demonstrates to all, who care to read it, a primary concern for productive utilization of human and nonhuman resources, is to stand indicted as a theoretical writer who has deliberately devised an instrumentality which is intended to bring about an obscuring

261

of the problem-complex of deemployment. Ricardo, who in his "Principles of Political Economy" has placed the aspect of reproduction and reemployment in the very center of his discussion, is pillored as a literary figure who has indulged in an analytical obfuscation of the social and economic issues involved in idleness of either men or resources.

Keynes does not care to pay any attention to Smith's realization that the pre-classical proposition according to which the flow of production is analytically inseparable from the flow of money has brought about a deadlock in systematic social and economic inquiry. Keynes does not consider it opportune to take notice that Smith as well as Ricardo had decided to separate monetary and nonmonetary aspects of production in their analytical procedure because the experience of their predecessors had taught them that, without such analytical separation, an analysis of the social and economic intricacies involved in the production process was doomed to sterility.

What prompts Keynes to root for an undifferentiated approach to monetary and nonmonetary values is brought to fore when he proceeds to treat the subject of wages. The answer to the question what compels him to press for an undiscriminatory treatment of nonmonetary and monetary evaluation is clearly given by Keynes' admision that such undiscriminatory treatment is regarded by him as a welcome vehicle for the discarding of the differentiation of real and money wages. Continued use of the term real wages, Keynes insists, precludes an unadulterated reference (as he chooses to call it) to what should be known by the name of productive service.

Without in any way acknowledging it, Keynes is echoing Bastiat. It could have hardly escaped Keynes' knowledge that Bastiat had taken recourse to the term service for the sake of blunting the distinguishing characteristics of social values. Keynes could hardly be remiss of knowing that Bastiat had treated use and exchange value in an undiscriminatory manner, in order to make it methodologically unfeasible to distinguish between productive and nonproductive utilization of human and material resources.

In an effort to rid the term productive service of any link with

262

the respective denotation of Bastiat, Keynes addresses himself to an improper addressee. He has no hesitancy in denouncing the Ricardian conception which holds real and money wages apart for the very faults Bastiat's deviation from that conception had deliberately invited. The classical delineation of real wages, Keynes feels not the slightest scruple to proclaim, is designed to throw a veil over the social and economic issues of work remuneration. The conceptual distinction of real from money wages which the classicists had maintained, Keynes has no hesitancy to assert, consitutes a procedure which cannot but lead to the impediment of a separate as well as a contrasting consideration of the social and economic issues connected with work compensation. The holding of money and real wages terminologically apart, Keynes does not shrink from an outright misrepresentation, is branded by the author of the "General Theory" as a way of mixing up the social and economic issues involved in the analysis of work payment.

In lieu of a social and economic explanation, Keynes proceeds to pile adjectives upon adjectives in a barrage of denunciations. The differentiation of monetary and nonmonetary remuneration which helped Ricardo to wrest his exposition from an analytical morass, is saddled by Keynes with the adjective, "grossly misleading." The keeping of money and nonmoney wages as specific identification marks which rated to Ricardo as the most distinctive feature of the acquisitive nexus, is denounced by Keynes as a scheme for making it impossible to discern the distinctive features of a social and economic system.

The realization of money wages, in terms of immediately realizable nonmonetary values, in other words, the criterion by which the wage receiver is able to judge whether and to what extent he has been offered a real share in the social product, is without any further qualification adjudicated by Keynes as the "most misleading factor," in any evaluation of deutilization. The monetary earning of labor when it is linked to presently available goods, constitutes the most improper causal linkage in any investigation of unemployment, in the light of the castigation to which Keynes devotes the first chapters of his "General Theory of Employment."

The classical theorists, Keynes continues to be in the mood for denunciation, are to be made to hear that even more glaring misconceptions are chargeable to them. The classicists, Keynes would like to make it sound horrible, have guarded themselves against overstepping the social and economic frame within the confines of which they have committed themselves to argue. Classical theorists, Keynes would like it to appear objectionable, have not considered it methodologically proper to indulge in a willful changeover from one range of argumentation to another. The classical conceptualizers, Keynes would like to create the impression that such a procedure is not permissible, have refused to attach socially and economically congruous attributes to socially and economically incongruous categories. The classical conceptualizers, Keynes would like to have it labeled as a reprehensible attitude, were quite adamant in refusing to engage in an arbitrary shifting from one proposition to its contrary, without any qualification. The classical conceptualizers, Keynes would like to leave it unnoticed, were stringently opposed to the violation of the principle of contrariety, on the ground that a reasoning which attempts to square contraries can hardly advance any understanding. The classical theorists have found it logically and methodologically unfeasible to dispose of the contrasting of personal notions and apersonal objectifications, although Keynes was inclined to look upon such a logical and methodological restraint with disfavor. The classical systematizers have expressed consistent opposition towards the foregoing of the drawing of a cognitive line between value postulated as a social ultimate and value conceived as a personal predilection, though Keynes regards such a cognitive division with misgiving. The classical systematizers were not at all prepared to forsake the delineation between value as common bond among individuals and value as a whim of a single person, though Keynes is not disposed to look kindly upon such cognitive scrupulousness. The classical systematizers were fully cognizant that by holding value as a socially objectified factor and value as a personal attitude apart, they welded a cognitive weapon which protected their respective social and economic inquiries from deteriorating into the presentation of social and economic irrelevances, although Keynes could not keep himself from expressing resentment to such an analytical approach.

The classicists were firm in their opposition against having the category of value reduced to social and economic inconspicuousness because they saw in the preservation of value as a focal category a factor which lent significance to their entire reasoning, no matter how disconsolate Keynes tends to become about it. The evolvers of classical economic thought were fully determined to maintain value as a category per se, they were not at all amenable to the proposition to have the category of value treated as interchangeable with categories known by any other name, because they saw in the renunciation of the distinctiveness of specific categories a means for avoiding clarification of respective social and economic issues, though Keynes appears to be very disdainful of the stated performance of the classicists. The initiators of classical economic thinking persisted in viewing value as an ultimate social determinant because they did not care to indulge in an evasion, when called upon to identify social and economic groups, no matter what irritation such distinctiveness in social and economic reasoning, causes Keynes.

The classical theorists were, moreover, adamant in maintaining a distinction between value as expression of the general as against value as an indication of the incidental, as a matter of analytical discernment, although such methodological strictness evokes a distaste in Keynes. The classical theorists were particularly careful in drawing a line between fleeting individual characteristics and definite attributes of a collective, though Keynes is not at all in sympathy with such a conceptual division. The classical theorists recognized the relevance of social and economic dimension, though Keynes considers such an acknowledgement superfluous.

The classical theorists, in spite of the variation in their views on conceptualization, have been particularly careful in keeping the discussion of supply and demand within a uniform social and economic range, though Keynes considers such a uniformity as unnecessary. The classical theorists have thought it logically and methodologically improper to deal with supply in an objective form and treat demand in a subjective manner, though Keynes utterly regrets such discrimination. The classical theorists were specifically opposed to have value and costs analyzed as if there was nothing distinct in either of the two factors, though Keynes considers that the classical thinkers have brought upon themselves discredit by such opposition. The classical theorists implied that a clarification of the respective social and economic aspects cannot be in any way advanced, were the delineation of value to be submerged with the denotation of costs, though Keynes undertakes to deny that the classicists were in any way concerned with making any contribution to a social and economic understanding by contrasting value and costs.

The classicists committed themselves to an upholding of a distinction between value as the predominantly abstract and costs as the predominantly concrete, though Keynes regards such a commitment with unmistakable displeasure. The classical theorists did not leave costs without the social and economic direction of value and did not, in turn, leave value socially and economically uncontested by costs, though Keynes is apt to become disconsolate about such contest. The classicists persisted in keeping value and costs cognitively apart since such separation permitted a contradistinction between reoccurring regular costs and irregular occasional expenditures, though Keynes expresses contempt for such a discernment. The classicists consistently opposed an unqualified intermingling of costs of production, postulated as an expression of a determinable relationship of social and economic groups and costs of production conceived as a reflection of indeterminate individual manipulations, though Keynes does not hide his dismay about such method of procedure.

The classicists fail to show any signs that they could ever be made receptive to a scheme by which costs of production designed as a factor of social evaluation and costs of production devised as managerial hunches are to be treated as undistinguishable, no matter how lamentable Keynes tries to present such disinclination. The classical theorists, Keynes notwithstanding, were very particular about not using the categories of costs and value in a manner which could lead but to an obscuring of a social and economic vision. The classical theorists could not have fallen for Keynes' allusion that costs and value distinctions are to be disregarded since the classical theorists have built the classical theory on the proposition of having production as well as distribution of goods and services analyzed as a part of a discernible social and economic process. Their firm stand on the sustaining of a social and economic distinction between value and costs makes it highly improbable that the classicists could ever have succumbed to the institution of a device, as the one which is given currency by Keynes, which is to have supply treated as a function which falls within the range of social causation and has demand referred to the scope of an unaccountable imputation. The classical theorists persisted in analyzing supply as well as demand as socially determinable as well as socially verifiable factors, irrespective of Keynes belated consternation. The classicists realized that nothing could be gained, in regard to a clarification of the social and economic issues involved, by having the analysis of demand lost in the untraceable speculations of an individual mind, despite Keynes' implication to the contrary.

The classicists and those who keep their record clear, are, moreover, apt to ask what, if any, understanding of the social and economic complexities involved in demand can be advanced should, as Keynes suggests, the analysis of demand be in part linked to presumptive spending schemes which are not supposed to be effected at the time when the analysis is undertaken and, for all that the analyzer is permitted to know, will presumably never be realized. The classicists who persisted in viewing supply as the embodiment of effected wage goods could be expected to be utterly resentful of Keynes' proposal to have demand related to unrealized production. The classical theorists, there should be little doubt about it, had a keen enough perception to suspect that a correlation of demand to something which is not there, as it is suggested by Keynes, constitutes a move which is designed to leave the question of the social and economic relevance of demand unanswered. The classical theorists who insisted on an interpretation of supply in terms of priced wares, can be depended upon to have a clear understanding that a conception of demand in terms of nonexisting goods can be advanced only by a theoretician who is bent on an evasion of a social and economic explanation of demand.

The classicists were committed to an analysis of the socially and economically existent and could, therefore, not be expected to adapt Keynes' device to have demand linked to some indeterminate and, for all intent and purposes, indeterminable individual speculation. The classicists, who were bent on gaining a balanced view on demand as against supply, could not be expected to be responsive to Keynes' allusion which favors the creating of an unbridgeable analytical gap between supply presented in an objectified form and supply treated in a subjectified manner. His proposition to have demand and supply treated as socially and economically incommensurable factors, Keynes ought to know it, could hardly be squared with the classical analytical approach which is based on the realization that supply and demand present but two manifestations of a given set of social and economic relations.

In contradistinction to the determination of the classicists, to bring demand into line with supply and vice versa, Keynes is set to prevent, under any conditions and circumstances, an equation or even a near equation between demand and supply. He does not employ quantitive devices to effect a balancing or near balancing of demand and supply. He is out to render adjustment of demand and supply inconceivable. He is determined to have demand and supply confined to cognitively incongruous ranges.

First, he undertakes to divide supply into two incongruous parts, the conception of supply is to be split into a supply conceived as an agglomeration of goods and a supply conceived as a "dreamed for supply." The split supply is on its part made to face a conceptually split demand, with the attendant result of creating a cognitively ambiguous situation. The demand for the supply conceived in terms of nonexisting goods is looming as large, if not larger, in Keynes' conception than the demand for a supply conceived in terms of goods which are readily available.

Keynes' demand and supply scheme is slated to serve as an instrumentality for dream-like projections in which the individual projector is supposed to be free to indulge. Torn by inner conflicts, uncertain of what he wants, and unmindful of what he could really get, the individual on whose decision the operation of the demand and supply scheme is to depend, is not expected ever to reach any conclusion. No specification, no concretization of demand and supply could ever be attained were Keynes' demand and supply scheme to be put to a test. Social and economic analysts who might fancy themselves that they can devise a procedure for spelling out in numbers the operation of Keynes' demand and supply scheme are sure to learn that they have set out to seek a will-o'-the-wisp.

In following up his sniping attacks on the postulates of the classical theory, Keynes tries to make a case for sheer limitless abstractions. Unnecessary qualifications, Keynes infers, are likely to become obstructions to an overwide range reasoning. Superfluous categories, the neo-classical theorist of deemployment implies, make the sustaining of an overlarge perspective unfeasible. The upholding of price as a separate category, Keynes proffers an exemplification, stands in the way of an oversimplification of questions of demand and supply. The sustaining of real and net output as terms with a specific meaning, Keynes appears to be ready with another demonstration, presents a cognitive deterrent to having production treated as a superabstraction.

Take, in turn, prices and real output, Keynes continues his argumentation, should each of those two denotations continue to rate as meriting a specific social and economic signification, such signification could hardly be squared with a demand category in the signification of which realized output and existing prices are *not* to be permitted to play any socially and economically specifiable role.

To remedy the methodological and terminological situation which precludes the drowning of the conception of demand in a maze of sheer limitless subjectivistic speculations, Keynes is ready to take drastic measures. Keynes does not hesitate to decree that prices and real output are to be ruled out as effective social and economic norms. He does not shrink from ordering that prices, real and net output, cease to be used as terms which refer to specifiable social and economic factors.

Should prices, real and net output, be regarded as lacking social and economic distinctiveness, Keynes reasons, a methodological and terminological objection to the formulation of demand in a socially and economically indistinctive manner could hardly be raised. The social and economic designification of prices, real and net output, Keynes wants to make it sure, is in particular to disqualify those designations from serving as effective leads in the determination of the demand for employment and the demand for wages.

The demand for employment as well as the demand for wages, Keynes finds it opportune to stress, are not to be viewed as expressing any ascertainable aspect of social and economic life. The demand for employment and the demand for wages are not supposed to express a factor which could reasonably be expected to materialize. The demand for employment as well as the demand for wages are not to be allowed to express the impact of any particular object. The demand for employment as well as the demand for wages are to be considered as but phases in the flow of something indeterminable. The demand for employment, as well as the demand for wages, Keynes wants to have consigned to the realm of the unaccountable, and uncountable.

After having satisfied himself that his drive for the acceptance of overgeneralizations has led him to plead for a terminology which is not to mean anything particular, if it is to mean anything at all, Keynes turns around and launches an attack on a focal concept on the ground that it presents too large an abstraction. He girds himself for leading an onslaught on the general category of time. Keynes is particularly concerned with having to honor the aspect of time sequence, in view of his reluctance to acknowledge a succession in the phases of production. Were he to continue to grant recognition to the distinction of the preceding and succeeding aspects in the general run of time, Keynes is aware he could logically not deny that the phase which he terms as current production constitutes but the preceding stage of what generally has been referred to as a future production phase. Should he retain time sequence as analytical medium, Keynes is very conscious, he could hardly present it as being open to questioning, that the phases referred to as current and future production are, on their part, but succeeding phases of a production which is being linked with the past. Should he uphold the conception of time sequence and adhere consequentially to a signification of a distinction between current, future, and past production, Keynes fully realizes, he could by the same token not refuse a distinct signification to present, (or in his terminology, current) future and past demand.

Should he accept the conception of a definite time sequence as a prerequisite of reasoning, Keynes expresses apprehension, he cannot reasonably prevent time sequence from asserting itself in any analysis of a given demand situation, he Keynes, is prone to undertake. Should a definite time sequence be considered ascertainable, Keynes fears, the assertion that such a sequence stops short of manifesting itself in any correlation of demand with supply, could hardly be made plausible.

To safeguard the presumption of social and economic unmeasurability of demand, to the sustaining of which he has pledged himself, Keynes proceeds to block an integrated view on time. To guarantee the social and economic incommensurability of demand as related to supply, the neo-classical theorizer of deemployment is determined to render time sequence well nigh incomprehensible. In an effort to underwrite the social and economic incongruity of demand and supply, Keynes is in particular bent on having time sequence disqualified as a relevant analytical factor.

The present and the past, Keynes lays down his dictum, are not to be regarded as ascertainable time aspects. All time phases but that of the future, Keynes orders, are to be refused any recognition as an analytical factor. The future on its part, is to undergo what can be characterized as individuation. The future is to be treated as if it were nothing but a form of personal expectation.

A personal expectation, Keynes amplifies, does not lie within the range of any specific time period. A personal expectation is in particular not supposed to have any relation with any conceivable conception of time sequence. The designation of personal expectations is supposed to refer to nothing but a maze of the indeterminate. The designation of personal expectations, by Keynes, is supposed to denote nothing but a race with a time element which had been turned loose.

Personal expectations are to Keynes nothing but unpredictable eruptions. Personal expectations present to Keynes but a stream of an otherwise unidentifiable individual consciousness. On the record, Keynes is amenable to have a distinction maintained between short term and long term expectations. He is prepared to distinguish, so he says, between personal expectations which refer to the use of capital actually invested and personal expectations

271

which refer to capital the investment of which is anticipated. He is, moreover, willing to differentiate, so he claims, between personal expectations which refer to existing equipment and personal expectations which are referred to nonexisting equipment.

Keynes is i.e. forced to admit that subjective expectations which have an objective foundation, differ somewhat from subjective expectations, which are based solely on subjective speculations. His admission, however, does not present any move in the direction towards the revalidation of the determinable in the signification of expectations. Keynes is but making preparations for a terminological fence ride. He suggests the terming of expectations which contain some reference to objective factors as short term expectations and the terming of expectations with no reference to objective considerations as long term expectations. Since neither of the two kinds of expectations is to be held determinable to any appreciable degree, the terminological distinction Keynes offers between short term and long term expectations does not constitute a move which could conceivably lead to a comparatively greater differentiation. The term short term expectations remains, by and large, as indeterminable as the term long term expectations, within the range of Keynes' formulations.

To erase any doubt that the terms short term and long term expectations are advanced by him in an effort to bring about a less pronounced social and economic distinctiveness in his conception of time, Keynes burdens the terms of short term and long term expectations with some qualifying clauses. The term short term expectations is to be made to refer to effected production equipment under the condition that such reference is to be regarded as subsidiary. The denotation of short term expectations is to be held as having a relation to realized production, provided such relation is to be regarded, as having a transitional character.

Short term expectations, Keynes wants to make it sure with the qualification he advances, are to be prevented from acquiring any social economic distinctiveness of their own. Short term expectations are to be conceived in a manner which is to provide for their submerging in the maze of long term expectations. Short term expectations, and their implicit link to objectified conditions, are to be so framed as to insure their merging with the subjectivistic conception of long term expectations.

The differentiation between short term and long term expectations is not to become more than nominal, Keynes makes it certain, with the qualifications he is putting forward. As far as their social and economic ascertainability is concerned, short term expectations are not to differ from long term expectations. Expectations, whether they are called long term or short term expectations, are not supposed to express expectations which can be assayed in any specific manner. Expectations whether they are called short term or long term expectations, are not supposed to express expectations which are realizable in any length of time. In trying to make a case for a nominal distinction between short term and long term expectations, Keynes is but engaged in creating the impression that something can be made known about nothing.

Keynes' scheme to have the ascertainment of social and economic factors involved in production and employment blocked, could hardly be considered complete, were he not to undertake to becloud the social and economic aspects of costs. Costs, after all, occupied a focal position in the postulations of the classicists. In assigning costs a key role in his argumentation, Ricardo was able to solve quite a few social and economic riddles which had hitherto beset the analysis of production. In placing the discussion of costs in the center of his discourse, Ricardo attained an unprecedented high level of systematization. The cost category presented therefore a quite tempting target for mutilation for one who has become engaged in a drive to dispose of conceptual means of social and economic identification.

Keynes does not disappoint those who expect him to dismantle the cost category. He is quick to express great misgivings about the placing of costs within a national economic range. The treatment of costs as a uniform category is distasteful to Keynes. He is horrified by the thought of having a socially integrated view on costs prevail. He is determined to make shambles out of the classical cost category. He pledges himself to the task of having the cost analysis lose itself in a maze of unrelated details.

The classicists, Keynes complains, have been opposed to the

273

splitting of the cost category. If it would have been left to him, he, Keynes, would have forced the classicists to reserve the rating of objective costs for costs which refer to purchase of equipment and material. As for himself, Keynes is determined to refashion the classical view on costs by granting only those costs an objective i.e. a social signification which are calculable without any direct relation to actual production. In turn, Keynes sees himself in the role of forcing the classicists at this late date to accept a completely subjective rating for those costs which are incurred by way of actual production expenditures.

If Keynes is to have his way, the costs of actual production, i.e. the costs which have been treated by Ricardo as the supreme indicator of social factors involved in the process of production, are to be left to the appraisal by individuals who are supposed to plead innocent of knowing anything about the impact of social relations on costs.

The analysis of costs of production can result in nothing but a maze of socially unrelated figures, should an individualistic conception of costs of production, as the one Keynes proposes, to be applied throughout. The appraisal of production costs within a subjectivistic framework, as the one suggested by Keynes, can lead but to an enmeshment of the analytical procedure in a mosaic of indeterminate detail.

Keynes has a special reason to preach evasion of the social signification of production costs; should he be successful in his attempt to distort the classical view on costs, he fully realizes, he could furnish himself with a convenient springboard for the subjecting of the classical conceptualization of income to a successive undermining venture. Should his suggestion to prevent a unified outlook on costs be accepted, a socially integrated view on income could hardly be maintained. Should his scheme of the splitting of costs into two conceptually incongruous parts be followed, Keynes is fully conscious, the conception of income, as the focal expression of social and economic division, would be dealt a hard blow.

The classicists, Keynes observes with particular displeasure, attached their conceptualization of income to a socially projected production. The classicists, Keynes notices with distaste, had made a radical conceptual step in the direction of having income explained in terms of other than exchange factors. The classicists, and Smith in particular, have signaled their frontal assault on mercantilistic conceptions by denying exchange factors a direct access to the signification of income, Keynes becomes greatly disturbed. The classicists have made it a keystone of their social and economic comprehension, to have the exchange factor consigned to the sphere of the apparent, Keynes is disconsolate. The author of the "General Theory" regrets that he had not been present to favor the classicists with the advice to fall back on mercantilistic conceptions. Keynes is full of remorse that he was not available at the proper time to order the classicists to postulate aggregate income as an exchange category.

Keynes at any rate wants aggregate income formulated in a manner in which a relation of income to the social effects of the production process is not to play any role. Production, in turn, is to be prevented from manifesting any social effects in the comprehension offered by Keynes. Production is, by direction of Keynes, to be made to relate nothing but managerial skills. The conception of production is to be reduced to the range of an individual managerial efficiency.

The classicists would they have been permitted to come in at this stage of Keynes' deliberations, could surely be expected to point out to their latter day detractor that they, the classicists, set themselves the task of analyzing production within as wide a range as possible, in order to promote a clearer understanding of the social implications of the production process. Adam Smith as the mastermind of the classicists, were he be given an opportunity to face Keynes and argue in favor of his, Smith's, conception of production can, in turn, be expected to remind his belated critic that he, Smith, was greatly concerned in his "Wealth of Nations" with the proposition of overcoming the limited onesided view of the physiocrats on the nature of production.

Smith and Ricardo are to be considered as being fully within their literary rights, were they to present their side of the controversy with Keynes by pointing out that their persistence in bringing out social factors in all stages of production, as well as in all the spheres of production (agricultural as well as nonagricultural) constitutes their major contribution. Smith and Ricardo can well rely upon their literary record were they be given the opportunity to make it known to Keynes that the inclusion of social factors along the entire line of their argumentation in which production in all its spheres is linked with income in all its forms. had cleared the way for an accounting for the social preconditioning, as well as the social effects of the new technology.

Had they, the classicists, not included the social factors in their analysis of production in all its spheres and aspects, Smith and Ricardo can, furthermore, argue on the basis of what they had to say, in their time, the social impact which led to the industrial revolution as well as the social impact which was brought about by the machine could not have been fully recorded and therefore could hardly have been understood.

The limiting of the analysis of production to the manifestation of managerial skills, as insisted upon by Keynes, the classicists would not have failed to find out, is obviously intended to clear the conceptual ground for a social designification of income in all its forms with respect to all its analytical stages. Keynes himself, makes it dawn upon anybody who tries to grasp what he, Keynes, expects to attain by his underhanded attacks on the classicists. His, Keynes', verbal barrage against classical conceptions can in the main be viewed as a means by which he seeks to clear the conceptual road for his design to create an unbridgeable analytical gap between the conceptualization of aggregate income and the conceptualization of net income. There should be little doubt that Keynes expects to furnish himself with an authorization by his lefthanded assault on the approach of the classicists to the analysis of production and income, to render the linking of net income and aggregate income analytically inconceivable. Any social and economic theorizer who, in pursuing the classical tradition, continues to maintain that net income is derived from gross or aggregate income, is most certainly to draw Keynes' ire. The classicists are most guilty, in the eyes of Keynes, for not allowing a conceptual incongruity and a social and economic incommensurability of aggregate and net income to be recorded in their respective theoretical discourses.

Keynes makes it appear, as if he is at a loss to understand why

276

the classicists had failed to disestablish any conceivable analytical link between aggregate and net income. Why did the classicists insist on the social signification of all forms of income, Keynes poses a naive question. Why did the classicists persist, Keynes pretends he does not know the answer, in conducting their systematic analysis in a way in which income in all its forms came to be related with the kind of social relations framework out of which the specific income forms have come to arise.

Had they listened to him, Keynes gives the impression of grieving, the classicists would have desisted from embracing a conception in which social and economic stratification is laid at the core of all income division. The classical thinkers have made a fundamental error in Keynes' presumption, by having conducted a socially relevant analysis of all forms of income. Had the classicists consented to compress income derived from production into a managerial frame as he, Keynes, has suggested, the author of the "General Theory" sounds off with a devious argument, they the classicists could hardly have advanced any methodological or terminological objection against having the determination of net income perceived as a mere bookkeeping feature as he, Keynes, proposes to do.

The classicists, Keynes voices a particular objection, should have equated gross income and trading profits. Had the classicists treated the categories of gross income and trading profits as interchangeable, Keynes suggests the inference, profits could not have been made to play the role of a general income category. The classicists, Keynes is once more ready with a belated advice, should not have permitted profits to become a focal social and economic category. The classicists should have indicated that profits in their general aspect are neither socially nor economically determinable, to please Keynes. Had the classicists been willing to regard gross income and gross profits as interchangeable, Keynes remonstrates, they would have demonstrated by such treatment that profits do not present any overriding social and economic factor.

By subsequently insisting that net profits are to be regarded as arrived at by way of a personalized accounting device, Keynes reveals that the twin conceptions of gross income and gross profits which he is trying to advance, are not supposed to be any wider in range than a conception which can be placed within a managerial range. Net profits emerge from Keynes' treatment in the form of an individualized accounting of firms with reference to gains made by their trading practices. Keynes but underscores by such treatment of the factor of net profits that he is not willing to recognize a general category of profits in a societal dimension. The kind of category on which the classicists had based their reasoning remains unacceptable to Keynes. Profits do not rate more than a peculiar device for the reading of the cash register of certain trading enterprises, in the formulation insisted upon by Keynes.

Keynes' subsequent injection of a quantitative note is to create the impression that the quantitative methods of the classicists have been found wanting. Actually, Keynes sets out to criticize not the stand on quantification which the classicists had taken, but the position which he considers the classicists should have taken. He thus becomes engaged in what can be termed as knocking down of a straw man. Keynes' criticism of the methods of ascertaining the degree of approximation which is ostensibly directed at the classicists, constitutes but an attack on his own preconception in regard to quantification.

Keynes argues under the presumption that the classical postulation of aggregate income which is derived from the employment of productive resources, had given way to his, Keynes', conception of aggregate income in the sense of an aggregate of traded goods. He announces in consequence, his resolution to exert a rigorous exactitude in the determination of aggregate income the conception of which, he fancies himself, he had forced upon the classicists.

While the presumption that the classicists have been posthumously made to change their mind on their conception of aggregate income on Keynes' insistence. can hardly be considered credible, Keynes' plea and promise to attain more exact results with reference to his own conception of aggregate income, does not sound unconvincing. After all, it is quantitatively less of a problem to get exact figures on the turnover of specified goods in specified enterprises, to which Keynes' own conception of aggregate income refers, than it is to get exact data on all goods and services which are produced as well as traded in any number of and any

278

kind of enterprises to which the unfalsified classical conception of aggregate income makes reference.

Keynes further argues under the presumption that the classical postulation of net income in the sense of net national economic gains from the development of productive resources, has been supplanted by his own conception of net income in the sense of net gains which are to be derived from personal managerial skills. In consequence, Keynes pleads for the acceptance of the inaccuracy in the accounting of net income as a deficiency which cannot be corrected.

While again Keynes' presumption that the classicists have been posthumously made to change their mind in regard to the conception of net income on the basis of Keynes' prodding, can hardly be granted any credibility, Keynes' resignation to inexactitude in the ascertainment of what he conceives to be net income, is not entirely unfounded. Conceivably it is a quantitatively more perplexing problem to furnish exact data on income which is derived from such elusive a factor as personal managerial skills to which Keynes' formulation of net income refers, than it is to provide accurate data on net income in the sense of determinable national and international economic gains attained through the development of clearly ascertainable productive resources (human and nonhuman) to which the undistorted classicists' conception of net income makes reference.

Keynes continues his misplaced criticism of the quantification methods of the classicists by pretending that the classical postulation of gross profits, in the sense of gains scored by owners of productive property, has given way to his own designation of gross profits conceived solely as trading gains. In consequence, he advances a proposition that gross profits lie within the range of the foreseeable.

The classicists' conception of gross profits has not of course disappeared from their discourses, to deliver Keynes the rebuke he deserves. In giving Keynes what is due to him and the classicists what is due to them, it does not appear unplausible, to give Keynes the proper weight, that gross profits conceived as mere trading gains, the conception which Keynes favors, are more likely to fall within the scope of the foreseeable than the gross profits conceived as gains scored by owners of productive property, a conception to which the classicists had continuously adhered.

A much simpler mathematical procedure is no doubt required to calculate the amount of gross profits of trading enterprises for not too distant a future to what Keynes' formulation refers, as compared with the quantification devices which are necessitated for foretelling of the amount of gross profits of productive enterprises with a due consideration of the technological development and the interplay of the social and economic forces which prompt such development which are referred to in the classical formulation.

Keynes, on his part, argues under the presumption that the classical postulation of net profits, in the sense of net gains scored by owners of productive property, has been displaced by his, Keynes', conception of net profits which refers but to a bookkeeping device. On the basis of the stated presumption Keynes argues that net profits are unpredictable.

In spite of Keynes' presumptuousness, to put the author of "The Theory of Employment" in his place again, the classicists' version of net profits has not been removed from the treatises of the classical writers. As far as Keynes' insistence is concerned, that net profits, which he conceives as a bookkeeping figure, are unpredictable, such assertion appears without much foundation at first glance. Since Keynes asserts that gross profits conceived by him as trading profits are foreseeable, and that assertion comes to be warranted to some extent, his subsequent insistence on having net profits of those trading enterprises regarded as unpredictable is not at once explicable. Since Keynes shows no indication of challenging the regular bookkeeping procedure which arrives at net profits by way of deductions to be made from gross profits, it can be but assumed that he is staking the case for the unpredictability of net profits on the presumption of the indeterminability of the deductions which are to be made from the gross profits. That such is the case, can be inferred from Keynes' insistence on the uncalculability of deductions from gross profits, when he refers to net profit gains as unpredictable. He is even setting out to demonstrate the uncalculability of deductions from gross profits when he proceeds to relate quantification with regard to output.

Following his by now customary procedure, Keynes advances

the presumption that the classical postulation of output as a social product has been superseded by his, Keynes', designation of output as an asocial product. Consequently, he argues, output presents nothing but a ceaseless stream.

Once more Keynes has to be put in his place by having it made known to him that the classical treatment of output as a social product, constitutes one of the conceptual landmarks of classical thought, in spite of any attempt by any theoretical latecomer to give the impression that the stated approach of the classicists had been reversed. With regard to the strictly Keynesian conception of output which conceives output as exclusively current output, Keynes' inference that no time limit can be set with regard to such output cannot be challenged on logical grounds. The classical conception of output which, by contrast, makes a distinction between output effected in the past and output effected in the present warrants, in turn, the reference to limited time periods in any analysis of output, no matter how disturbing Keynes would like that kind of definiteness in the conception of timing to appear. Even if the classicists could have been prevailed upon to abstain from making a direct reference to periods of production, as Keynes would have liked them to do, a specific designation and definite timing of output would still have been feasible within the analytical range of their conception. Had the classicists continued to use the term of investment and consumption in the sense in which they have treated these terms in their discourses, a complete resignation on their part to a social and economic untraceability of the disposition of output would not have been logically and methodologically called for within the framework of their systematic reasoning.

It is only the substitution of Keynes' view on investment and consumption for the classical conception of investment and consumption which predetermines an analytical deadlock with regard to the tracing of the disposition of output. Within the classical conception of consumption in which output was conceived in terms of material goods, the designation of output for consumption remained socially and economically identifiable. It is only within Keynes' own characteristic conception of consumption that the designation of output for consumption loses its social and economic definiteness. It is Keynes' objection to viewing consumption in terms of material goods, it is, moreover, Keynes' insistence on viewing consumption in no other terms but spending, which furnishes the terminological as well as the methodological basis for a complete disruption of any attempt to explain the realization of consumption.

The terminological undifferentiation of consumer and producer's goods on the part of Keynes is obviously intended to predetermine the social and economic undistinguishability of the use of producer's goods from the use of consumer's goods. In the face of his refusal to uphold even a terminological separation between means of production and means of consumption, little, if any sense, can be attributed to Keynes' elaborate discussion of obsolescence and depreciation.

How is the factor of obsolescence to be applied to something which is supposed to be indeterminable, Keynes should be asked the direct question. What procedure is to be used, Keynes should be queried, for the assessing of depreciation of a product which is to be considered unspecifiable in either terms of production or terms of consumption.

In his dealing with obsolescence and depreciation, Keynes should be forced to admit, he has been caught in the web of his own preconceptions. By having refused to recognize time as a specifiable factor, Keynes should have realized he has committed himself to a nonrecognition of a conceptualized distinction between regularity and nonregularity. By having denied the existence of a specifiable materiality with regard to goods, Keynes should have been aware, he has made it conceptually unfeasible for himself to distinguish between objective and subjective factors in depreciation.

As an expounder of an extreme personalization of time, and a proponent of indeterminable materiality,—it does dawn upon Keynes,—he has made it compulsory for himself to emphasize the irregular in what he presents as a calculation of depreciation. He has to take recourse to turns and twists in argumentation, it does impress itself upon Keynes, to have objective factors submit to the most subjective considerations in the ascertainment of the kind of depreciation charges which he advances. Keynes did come to appreciate that the disqualification of regularity and accountability at which he had arrived was by the very logic of his argumentation, to lead him to the depreciation of the very meaning of depreciation. Keynes, nevertheless, does not show any signs of being in any way disturbed by the impasse at which he has arrived. He shows signs of perfect satisfaction with the chaotic condition of social and economic analysis which he has brought about.

He is, moreover, delighted with the prospect of leaving consumption within the range of the indeterminable. He is but extending his designs of deconceptualization by having the conception of investment included in his deconceptualization effort. He is fully cognizant that, by having investment rendered as indeterminable as consumption, he can make his entire consumption investment scheme,—the keystone of his entire employment theory,—mean next to nothing.

His formulation of investment, Keynes wants to make it sure, is to steer clear of specifying the use which is made of investment. Any defining of investment on his part, Keynes is quite outspoken about it, is in particular to avoid any reference to a material realization. In his conception of investment, Keynes boasts, he wants to be careful not to succumb to the classicists' position on investment.

The classical position which approached investment as but an extraneous aspect of production, is scrupulously eschewed by Keynes. Investment, Keynes decrees, is not to be viewed as referable to a specific time sequence. To conceive of investment as analyzable within the framework in which a distinct and distinguishable present follows a distinct and distinguishable past, is to be labeled as a misconception, on the strength of Keynes' directive.

The delineation of investment, in the way it had been undertaken by Smith and Ricardo, is to be avoided, under any circumstances, Keynes demands. The formulation of investment in a manner which makes allowance for a correlated signification of socially and economically identifiable production periods, is to be termed as singularly misleading, on orders from Keynes.

The contrasting of past and present investment is placed by Keynes beyond the realm of the comprehensible. A conceptualized distinction between past investment and present investment, Keynes lays down the law, is to be regarded as inconceivable.

Were he to consent to a contradistinction of past and present investment, Keynes can be overheard reasoning with himself, he would jeopardize his aim to avoid having to contend with an analysis of investment in terms of recognizable causes and identifiable effects. As a precautionary step against such unwelcome contingency, Keynes rules out any respective direct reference to past and present. To exclude the feasibility of any consecutive analytical distinction Keynes is not even prepared to accord past and present investment specific terms.

The denotations past and present are slated to disappear from the vocabulary, as far as their reference to investment is concerned. As far as the delineation of the past and present in regard to investment is concerned, Keynes is not willing to have it specified in any other form than by an indeterminate reference. Current investment is to be considered as the only legitimate term for referring to past and present investment.

The very indefiniteness of the term current investment which Keynes lovingly embraces, is fully in keeping with his determination to cultivate indistinctiveness, as far as the realization of investment is concerned. With the term current investment, Keynes wants not only to remove distinctive time factors from any investment analysis; the term current investment is supposed to serve him as a terminological device in his drive to have objective considerations denied any signification with regard to investment. The denotation of current investment is slated to be used by Keynes as a terminological vehicle for the rendering of all investment deals socially and economically meaningless.

Keynes finds it greatly convenient to take refuge in the term current investment when he is confronted with the proposition of stating, whether all investment is made out of personal whims or whether any rational calculations might also enter into an investment deal. Keynes finds it opportune to invoke the term current investment when he is faced with the problem of ascertaining whether investment transactions reflect nothing but fleeting personal moods, or, whether, some long range objective planning has also some bearing on the investment flow.

The very indeterminability of what current investment is made to refer, predestines that term to play the role of a terminological instrumentality by a reference to which any interrogation whether investment has or has not any wider social and economic implications, can be effectively blocked. The very indeterminability of what is supposed to constitute current investment makes the term well fit to serve as a screen for Keynes' refusal to answer the question, whether all that an investment analysis is to be concerned with is supposed to be limited to the range of personal investment manipulations, or, whether, an investment analysis is to be conducted with a view of providing an understanding of some of its respective wider social and economic ramifications. The very unspecifiability of the scope and range of "current investment" is designed to furnish an obstacle, through a reference to it, to the attainment of any meaningful account of what investment is all about.

The denial of social and economic signification to investment, to which Keynes is committed, goes hand in hand with his refusal to advance a social and economic understanding of what is involved in the refraining from investment. The designification of the utilization of investment on the part of Keynes, finds its counterpart in his disqualification of the factor of nonutilization of investment to serve as a meaningful link in an explanation of what the author of the "Theory of Employment" wants to be known by the term de-investment. The separation of investment in the analytical procedure from any socially and economically significant contact with production on which Keynes insists, finds its pendant in his insistence on the detachment of an attempted encompassing of de-investment from any socially and economically meaningful relation with the production process. Keynes' discounting of the material aspect of investment is being fully matched by his disregard of the material aspects as far as they affect non-investment.

The case he has made against honoring sequence and causation with regard to investment, Keynes takes a selfassertive attitude, absolves him from paying any attention to sequence and causation as far as non-investment is concerned. His effort to undifferentiate time elements in respect to the investment sphere, Keynes presumes, entitles him to abstain from differentiating the run of time as regards non-investing.

Keynes is particularly on guard against making any specific reference to one of the time elements when he deals with non-investing. He is very meticulous in withholding any social and economic signification of the future from his formulation of non-investment. He is determined not to permit the future to become more than a glimmer in the view of de-investment which he is set to expound. Keynes is fully committed to the task of preventing the time element future, as well as any other time elements, from becoming distinct in the comprehension of non-investment which he is set to propagate.

As a concomitant of his barring of time sequence from playing any signified part in the comprehension of non-investment, Keynes sets up roadblocks against the effectuation of social and economic causation. The compounding of the indeterminability of time with the unspecifiability of causation, Keynes appears to feel sure, insures a sufficient disorientation in conceptualization to make his, Keynes', assertion that non-investment is due to nothing but the vaguest of individual premonitions acceptable without any serious challenge.

The maze of indistinctiveness into which he makes non-investment submerge, Keynes assumes an air of selfsatisfaction, is as lacking of social and economic contours as the maze of indistinctiveness in the web of which investment is to be enmeshed. His denial of a distinctive social and economic identification to investment, coupled with his refusal to accord a distinct social and economic identification to non-investment, Keynes is extremely pleased, makes it conceptually unfeasible for him to arrive at a social and economic contradistinction between investment and non-investment. Since he rules out a definite social and economic delineation for either investment or non-investment, Keynes is proud of his tour de force, he is free to leave the determination of what is invested and what is not invested, to individual hunches.

He frankly does not expect that a personal guess can be of any great assistance in an effort to set the comprehension of investment apart from the comprehension of non-investment. By leaving it all to a hunch, Keynes realizes, he is but advocating a course which is to lead to an analytical dead end. An attempt to determine by hunches what distinguishes investment from non-investment, Keynes is keenly aware, is bound to be utterly futile. Hunches are to prove so unreliable in regard to any attempted social and economic differentiation between investment and non-investment, Keynes is fully cognizant, as to drive the individual guesser into despair.

In anticipation of such a contingency, Keynes is ready to take a most radical step. Without waiting for the guesser to dissipate himself by fruitless guesses, Keynes is ready to draw the conclusion that the reference to investment and non-investment by separate terms, is bound to become senseless in the absence of any objective social and economic criterion for the determination of either of the two factors. To bolster the case he is making for the indeterminability of investment and non-investment, Keynes wants another feature added. To strengthen his defeatist position, Keynes goes on record in favoring indeterminability in regard to what makes for a change from investment to non-investment and vice versa. The reason for turning investment into non-investment, and vice versa, is, Keynes asserts, bound to remain indefinite. A change from the invested status to the status of the non-invested, and vice versa, Keynes insists is to be regarded as wholly unpredictable. A transition from investment to non-investment is to be held as socially and economically unaccountable as the very factor of investment and de-investment. A changeover from investment to non-investment, and vice versa, Keynes reapplies his personal guess theory, is to be considered as a manifestation of nothing else but a change in a person's mood. The changeover from investment and non-investment, Keynes wants it to be inferred, can be as little guessed as the situation in the investment and non-investment spheres which preceded the respective changeovers. Hence, an attempt, Keynes wants it restressed, to identify a change from non-investment (or to use Keynes' term, de-investment) as well as the change to non-investment (read de-investment) in any specific form, has to fall short of realization. Hence, the very term of non-investment—read de-investment—becomes devoid of any specific meaning and is thus rendered useless by Keynes for the gaining of any social and economic understanding of investment factors.

Since the fundamental social and economic factors which account for investment, as well as the basic social and economic considerations which account for non-investment, are to be eliminated from the range of the knowable, Keynes advances a devious argument, the continued reference to non-investment as saving is to become socially and economically meaningless. Saving, Keynes throws another barb at the classicists, refers to a socially and economically identifiable aspect of human activity in its presentation by the classicists. Saving is not undertaken by anybody, the classicists make Keynes realize, without a determined effort to get a clear picture of the predictable as against the unpredictable factors which loom in the future. Saving, the classicists make Keynes concede, involves an effort to relate in the most distinct form as possible, the presently existing social and economic conditions with those conditions which are expected in the future. Saving, the classicists make Keynes aware, is predicated upon the clarification of the past and present in their correlation with the future, in the most distinct social and economic terms.

Lest he be suspected that he might be willing to make some concession to a more distinct social and economic formulation of non-investment, Keynes denounces the word saving. He declares the word saving as useless, since he is keenly aware that the very pronouncement of that word makes it incumbent upon its pronouncer to grant ascertainableness of time elements and allow for a determination of causes in the flow of social and economic life. Lest it be implied that he would be willing to go along with an objective interpretation of saving, Keynes wants to be excused from uttering that ominous word. Instead of the denotation of saving, Keynes suggests the use of the term de-investment. His suggestion implies that he does not care to dignify the factor of saving by the use of a positive denotation.

He does not want, by the same token to recognize saving as a social and economic phenomenon of its own. He is bent on having social and economic indistinctiveness pervade the sphere of non-saving, no less than the sphere of saving, Keynes is as much bent on having social and economic signification of saving precluded as he is determined to have saving deprived of any specific social and economic meaning.

An added note of obfuscation is brought into the picture by Keynes' refusal to sustain a recognizable contradistinction between fixed and liquid investment.

Keynes' insistence on having the terms investment and deinvestment used solely for the indication of the purchase and sale of titles of securities can hardly be considered as a contribution towards the delineation of the social and economic issues which arise out of investment. He is but promoting formulations within the range of which investment is to be made to mean nothing but investment and deinvestment is to allow for no other signification than the one that it represents deinvestment.

Keynes' asseveration that investment and deinvestment do not lend themselves to any but tautological interpretations can hardly bring about a more distinct social and economic understanding of what is involved in either.

Keynes expresses his determination to envelop the social and economic role of investment in as deep a terminological tangle as possible. There is nothing more Keynes would like than to have investment and deinvestment appear as but forms of individual self-realization. In their ultima ratio investment and deinvestment, are destined by Keynes to play the role of differing degrees of selfgratification.

Investment and deinvestment emerge out of Keynes' presentation as instrumentalities of an inner drive. Investment and deinvestment come to rate in Keynes' treatment as manifestations of speculative desires. Investment and deinvestment come to reflect a variation in personal satisfaction with gambling devices, in the presentation proffered by Keynes.

To reaffirm his negation of a social and economic contradistinction of investment and saving, Keynes rules out the drawing of a distinct social line between the individual who is a saver and the person who is an investor.

He thus crowns his obfuscation of the function of investment and saving to which he devotes a major part of his literary labor by his refusal to make any socially and economically relevant distinction between real and apparent ownership as far as investment and saving are concerned.

For their persistence in sustaining a social and economic contradiction between borrowing and lending, Keynes throws another barb at the classicists. The classical insistence on having creditors and debtors presented as exponents of a really existing social and economic division, draws fire from the author of the "General Theory." The neo-classical innovator prefers to have borrowing and lending pictured as a means of intra-personal gratification.

Borrowing and lending, Keynes is particularly sensitive about it, are not to be regarded as taking place in an acquisitive nexus. Keynes would like to leave the impression that lending and borrowing transactions are but means to sustain consumption.

Consumption, in turn, is not conceived by Keynes in any socially or economically definable form. Consumption, Keynes makes it sure, is to remain but a vague notion in any reference which is made to it.

He rests content with a side-tracking of the issue of social and economic identification, regardless whether the reference is made to borrowing, or lending, or consumption. He is satisfied with linking borrowing and lending with a kind of consumption which cannot be clearly comprehended.

The neo-classical innovator gratifies himself, moreover, with forestalling of a balanced view on the social and economic effects of borrowing and lending. It pleases Keynes to deny that the net effect of borrowing presents as real and significant a condition as the net effect of lending. It serves his fancy to regard only the lending transaction as something more or less ponderable.

Keynes takes it upon himself to permit only the role of the creditors to retain a certain degree of social and economic identifiability. He shows, in turn, signs of determination to have borrowing transactions committed to the range of imponderables. He is not willing to pursue a more than hazy discussion of the social and economic role of the debtor. The net social and economic effect of lending is graced by Keynes by having it accorded a certain measure of reality. The net social and economic effect of borrowing is on its part discarded by the author of the "General Theory," by having it labeled unreal.

Keynes lets only the net effect of lending have some real social and economic significance. He is dead set against having the net effect of borrowing granted more than an apparent social and economic import.

The net effect of borrowing is in Keynes' dictum to be viewed but as an outer manifestation of the net effect of lending.

What lies behind his literary effort to have the social and economic impact of borrowing obscured is not readily disclosed by the author of the "General Theory." The suspicion of the reader that the relegation of borrowing to the sphere of the merely apparent on the part of Keynes, is designed to prevent a realistic social and economic appraisal of what the borrower does with the funds he borrows, is not alleviated in any way by the neo-classical innovator.

Keynes prefers to leave things unsaid. Following his general device, he is utterly unwilling to come out with any distinctive formulation.

Keynes chooses to hide his preconceptions behind insinuations and innuendos, with the classicists serving as his favorite target. He chooses to keep his argumentation as equivocal as possible, in order to lure the reader into reading anything and nothing, into his presentation.

Keynes' evasiveness stands out in bold relief when he reaches the subject of interest. Ostensibly, once more, he raises objections to the classical conception. He finds it opportune to throw it up to the classicists that they have treated interest as a distinct social and economic category. He cites with misgivings the factor that the classicists had drawn a distinct social and economic line between secured and unsecured investments.

The classicists Keynes insinuates, have to be disavowed, since they presented interest and risk premiums as denotations which are socially and economically distinguishable from each other. He posts himself in this instance as a disavower of any specifiability of any social and economic claims. He is gearing himself to the using of social and economic indistinctiveness in interest and risk premiums as a means for the effecting of a reduction of the social and economic claims of the borrower to as vague a notion as the one to which he had reduced the social and economic position of the lender.

In the promotion of deliberate indistinctiveness, in the cultivation of vagueness in his propositions, which form a general characteristic of Keynes' exposition, the author of the "General Theory" provides himself with an authorization for the treating of any generalizing factors at will.

In making unexplained omissions in the sequence of argumentation, Keynes furnishes himself as a rule with a legitimization for the shirking of causative links.

The author of the "General Theory" does, to be sure, not openly disavow the rules of logic. Keynes, to be sure, does not go on record in rejecting methodological restraints. Formally he maintains a given line of reasoning. Nor does he outwardly disclaim precision in advancing his formulations.

It is only when the question is raised, what social relevance has his line of argumentation, when Keynes' reasoning comes to show gaps. It is only when an attempt is made to find out whether his formalistic argumentation has any specific social and economic meaning that the point which Keynes purports to discuss tends to get lost.

It is only when an effort is made to attach any social and economic significance to Keynes' formulations when the "General Theory" comes to stand out as a testing ground for incongruities and inconsistencies of Husserl type alogisms, which can be characterized as logical propositions which are placed within a non-logical cognitive framework.

Since Keynes demonstrates an utter disregard for socially relevant features of economic life, he is bound to lose himself in irrelevancies. Since he expresses an utter disrespect for a socially meaningful conceptualization his exposition cannot acquire any definite social and economic meaning, in spite of the air of respectability of logical reasoning which he tries to maintain.

Since he dedicates himself to the sustaining of a studied social and economic vacuum, his "General Theory" cannot contain much, if any, pertinent social and economic content.

Though Keynes outwardly maintains the validity of logically

arrived inferences, he does not, it should be noted, postulate logic as a normative frame of reasoning. Logic is being posited by the logico-positivistic innovator as but an individual frame of mind.

In his psychologizing of logic it should be granted, he somewhat shies away from fully endorsing incoherence and inarticulation. Keynes, it should be admitted, is somewhat reluctant to have the subconscious endorsed as primary source of social and economic understanding.

The author of the "General Theory" does stay away from directly subscribing to a view which holds that knowledge which is ascribed to intimations of the subconscious is as socially and economically valid as knowledge which is derived from conscious articulation.

Keynes, as contrasted with Schumpeter, avoids the extending of an open invitation to disavow reasoned social and economic accountability. In contradistinction to Schumpeter, Keynes does not advocate the wedding of economic concepts to a socially and economically unaccountable intuition.

The neo-classical innovator does not openly espouse unreason. Keynes holds on to at least a semblance of rationality throughout his entire exposition.

The inner contradiction, the inconsistency of Keynes' presentation, arises out of his implied acceptance of subjectivistic preconceptions. The ambiguities which are found in Keynes' discourse, are largely due to his failure of distancing himself from Menger's and Wieser's presumption that sensualistic vibrations lend themselves to a coherent social and economic explanation.

The presumptuousness of the feasibility of turning every twist and turn in personal sensitivity into a socially and economically measurable factor accounts in large measure for the disabilities from which Keynes' discourse comes to suffer.

It is his siding with the presumption that minute observations of individual hopes and desires constitute an adequate analytical device for the assaying of all the vicissitudes of social and economic life which makes the logico-positivistic innovator conceptually incapable of providing any real social and economic guidance by way of his exposition.

When he accepts the presupposition that a minute recording

of individual anxieties and frustrations can be used as a means for the clarification of crucial social and economic issues, he but reveals in a most glaring fashion his own theoretical inadequacy.

When he suggests reliance on an instrumentality for the quantification of the anxieties of would-be consumers, in regard to investment they wish for and employment they dream of—to be called multiplier—to serve as an indicator of the degree of a general social and economic dislocation, he but testifies to the reaching of a theoretical impasse. By presuming that compounded wishes and dreams can provide a clue for a proper social and economic understanding of the vexed problems of production and employment, Keynes himself furnishes a devastating indictment of his utter theoretical helplessness, if not bankruptcy.

Part 4

The Anti-Anti-Climax of Extreme Subjectivism

CHAPTER 10

MYSTICISM

KEYNES' adherence to the principles of formal logic presents but a thin line of defense in the battle against unreason. His attempt to maintain a front of logical positivism forms a rather pathetic effort to stem the tide of irrationalism. In the revolution of economic thought, Keynes' performance constitutes but a passing gesture.

Schumpeter, not Keynes, foreshadows the ultimate fate of economic fictitiousness. Schumpeter, not Keynes, presages the destination of economic subjectivism. Schumpeter, more than Keynes, sensed the basic destructiveness of individualistic preconceptions. Schumpeter, more than Keynes, recognized that the piling up of inanities upon inanities can hardly be explained in rational terms. Schumpeter, more than Keynes, is aware that the adding of conundrums to conundrums, does not fully square with the rule of reason. Schumpeter, more than Keynes, has come to realize that the cumulative twists of designification can hardly be used to prove anything.

Schumpeter, more than Keynes, has come to know that a mass of conceptual debris can scarcely be made to serve as an effective barrier against nonsensical propositions. The evolvers of marginal utilitarianism, Schumpeter came to adduce, have reduced social and economic inquiries to all but senselessness.

Economic theorizing, Schumpeter was not unmindful, has been reduced to utter sophistry. Literary offerings in economic theory have come to contain not much more than empty phrases, Schumpeter could not help noticing. The form of literary presentation which had been sired by Menger has brought in its wake collections of meaningless expressions. The theoretical formulations which have been impregnated by Wieser, have come to be typified by an assortment of unsignifiable impressions. At the time, Boehm-Bawerk, John Bates Clark and William Stanley Jevons have made their entry on the literary scene—Schumpeter was not uncognizant—the stage has been set for economic theory to become a play with words.

Schumpeter expresses a disquietude over the presumed effectiveness of a barrage of reasoned subterfuge. He prefers to assign reasoned inanities to a subsidiary role in social and economic analysis. He lets unreason take over the analytical mainstream.

In sanctioning the irrational, as the major factor of social and economic comprehension, Schumpeter brings a highly explosive issue to the fore. In having the irrational take precedence over rational conceptions, Schumpeter commits an act of an epistemological counter-revolution. In dethroning rationality as criterion for social and economic validation, Schumpeter invalidates the major precepts of all the social and economic reasoning which went before him.

In placing his major reliance on the irrational, Schumpeter, in turn, foreshadows a further drastic deterioration in social and economic comprehension. The irrationality to which Schumpeter makes social and economic theories succumb, is not far removed epistemologically from the arationality which has come to be expounded by Spann. From the emphasis of the irrational, as an antidote to the rational, there is epistemologically but one step to the emphasis of the arational as antidote to the rational as well as the irrational.

If extreme subjectivism is not to be granted more than an irrational authorization, there arises the legitimate question which has been asked by Spann, whether subjectivistic conceptions have any validity at all.

Othmar Spann to introduce the author of "Tote und Lebendige Wissenschaft" has nothing but scorn for subjectivistic projections. Othmar Spann is full of resentment against the individualistic approach. Othmar Spann does not mind saying it aloud that "marginal utilitarians" are laboring under a fundamental misconception. Othmar Spann speaks his mind in divulging that the exponents of marginal utility theory have misconstrued the pattern of their observation of social and economic life.

Othmar Spann states it most directly that the evolvers of the marginal utility theory have themselves abdicated from the post of a social and economic guide by propagating a distorted view of social and economic reality. Othmar Spann proclaims without any equivocation that the marginal utility theoreticians have busied themselves with the perfection of means for a deliberate omission of relevant aspects of social economic experience in the analytical picture they have devised.

Quantification of personal attitudes which Menger and Wieser posited as an analytical clue, constitutes an unrealizable proposition, Spann discloses. Consequently, Spann reveals, the analytical apparatus which the marginal utility school has set up, cannot but result in a futile attempt to advance any real social and economic understanding.

Subjectified wants, as the marginal utility theoreticians themselves admit, cannot be clearly delineated. Subjectified satisfactions, the marginal utility theorists do not deny, cannot be definitively ascertained. On the strength of what, Spann asks, do the proponents of the marginal utility scheme propose to measure individual wants and satisfactions which they themselves place in the realm of the unspecifiable. Can a something which eludes even a clearcut formulation be quantified, Spann queries. Can a something which can conceivably be termed as nothing, be made subject to a quantitative correlation with another something which can conceivably be termed as nothing, Spann is prompted to ask.

In the conception of marginal utility theorists, Spann is led to observe, any single individual differs in his emotional makeup from any other individual. Any single person is presented as reacting differently to the satisfaction, of what that person is made to regard as his own want, by the proponents of the marginal utility scheme, Spann continues his observation. The reaction of any single person is, in turn, pictured by the marginal utility theorists as being wholly unpredictable in the variation of his individual emotional reactions, Spann notices. No two reactions of the same person to the satisfaction of what that person is made to regard as his want are treated as alike in the marginal utility scheme, Spann comes to know. Each individual, moreover, is denied certitude by the marginal utility schemers in regard to what exactly he is to regard as his want, Spann comes to realize. Subjectified satisfactions become as indeterminable under the postulations of the marginal utility schemers as subjectified wants, Spann is fully cognizant.

How the promotion of the irregular and the nonuniform by the marginal utility schemers can be squared with their effort to demonstrate regularity and uniformity, Spann appears at a loss to understand. How the persistence with which the marginal utility schemers compound the unspecifiability with indeterminability with reference to the comprehension of individual wants and their respective satisfaction is to be brought in line with the professed determination of the marginal utility theorists to evolve an economic law on that basis, Spann finds hard to explain.

Since any definition to which the marginal utility schemers subscribe testifies to the fluidity of subjective manifestations, since, moreover, the very postulation which the marginal utility school advances presupposes that any given subjective manipulation is analytically inseparable from numberless other subjective implications, the delineation of a unit of subjectified reaction within the marginal utility framework is precluded, Spann is justified to state. Since in the marginal utility preconception any given subjectified social and economic consideration flows into any other subjectified consideration, social, economic, or other,—a social and economic entity cannot be evolved within the marginal utility range, Spann has good reason to conclude. Since the marginal utility schemers do not expect a person to have a definite sensual reaction to any given substance, since, in turn, any person's emotional reaction to any given materiality is ruled indeterminable by the marginal utility schemers, the determination whether a said personal reaction does reoccur, or not, comes to present an analytically unfeasible proposition, Spann correctly infers. Since the marginal utility schemers want any person to be considered free to change his sensual reaction to a given material factor at will, they deny by the same token the permissibility of regularity in either impression or expression of a person's sensitivity towards material particles, Spann has grounds to charge.

Since the marginal utility doctrinaires expound the proposition that in a subjectified view on personal satisfactions, any material factor comes to be regarded as undetachable from innumerable other material factors, they deny the feasibility of a subjective comprehension of a separate material unit, and thus place the relation of one material particle to another with regard to their impact on personal satisfaction within the realm of the inconceivable, Spann is fully justified to state in his indictment. No two material particles are comparable with regard to their utility in the subjectivistic conception to which the marginal utility schemers give currency, a marginal utility cannot be conceived of within the limits of a subjectified comprehension, Spann is well advised, in directing his blow at the very preconception of the marginal utility doctrine.

Spann, to be sure, has his own axe to grind. The professed reawakener of social and economic science is not demonstrating the untenability of subjectivistic conceptions in order to point the way back to social and economic objectivity. Spann does not make a case for the reembracement of classical conceptions of social and economic thought. The author of "Tote und Lebendige Wissenschaft" did not consider that by divulging the self-contradictory character of the premises on which the marginal utility theory rested its case he is writing a brief for the restoration of the conceptual framework of Adam Smith and David Ricardo. Spann wants his body blow at the preconceptions of the marginal utility school to serve as a side attack on the premises of classical social and economic thinking. The self-professed awakener of social and economic science would like his assault on the form of validation to which the school of Menger and Wieser came to rely, to be interpreted also as an attack on the criteria of validity to which the school of Smith subscribed. Spann wants to give rise to a clamor that he has not only demonstrated the logical and epistemological untenability of the manner of validation to which the marginal utility school had laid claim, but that he had by the same token furnished a proof that the validation procedure used by the classicists presents a logically and epistemologically unworkable proposition.

In advancing such an over extended claim, Spann fails to notice that he is laboring under a fundamental misconception of his own. He is particularly unaware that the marginal utility schemers and the reasoning framework of classical economic thinkers do not rely upon identical conceptions of reality. The author of "Tote und Lebendige Wissenschaft" obviously assumes that the deliberate fictitiousness to which the marginal utility schemers had to take recourse does not merit any special attention. Spann does not care to acknowledge that the projecting of the individual by the marginal utility theorizers into a social and economic void requires very special consideration. Spann does not concede that the presumption espoused by the marginal utility schemers which pictures the individual as operating in complete social and economic isolation calls for a very specific appraisal. The classicists, by contradistinction, Spann does not want to know, drew their analytical picture in a form which placed the individual within the interplay of social and economic forces of which the individual himself forms a part.

Spann appears to think that the relation of an individual to other individuals does not have to be defined. Spann seems to be of the opinion that the place of the individual in the social and economic matrix does not have to be formulated. Spann apparently considers that the social and economic context in which the individual operates is of no relevance. Spann obviously holds that the word individual is self-explanatory. Spann is obviously satisfied that the mere uttering of the word individual is quite sufficient to account for its meaning. The conceptual problem of setting a criterion by which one individual comes to be distinguished from another individual leaves Spann wholly unconcerned. It does not occur to Spann that he could hardly hold the title of a fundamental reappraiser of social and economic science without giving any thought to the contradistinction between the conception of an individual who is not required to offer any other proof for his, the individual's, social and economic claims than his, the individual's, assertion that he feels psychologically predisposed to make such claims and the conception of an individual who is called upon to establish his social and economic claims in a social and economic contest with other individuals.

It is a matter of complete methodological and epistemological indifference to Spann, whether the individual is conceived as a willfully acting person who is considered free to discount the existence of any other individuals with a view of making socially and economically uncontested claims, or whether, by contrast, the individual is conceived as being by his very existence dependent upon the existence of other individuals whose social and economic claims are established and sustained in a continuous and most real interaction with other persons. The vital analytical distinction between the socially and economically irresponsible way in which the marginal utility theoreticians approach the subject of conceptualization of the individual and the socially and economically responsible form in which the classicists conceptualized the individual, is nowhere registered by Spann.

Spann's disregard for the distinctions in the conceptualization of the individual is matched by his disinclination to pay any attention to conceptual differentiation in other projections. The distinction between the subjective formulation of goods and an objective formulation of the concept of goods, goes likewise unregistered with Spann. Nothing is mentioned in Spann's exposition which would indicate that he was cognizant of the conceptual incongruity of goods perceived as nonmaterial factor and goods conceived as realized matter.

In approaching the subject matter of goods, the author of "Tote und Lebendige Wissenschaft" outdoes the marginal utility schemers in his unwillingness to proffer a social and economic explanation. He refuses to consider any kind of meaningful signification. He proceeds in a manner which gives the impression that he never heard that a struggle has ever taken place in the history of human thought between a meaningful and a meaningless use of words.

When he reaches the subject of goods, he makes it appear, as if the usage of words has never been considered as signifying anything else but a juxtaposition of vowels and consonants. In approaching the subject matter of goods the professed reawakener of social and economic science seems to be imagining that a relation of one word to another has in all literary history meant nothing more than a relation of one sound effect to another sound effect. He obviously considers that he can save himself the trouble of accounting for the difference between the socially and economically relevant and the socially and economically irrelevant in the formulations of goods in the history of social and economic conceptualization, by indulging in a wholesale condemnation.

Instead of trying to analyze and explain in a socially and economically comprehensible way the distinct differences in representative formulations of goods, Spann indulges in the game of placing a word on an index on the ground that the sound effect of that word does not appeal to him. In an effort to avoid answering the question why he is so eager to create a social and economic void around the subject matter of goods, he proclaims a ban on the explosive word, reality. He wants the word reality completely barred. The very mention of the word reality appears to have a disturbing effect on Spann.

He does not care to make a distinction between the use of the word reality in a qualified or unqualified form. He abstains from pointing out the difference between the word reality as applied with regard to material substances and the sound complex of reality uttered in disregard of material factors. He carefully refrains from acknowledging that the word reality is most potent when used as a means of contrasting the unreality of fiction.

Spann follows up his edict against using the word reality by making the paradoxical statement that the postulation of reality of individual life as well as the assumption that specific goods are real, has led to a basic misinterpretation. With this paradoxical pronouncement, Spann seems to imply that the postulation of an objectified approach to reality as it had found expression in the conceptualization of the individual by the classicists, is as meaningless as the subjectivistic reality practiced by the marginal utility schemers in their formulation of goods. His indiscriminate treatment of contrary approaches to reality has obviously brought him to a point at which he squares meaning with meaninglessness. From his professed struggle against meaninglessness Spann emerges as a propounder of the expurgation of the very epistemological criterion of social and economic meaning. By placing the contrasting of reality and unreality beyond cognitive limits he has rendered social and economic comprehension inoperative.

Spann is not conscious that by eliminating any conception of reality as factor of social and economic validation he is lending an air of unreality to his entire subsequent argumentation. Wholly unconcerned about the validity of his claim that the factor of reality is of no relevance in regard to the answering of the question what constitutes an individual and what forms a good, Spann proceeds to root for a social and economic disqualification of the process of exchange. In reapplying his device of indiscriminate condemnation, Spann refuses to differentiate between the two basic conceptions of exchange. Spann is unwilling to acknowledge that there is a distinct difference between the formulation of exchange as an integral part of an objectively conceived social and economic process and the formulation of exchange as a subjectively perceived means for the supplementation of personal consumption. Spann is not prepared to admit that it makes quite a difference whether exchange is presented as a factor which plays a part in the interrelation of social and economic forces as it had been done by the classicists or whether exchange is presented as a factor which is merely related to wishes of an individual in regard to his consumption. Spann, moreover, remains wholly insensitive to the distinction between a formulation of exchange which makes specific reference to the market nexus and a formulation of exchange which refers, whether implicitly or explicitly, to an exchange in kind.

Spann is, furthermore, not disposed to take any notice in his drive for a social and economic disqualification of exchange that it makes quite a difference in any critical evaluation of the exchange factor whether such evaluation refers to an objective appraisal of material elements—the course taken by the classicists—or, whether, such evaluation relates a subjectified evaluation of material particles to which the marginal utility schemers take recourse.

The basic division which sets the classical proposition of a cause and effect relation of objectified factors apart from the marginal utility view which limits the cause effect relation to a correlation of personal feelings goes largely unnoticed with Spann. The wide methodological and epistemological gap which separates the classical proponents of causation from the marginal utility promoters of imputation does not appear to exist for Spann.

His subsequent objection to what he terms the undue significance which has been placed on personal motivation brought about by the embracing of material causation and his chiding of the undue attention which had been paid to individual actions which had come to be directed towards material particles, serves but as confirmation that Spann's understanding of the respective positions taken by the classical systematizers and the marginal utility schemers in regard to the subject of sequence is sadly wanting. Spann does not seem to realize that the classical position is characterized by an emphasis of material causation and a respective deemphasis of personal motivation. Nor does the author of "Tote und Lebendige Wissenschaft" appear to recognize that the marginal utility stand places an overemphasis on personal motivation at the exclusion of all material causation. In his denunciation of personal motivation which towers over material causation Spann misrepresents the position of the classicists. In denouncing individual actions for being directed towards material particles Spann gives a misleading impression of the marginal utility stand. Spann's condemnation of the classicists who are known to be mechanical materialists for an overemphasis of willful subjectivity in their position with regard to sequence can only be classed as an absurd indictment. No less absurd is Spann's denunciation of the marginal utility theorizers who for the most part are known to be metaphysical idealists for the large part which objective material factors are permitted to play in their stand on sequence.

The irresponsibility with which Spann proceeds in his denunciations is carried over into his enunciations. Spann's disqualifications are as arational as his qualifications. His denial of a quality is as much devoid of reason as his espousal of a quality.

Spann does not deny that trading of individuals with individuals does take place. He does not undertake to refute that goods are traded for goods; he nevertheless accompanies the respective enunciation with a major qualification. He insists on having the role of the individual subdued, as far as trading is concerned. What an individual intends or does not intend, is not to merit any attention. Motivation, whether in its individualistic extreme, or, in a socially projected form, is to be viewed as equally unimportant. Nor is much significance to be attached to what a person does or does not do. Personal action or inaction, whether such action is subjectively conceived or objectively projected, is to be regarded as equally insignificant.

Mutual transfers of objects where they take place, trading of good for good, where it does occur,—Spann specifies his qualification—is not to be appraised as more than an incidental factor. Person to person exchange of material objects, even if such exchange constitutes an operation which is representative of the working of a social and economic system, Spann wants to be termed as an inconsequential occurrence.

A person to person exchange is not to merit an investigation which could conceivably determine whether such exchange is non-acquisitive or acquisitive in its design. A person to person exchange, whether it is undertaken in order to supplement the supply of a self-sufficient householder, or, whether it is devised as a means of exchanging supplies among traders, is regarded by Spann as but a minor incident.

The actual phase of turning over of objects from the possession of one trading party to another is to be granted an even lesser significance. The passing of single objects from one trading party to another is to be taken as being merely accidental. The change in ownership of traded goods is, in other words, posited as a wholly unessential factor, in Spann's deconceptualization of exchange. Only accidentally, Spann indirectly concedes, can it become evident that a person to person exchange is predicated upon the transfer in the possession of objects.

Spann goes out of his way to draw attention away from a shift in ownership. The author of "Tote und Lebendige Wissenschaft" makes a supreme effort to bring another kind of shift to the attention of the reader. Foremost attention is to be accorded to the place which exchanged parts take in the interrelation of all parts. Major consideration is to be given to what Spann terms as the shifting of particles within the whole. Spann is not prepared to state, however, what, in his view, forms a particle. Nor, is he willing to disclose what criterion he would like to have applied to determine what constitutes an exchanged part. It remains, moreover, a complete mystery what precisely Spann considers as the course of the movement of the particles.

Any explanation which could conceivably attempt to place the causing of the movement of the so-called particles within the range of the human motivation which prompts the exchange act, Spann obviously wants to avoid. He also shies away from any explanation which could conceivably undertake to interpret a change in the position of the particle, in terms of an effectuation of a human effort which had come to be consummated by an exchange act.

Spann is determined to eschew any inquiry which could conceivably lend a human touch to the unascertainable physical reverberations as which he presents the exchange act. He is set to bar any socially relevant cause from entering into any discussion of operation of exchange. He is utterly opposed to the granting of any socially significant effect to a trading act.

In the presentation he offers, Spann sees to it that the exchange transaction remains bare of any social meaning. In the formulation he advances, Spann makes it sure, an exchange transaction refers to an activity in which those, who engage in it are invariably to suffer from a loss in the sense of social direction. The human parties to the exchange act are destined to remain socially blind in Spann's conception.

Nothing more is to be considered ascertainable about an exchange transaction, Spann is at pains to emphasize, than the gaining of an assurance that the exchange act forms an operation in which each part involved in the respective transaction has a chance to reassert its predestined tie-up with the whole. Those who expect that the assignment to the whole of a quality of a predetermining factor is to be accompanied by a provision for a greater intelligibility of the whole are in for a disappointment.

In referring to the whole, as the ultimate, Spann does not care to provide an analytical dissection of the whole. No other analytical clue is provided by Spann than the mere hint that the whole is not to be regarded as something which can be arrived at by adding up parts. Nothing is said about the identifiability of the whole, no mention is, more specifically, made about ways and means by which the whole could be socially and economically identified.

The whole is posited by Spann as something which is not subject to scrutiny, the whole is, in particular, postulated as something which defies social and economic scrutiny. The quality of predestination which is conferred upon it turns the whole into a kind of mystical preconception. The unspecifiable particle and the incomprehensible whole are offered by Spann as the major components of the exchange act.

He wants his designation of indeterminate particles vacillating around a mystical whole to take the place of a formulation which encompasses the exchange of specifiable objects by identifiable humans. His formulation which presents the exchange deal as an asocial and aeconomic process in which each part is sure to find its predestined location in the whole—Spann seems to infer,—makes it superfluous for him to respect the particular components which enter into a social and economic comprehension of the exchange act. He expresses his contempt for the social and economic delineation of the exchange act by contending that he cannot be refuted when he insists that in the final resolve an exchange deal entered into by two subjects cannot be distinguished from an exchange deal in which a single person is dealing with himself. Neither is it, in the final resolve, feasible, Spann asserts, to differentiate between an exchange deal which encompasses two objects and an exchange act which encompasses but one object. That the stated two contentions constitute nothing less than an inadvertent admission that the deprecation of all conceptual and perceptual safeguards in his formulation of exchange has made his comprehension of the exchange transaction vulnerable to the lures of an unadulterated solipsism is, of course, not recorded by Spann.

The cumulative disintegration of the exchange category at the hands of Spann does not constitute a chance performance on his part. His untiring effort to have the concept of exchange reach an advanced stage of decomposition forms but a well premeditated move. The replacement of the social and economic components of the exchange act by asocial and aeconomic factors presents part of a well devised plan.

The conceptual blinds which Spann places in the path of a meaningful interpretation of exchange are slated to play a suitable role in Spann's subsequent attempt to obstruct the signification of a socially and economically potent outlook on prices. The proscribing of any form of concretization of any single exchange act is well fitted to assume the role of a preparatory move in any disqualification of specification in any presentation of the relation of one exchange act to another. The placing of the spatial and material aspect of any given exchange transaction beyond the realm of comprehensibility is well suited to serve as a steppingstone for a subsequent disqualification of any conceivable procedure for the quantification of exchange acts.

In following up his designification drive, Spann remains true to form. He implements his conceptual sterilization effort by divesting the price category of any social and economic content. Price changes—Spann takes an uncompromising attitude—are under no circumstances to be linked to a relocation of social and economic forces. A price which is postulated as a projection of an objectively ascertainable supply and demand situation is labeled by Spann as socially and economically irrelevant a factor as a price which is perceived as nothing more than an individual emotional reaction to the feeling that a person has about what he is inclined to regard as a relative abundance or a relative scarcity.

Social and economic relevance Spann is prepared to accord to a price which defies any quotation. He is willing to consider the according of social and economic signification to a price which cannot be singled out for any specific recording. He is disposed to view a price, which cannot be determined, as a key to a social and economic analysis.

Pricing, Spann wants to be regarded as a running device, with no beginning and no end. Price fluctuations, he wants to have viewed as a pendulum with incalculable swings.

No single price can ever be comprehended as such, Spann wants to make it sure. In ruling that prices are not to have any recognizable cause and any ascertainable effect, Spann makes one price appear as meaningless as another. In Spann's perception, any given price of a given object becomes undistinguishable from any number of other prices of any number of objects. Consecutive price listings are transformed by Spann into an unidentifiable chain reaction of innumerable prices of countless objects.

The ambiguity of his stand with reference to the question what accounts for a price formation presents a well studied move on the part of Spann. The ambivalence of Spann's position in regard to a price formulation forms but part of a scheme which is to make any conceptualization well nigh inconceivable within the framework of Spann's reasoning. His attempt to render the specification of prices well nigh incomprehensible presents but a preliminary bid for a social and economic disqualification of costs. The case Spann is trying to make for the presumption that the determination of the social nature of prices lies beyond the realm of ascertainable human knowledge is extended by him to include a ban on the ascertainability of the social character of the cost category.

Spann accuses those who have postulated costs as a price determining factor as being guilty of a misconception. Spann i.e., is trying to cast discredit upon those theoreticians who postulated costs as a factor which has a definite social and economic bearing on prices. Those who expounded the conception that prices are dependent upon material expenditures are denounced by Spann as persons who have advanced a fallacious proposition. Spann, i.e., is attempting to bring into ill-repute those theoreticians who conceived prices as being socially and economically accountable to ascertainable cost items. Spann tries to present the classical position, within the range of which production costs constitute an essential price factor, as misleading, because he has good reason to believe that his whole effort of obfuscation might be brought to fall, were he to subscribe to the projection of Ricardo and his disciples in whose systematic reasoning costs constitute the key analytical factor in the shaping and reshaping of social and economic relations.

Prices, Spann asserts, are not determined by anything specific. Prices, Spann insists, cannot be considered as a derivative of anything particular. Prices, Spann halfheartedly concedes, are not entirely unrelated to costs. There might be some relation between price factors and cost elements, Spann seems to be willing to concede. Such correlation he wants to make it sure, however, is not to be accorded any definite meaning. The relation of prices to costs, Spann decrees, is not to be presented in any concrete manner. The price and cost relation, Spann takes particular pains to stress, is not to be subject to any quantitative interpretation. Prices and costs in their relation to each other assume, in Spann's formulation, the role of two unspecifiable factors which are left to float in a social and economic vacuum.

Spann takes pride in extending the range of the net of social and economic unaccountability into which his conception of price is placed to include the cost category as well. The inexactitude which characterizes Spann's formulation of prices is matched by the lack of precision which he displays in the form in which he presents costs.

Prices, as well as costs, Spann pleads, are to be considered inexplicable in any social and economic sense. Prices and costs, Spann clamors, are to be regarded as a manifestation of something which lies beyond any rational social and economic range. Prices and costs manifest themselves in a form of a revelation in the characterization of Spann. Prices and costs, assume the quality of emanations, in Spann's presentation. Prices and costs are transformed into inexplicable presuppositions by the author of "Tote und Lebendige Wissenschaft." Prices and costs are committed to the sphere of the preordained by Spann.

Prices and costs become in Spann's formulation representative indications of a flow of economic life which is analyzed under a presumption that the preceding cannot be distinguished from the succeeding. A price and cost analysis conducted by Spann is not supposed to allow for any provision which would make it feasible to separate more significant from less significant elements. Prices and costs are to be subjected only to such an analytical scrutiny, Spann would like to make it sure, which deliberately excludes any contrasting of rational and irrational aspects in the constitution of either price or cost. Prices and costs analysis, in Spann's prescription, is to be conducted only in a manner which rules out any contrasting or reasoned and unreasoned attitudes in regard to cost and price formation.

Spann does not mind to give the impression he is willing to recognize a more and a less in the indistinctiveness he is out to promote. The author of "Tote und Lebendige Wissenschaft" appears to be going out of his way to intimate that there is room for a more or a less of indefiniteness in the analytical conception which he is advancing. Though he opposes numerical determination, though he rejects quantitative scaling, Spann intones, he is making allowance for a more or a less of disqualification. The social and economic disqualification to which he subjects price and cost formation, Spann proffers a demonstration, makes for a more pronounced indistinctiveness than any social and economic disqualification to which he could possibly subject the general category of value.

The reader might be inclined to remain doubtful whether Spann really means it, when he offers to show that, when contrasted with a socially and economically disqualified wider generalization as represented by a socially and economically disqualified value category, a socially and economically disqualified narrower range of generalization as the one represented by the socially and economically disqualified concepts of cost and prices, assumes the mark of lesser indistinctiveness; such doubts appeared to be somewhat justified, when Spann suddenly decides to abandon the subject of the relation of costs to value without subjecting it to the promised comparative disqualification test.

Suddenly, forgetting that he was supposed to demonstrate how his disqualification technique was to make a relatively more concrete formulation (i.e., costs and prices) relatively more abstract and a relatively more abstract formulation (i.e. value) relatively more concrete by comparison, Spann attempts to show how his disqualification technique affects the relation of identical abstractions (i.e. value to value).

Values, Spann proceeds to relate, refer to qualitative judgments. Qualitative, however, the author of "Tote und Lebendige Wissenschaft" cautions, is not to be taken in this instance as indicating anything specific. Qualitative, in the stated connection, is not to be taken as referring to any qualifiable attribute. The word qualitative when used in connection with the category of value, Spann warns, is not to be regarded as providing for the expression of something identifiable. A qualitative distinction in regard to value, Spann wants it stressed, is not to be expected to bring out anything tangible. A qualitative distinction with reference to value, Spann finds it necessary to emphasize, is not to be regarded as presenting something ponderable.

313

A qualitative distinction which is not presented as an inseparable part of an indefinite chain reaction, Spann rules, is to be out of order. The detaching of an expression of any given qualitative distinction from the expression of any other qualitative distinction, Spann wants to have prohibited. Any given qualitative distinction which takes the form of a value judgment remains invariably linked in Spann's dictum to any number of qualitative distinctions which, in turn, take the form of numberless value judgments.

Distinctiveness, in the stated formulation, becomes indistinct from indistinctiveness. Qualitative distinctiveness is in effect turned into a compounded indistinctiveness. Instead of granting a degree of concreteness to value judgments, as he ostensibly sets out to do, Spann proceeds to deny value any kind of specifiability. A specific valuation of a given social and economic entity becomes inconceivable. The value of any given social and economic entity flows into the values of uncountable other social and economic entities in Spann's comprehension.

A value judgment which refers to a social and economic entity of a certain range cannot be singly conceived, were Spann's strictures to be followed. A value judgment which refers to a social and economic entity of a certain range becomes but an inseparable part of an endless chain of value judgments which refer to a number of social and economic entities of sheer numberless ranges.

A value which is attributed to a production unit, Spann implements his strictures, is to be regarded as wholly undistinguishable from a value which is attributed to a consumer's desire. A value which expresses an objective projection is viewed by Spann as indistinct as a value which expresses a subjectified attitude. A value which is attributed either to a production unit or a consumer's stockpile, Spann implements his strictures in another form, is to be considered entirely undistinguishable from a value which is attributed to a national economic entity.

Value in its expression of the concrete is viewed as indistinct by Spann as value in its references to the abstract. Value which is attributed to a national economic entity, Spann offers another implementation of his strictures, is not to be viewed as being in any way distinguishable from a value which is attributed to a

314

supranational economic entity. A value which expresses a comparatively lower level of abstraction is thus rated by Spann as indistinct as a value which expresses a comparatively higher degree of abstraction. The degree of abstraction is as irrelevant a factor in Spann's formulation as the degree of concreteness in any attempt to apply his respective form of social and economic evaluation. The concrete is rendered by Spann as meaningless, as the abstract in the procedure he suggests for the ascertainment or, more correctly, non-ascertainment of social and economic values.

In crowning his efforts directed towards obfuscation of social and economic valuation, Spann declares that a value which is attributed to a supranational economic entity is in no way distinguishable from a value attributed to a non economic entity. Value which expresses a societal entity is to be rendered by this declaration as indistinct as a value which forms the expression of a non-societal entity.

As far as indistinctiveness is concerned, Spann is quite frank in his proclamation, it is to be a matter of indifference whether a societal or non-societal entity is made subject to evaluation. He is much less frank when he is called upon to state what he considers to be an entity.

Whether Spann holds that an entity of any kind can be so formed as to permit some degree of ascertainability is not made quite clear. Whether he considers it proper that an entity be characterized by a property is not stated directly by the author of "Tote und Lebendige Wissenschaft." He prefers not to throw any light on the aspect of determinability in the formulation of an entity. He chooses to avoid answering the question whether an entity by its very definition does not express something finite. He would rather make it believe that an entity cannot be distinguished from a nonentity.

The degree of distinctiveness of value and, by implication, the degree of distinctiveness of any kind of entity to which value is made to refer, Spann does intimate in an afterthought, is never to reach a stage at which a distinction between an object and a subject can be clearly comprehended. The distinctiveness of value and, by implication, the distinctiveness of the kind of entity to which value is made to refer, Spann does drop a hint, is not to advance to a point at which the difference between a human and an ahuman factor could become discernible.

The distinctiveness of value and, by implication, the distinctiveness of the kind of entity to which value is made to refer, Spann does come out with it, is not to be permitted to advance to a range within which the differentiation between material and non-material factors could be recognized. The distinctiveness of value, and, by implication, the distinctiveness of the kind of entity to which value is made to refer, Spann does indicate, is not to be allowed to come within a range within which a division between the natural and the supranatural could be recorded.

The ascertainment of value and, by the same token, the ascertainment of an entity to which value is made to refer, Spann does offer a lead, is to have nothing to do with a sense of social and economic direction. The ascertainment of value and, by the same token, the ascertainment of an entity, to which values are made to refer, Spann does suggest, is to have no relation whatsoever to elements (whether human or ahuman) which are subject to a social and economic control.

The ascertainment of value and, by the same token, the ascertainment of an entity to which value is made to refer is, in particular, to have no connection with any observable uniformity in nature. The ascertainment of value and, by the same token, the ascertainment of an entity to which value is made to refer, Spann does consider it opportune to state, is, more specifically, to be wholly unsusceptible to the bearing of any laws, regardless whether such laws are socio-economic in character or not.

The ascertainability of value and, by the same token, the ascertainability of the entity to which value is made to refer, Spann does let it out, is to be kept within the range which can only be assessed through progressive introspection. The determinability of value and, by the same token, the determinability of the entity to which value is made to refer, is to be linked to individual suggestiveness (Eingebung).

The measure of value and, by the same token, the dimension of the entity to which value is made to refer, Spann does make a statement to the effect, is to be gathered only to an extent which is compatible with a comprehension which refers to an emanation.

316

The dividing line between reason and unreason, the distinction between rationality and irrationality, are slated for disappearance by Spann. The validation of a knowledge, analytically arrived at, is to be discounted. Understanding, in whatever cognitive form is to be superseded by an a-rational mystical elation.

Spann, to view his contribution in retrospect, started his literary venture with the pertinent observation that those who conceived of social and economic isolation as a major frame of reference for their theoretical expositions, had reached a dead end in social and economic conceptualization. He proved to be less perspicacious when he saw himself confronted with the task of taking a positive stand in regard to social and economic comprehension.

The contrasting of social and economic form and social and economic content in which the marginal utility theorists have been found wanting, can hardly be expected to be attained by a theorist who has a bent for losing himself in mysticism.

Underlying Fictions

In the end Spann's exposition forms but another step in the direction of extreme subjectivism. Spann's reference to emanation can be well taken as but an accentuated tune as compared with Schumpeter's advocacy of selfabandonment. Spann's motif of taking off for a nonentity can well be regarded as but an underscoring of Schumpeter's motif of leading to nowhere. Nor does Keynes' motif of paging the nondescript suggest a basically different tune.

Keynes' device to quantify investment moods, Schumpeter's scheme of innate go-getting and Spann's advice for mystical evaluation, it can well be realized, constitute defeatist positions. The respective reliance of Schumpeter, Keynes, and Spann, on the irrational, the alogical, and the arational, can well be interpreted as a sure sign that national and international social and economic conditions have become ungovernable in the view of the named theoreticians. When the inexpressible, the inexact, and the incomprehensible are elevated to heights of preception as well as cognition, it is not difficult to realize that answers to basic social and economic problems are wanting.

Schumpeter might well have considered that in placing profits within an intuitive range, he can furnish a protective social and economic device for the selffinancing of industrial enterprises. Keynes might well have found comfort in the thought that by discounting the distinction between money and real wages he could provide a protective social and economic frame for installment sales. Spann might well have fancied himself with the perspective that his mystical conceptions of exchange and value might prove helpful in taking popular social and economic pressure off monopolies. Schumpeter, Keynes and Spann, might have thought that their ingenious or better said disingenious devices could provide social and economic immunization for the special kind of enterprises they favored. Schumpeter, Keynes and Spann possibly assumed that they could uphold special business interests under the presumption that those interests are representative of the national society and economy in its entirety. Whether they themselves were convinced of the effectiveness of their rationalizations remains questionable.

BIBLIOGRAPHICAL NOTE

This volume refers to the focal aspects of the most representative books of the following authors:

Chapter 1

JOHANN HEINRICH VON THUENEN. *Der Isolierte Staat.* Neudruck. G. Fischer. Jena. 1910.

Chapter 2

KARL MENGER. *The Collected Works of Carl Menger.* V. 1-4. London 1933-36. London School of Economics. Volume 1. *Grundsaetze der Volkswirtschaftslehre.* 1871.

Chapter 3

FRIEDRICH VON WIESER. *Ueber den Urspung und die Hauptgesetze des Wirtschaftlichen Werthes.* Hoelder. Wien. 1884.
FRIEDRICH VON WIESER. *Der Natuerliche Wert. Einleitung.* Hoelder. Wien 1889.

Chapter 4

EUGEN VON BOEHM-BAWERK. *Capital und Capitalzins.* Abt. 1-2. Wagner. Innsbruck. 1900-02. 2 volumes. Second edition.

Chapter 5

JOHN BATES CLARK. *The Distribution of Wealth.* Macmillon Co., New York. 1899.

Chapters 6 and 7

WILLIAM STANLEY JEVONS. *The Theory of Political Economy.* Macmillan and Co. London and New York. 1888.

Chapter 8

JOSEPH ALOIS SCHUMPETER. *Theorie der Wirtschaftlichen Entwicklung.* Duncker und Humboldt. Leipzig. 1912.

Chapter 9

JOHN MAYNARD KEYNES. *A Treatise in Probability.* Macmillan and Co. London 1921.
JOHN MAYNARD KEYNES. *The General Theory of Employment Interest and Money.* Harcourt Brace Co. New York. 1936.

Chapter 10

OTHMAR SPANN. *Tote und Lebendige Wissenschaft.* G. Fischer. Jena. 1925.
OTHMAR SPANN. *Philophenspiegel.* Meyer. Leipzig 1933.

INDEX